APPROACHES TO THE DEVELOPMENT OF MORAL REASONING

Approaches to the Development of Moral Reasoning

Peter E. Langford
Graduate School of Education,
La Trobe University, Victoria, Australia

LEA **LAWRENCE ERLBAUM ASSOCIATES, PUBLISHERS** LEA
Hove (UK)   Hillsdale (USA)

MT

Lawrence Erlbaum Associates Ltd., Publishers
27 Church Road
Hove
East Sussex, BN3 2FA
UK

British Library Cataloguing in Publication Data

Langford, Peter
   Approaches to the Development of Moral
   Reasoning.–(Essays in Developmental
   Psychology Series, ISSN 0959-3977)
   I. Title II. Series
   155.232

   ISBN 0-86377-368-0

Cover design by Joyce Chester
Printed and bound in the United Kingdom by Redwood Books Ltd., Trowbridge, Wilts.

12/20/07

Contents

Acknowledgements

I would like to particularly thank the following people for their advice, inspiration and support during the course of the work described in this book: Carol Ammons, Leslie Claydon, Brian Crittenden, Ronald Goldman, Jacqueline Goodnow, J.V. D'Cruz, Robyn Langford, Margery Learner, Liu Ai Yun, Peter Tomlinson, Bishara Seif, Margaret Stevens, F.E. Trainer, and John Wilson. I am also greatly in debt to an anonymous Erlbaum reader who lavished far more than regulation care on the drafts. Needless to say, none of these people is responsible for the imperfections of the book or for the opinions expressed in it.

I am also particularly indebted to those many children and adolescents that I and my research assistants have interviewed over the past 10 years, on topics involving moral reasoning. In many cases they offered us far more of their time and involvement than we had asked for or were expecting. I particularly recall those undergraduate students at La Trobe University who became so engrossed in the topics of our interviews that they talked considerably beyond the estimated interview time in their eagerness to say everything they wanted to on the topic. I also recall the spirit of our interviewees of all ages, which was that this was an important topic that they took seriously. Those social philosophers who believe that all moral seriousness has evaporated, in what they are pleased to call a postmodern society, would do well to get in touch with the views of the average person by conducting such interviews, rather than intuiting their views by indirect methods.

I gratefully acknowledge the assistance of the University Research Committee and the School of Education Research Committee of La Trobe University for funding several of the studies described here. I also extend very sincere thanks for the unfailing helpfulness and courtesy of the librarians of: the Borchardt Library, La Trobe University; the Baillieu Library, University of Melbourne; Senate House Library and the Institute of Education Library, University of London; the British Library, Bloomsbury; and the Bodleian Library, Oxford.

CHAPTER ONE

Introduction

This introduction will begin by discussing definitions of moral reasoning and then provide a brief outline of the book.

DEFINITIONS OF MORAL REASONING

Formal definitions of moral reasoning tend to rely heavily on the notions of moral rules and moral norms, so some preliminary consideration of these is needed. A moral rule is usually taken to be any rule about human behaviour that is framed in moral language or has a moral intent. Such rules may be generally accepted rules, such as, in many societies, "You should not lie, cheat, steal, or murder." These are known as moral norms. It is usually thought that a norm is such for a given society. Thus, the rule "You should not offer human sacrifices" is a norm in most modern Western societies, but it was not a norm to the Phoenicians or the Aztecs. There are in addition many moral rules that are advocated by some people in a society, but rejected by others. In Western societies the rules "You should not have sex before marriage" and "You should not take soft drugs" have this character. These are moral rules that are not norms for our society.

Both Piaget (1932) and Kohlberg (1958) thought that moral reasoning focused on generally accepted moral rules or norms, such as the rules against stealing, lying, and murder. This involves some difficulties, as rules equivalent to "We ought to help other people", "We ought to promote the greatest happiness of the greatest number", and other expressions of the idea that we should act to aid others, occupy an ambiguous role in definitions of this kind.

Such rules about helping others are evidently moral norms in Western societies and are agreed to be so whatever definitional tack we take, but they are not usually taken as key examples of moral norms by Piaget and Kohlberg; and they occupy a rather different role within systems of moral reasoning from rules like those against lying, stealing, and murder. This is because they are often given as reasons for adhering to rules like those against lying, stealing, and murder. If asked why we should not lie or steal or murder, one common reason given by both children and adults is that these rules enable everyone to be better off, or that flouting them makes everyone worse off (see Chapter 8). On the other hand, few people will give "You should not lie" as a reason for not stealing, or "You should not murder" as a reason for not lying. For this reason, it is convenient to distinguish first order moral norms, like those against lying, stealing, and murder, from second order moral norms, like rules suggesting we should help other people. First order norms are generally agreed moral rules that are not usually used to justify other norms, whereas second order norms are generally agreed moral rules that are quite often used to justify first order norms.

In considering formal definitions of moral reasoning, it is useful to look first at some general definitional tactics and then at some particular definitions that have been influential in the psychological literature. It is most usual to approach the problem of definition either through the set of rules for regulating conduct that are held to define the topic, or through some kind of metaethical theory that explains why this set of rules is to be included (see especially Garner & Rosen, 1967; Hare, 1981; Mayo, 1986; McCloskey, 1969; Sanyal, 1970; Trainer, 1991). Philosophers usually distinguish between normative ethical theories and metaethical theories. Normative ethical theories tell us which kinds of things and actions are good. Thus, specification of a set of rules to define moral reasoning is closely related to one style of normative ethical theory.

Metaethics is concerned with the analysis of the meanings and logical functions of ethical expressions. Metaethical theories may involve a variety of tactics, including the purely descriptive analysis of the meaning of ordinary moral language. Here, arguments may be given that in such language the term "moral" has a certain extent (probably rather ill-defined) and that we should stick to the ordinary language usage of the term. Similar arguments may be applied to other moral words. Alternatively, a prescriptive metaethical theory may be put forward that aims to say why we ought to redefine the term in ways not sanctioned by ordinary language.

Some metaethical theories do not specify much about the content of normative ethics. Thus, the metaethical theory that what is good is that which is the will of God tells us nothing about what God actually wills. On the other hand, the metaethical theory that what is good is that which promotes the greatest happiness of the greatest number tells us a good deal about what is good. Metaethical theories, like the second one, that define what is good through a norm, tend to constrain what we should think about normative ethics to a greater extent than those that give more abstract definitions of what it is to be moral.

In considering the most influential psychological definitions of moral reasoning, it is convenient to begin with the way in which they use specification of a set of rules (the first kind of definitional tactic) to produce a definition. This is enough to specify what counts as moral reasoning and what does not. However, there is often also a prescriptive metaethical theory that at least in part motivates the selection of the chosen rules. We can understand more about the underlying reasons for adoption of the first kind of definition by an awareness of this theory.

Three definitions of moral reasoning will now be described, those of Kohlberg (1958), Piaget (1932) and that adopted by ego psychologists like Loevinger (1970, 1983, 1993) and Haan (1977, 1991). In considering the first two, a distinction needs to be drawn between the explicit and the implicit definition used by an author. Thus Kohlberg (1958) explicitly defines such reasoning as being about moral norms, but implicitly, as seen in the kinds of situation he chose to consider as involving moral reasoning, he nearly always restricts the norms considered to first order norms like those against lying, stealing, and murder.

Kohlberg's (1958) explicit definition is that moral reasoning is about the reasons for upholding norms that are under challenge, usually because in a particular situation they conflict with another norm. His implicit definition tends to restrict this to first order norms.

Piaget's (1932) definition, in its explicit version, is broader than that of Kohlberg and is that moral reasoning is about why we show respect for generally accepted moral rules. This is broader than Kohlberg's definition in two ways. First, it does not stipulate that the norm must be brought into question, including reasoning about norms that are not in question. Second, Piaget interprets the term "moral rule" to include conventional rules that people think they ought to adhere to, like the rules of games, as well as moral rules in the more usual sense, which is that such rules should involve moral language, or have a moral intent, and bear on human interests. This excludes conventional rules, like the rules of games, that may be discussed in moral language, but do not bear on human interests. Turiel (1983) and Turiel, Hildebrandt, and Wainryb (1991) were able to present considerable evidence that the development of thinking about conventional rules differs substantially from that of thinking about moral rules in the narrower and more usual sense. Piaget not only includes conventional rules in his definition, but assumes the development of thinking about them is similar to that of thinking about moral rules in the narrower sense.

Piaget's implicit definition of "moral rule" excludes second order norms, which he does not deal with in his studies.

The third and broadest definition of moral reasoning is that it is about what decisions we ought to make when these affect human interests. This definition is adopted in practice by Loevinger (1970, 1983, 1993) and Haan (1977, 1991). The most usual version states that the reasoning must involve moral language and the issues considered must bear on human interests. Reasoning of this kind may involve only second order norms, such as those relating to aiding others, with no reference to first order norms. It will always involve second order norms about aiding others, as these are always relevant when thinking about what we ought to do where human interests are at stake. First order norms may or may not be involved.

The adoption of the first two definitions given here seems at least in part to have been motivated by the prescriptive metaethical theory of Kant (1788). In his *Critique of practical reason*, Kant argued that the definition of morality should be based on his categorical imperative, which states that we should act according to rules that can be established as universal laws applying to everyone. Piaget and Kohlberg assume that most people have recognised this binding character of universalisable rules of conduct, and thus universalisable moral norms will also be empirical moral norms.

However, they are on somewhat shaky ground in making this extension of Kant's theory to ordinary people. For instance, Kant believed that the rule "You should not kill another human being" was a universalisable moral norm, although it is not an empirical norm of modern societies, which tend to adopt the rule "You should not murder another human being", excluding at least killing the enemy in war and also often capital punishment as well. Thus, Kant includes some rules as moral norms that are arguably not recognised as such by most people in our society. For this reason, moral norms will be understood here as empirical norms, rather than as rules that some philosophers think can be universalised. The aim of doing this is to avoid the conceptual confusion that can arise from the joint use of the empirical and universalisability criteria for being a moral norm. It also avoids the uncertainty that philosophers have about which norms are really universalisable in the philosophical sense, and what is meant by the ambiguous term "universalisable" (on the latter see especially McCloskey, 1969; Mackie, 1977).

It is worth adding that Kohlberg also claimed to have been influenced by the universalisability arguments of Hare (1963). These are intended to provide a descriptive rather than a prescriptive metaethical theory, saying what ordinary moral language *does* mean rather than what it *should* mean. This theory has been subjected to considerable criticism on the grounds of its ambiguity and tendency to pass off a positive commitment to particular normative values as descriptive metaethics (e.g. Mackie, 1977; Nagel, 1988; Singer, 1988). As it is widely held that the theory is really, for the second of these reasons, prescriptive and not descriptive metaethics, reliance on it in defining moral reasoning has many of the same problems as reliance on that of Kant.

Although it is less easy to make a direct connection between the definition of moral reasoning adopted by the ego psychologists (who in this respect followed their mentor Freud) and their metaethical position, it is reasonable to see a link between the liberal humanism of Freud and many of his followers and their preferred definition of moral reasoning. Thus Bentham and John Stuart Mill, who played a key role in the establishment of the liberal humanist tradition, both thought that morality ought to be based on maximising human welfare. This leads to a definition of morality that emphasises this rather than other kinds of moral rule.

In his later work, Kohlberg tends to define moral reasoning as the study of reasoning about principles of justice (Kohlberg, 1971, 1981; Kohlberg, Levine, & Hewer, 1983). In the first two of these sources, justice reasoning is thought of as general styles of thinking that can be used to balance conflicting moral claims. In the third (Kohlberg et al., 1983, p.91), he also says "Our starting assumptions led to the design of a research instrument measuring reasoning about dilemmas of conflicting rights or of the distribution of scarce resources; that is, justice concerns." However, the second part of this statement seems to represent something of an afterthought and is difficult to connect with the genesis or nature of the dilemmas that he regarded as so fundamental to the study of moral reasoning. There is no dilemma that deals with the distribution of scarce resources that does not at the same time involve the conflict of norms.

The notion of justice being invoked here, central to the later definitions, involves a kind of balancing of moral criteria that is only revealed by Kohlberg's particular way of analysing interview replies. As such analysis is controversial, this appears an unwise definitional tactic.

An important use of definitions in this field is to determine whether particular questions are likely to elicit reasoning that is moral according to the adopted definition or not. This means that definitions should focus on the less controversial issue of how to categorise questions, not on the more controversial one of how to categorise replies. If introducing the notion of justice into the definition is merely intended to say that norms should be put under challenge in the interview, to encourage reasoning that involves balancing moral criteria, then this leads us straight back to the earlier definition. For these reasons, the 1958 definition will be assumed sufficient here. In any event, the shift from the earlier to the later definitional emphasis brought about no discernible change in the content of the dilemmas used to study moral reasoning.

Work inspired by all three of the major psychological definitions will be considered here. This is partly because they all help to delimit aspects of reasoning that we call "moral" in everyday language. It will also be argued that consideration of the wider range of issues, involved in the third definition, helps to reveal aspects of reasoning of the two narrower kinds, which remain obscure if we consider only those two narrower definitions.

These definitions are still quite restrictive in relation to what are called moral issues in everyday language and are considered as such by some philosophers. Thus, issues such as blasphemy and sacrilege are moral in these everyday and philosophical senses, but do not fall under any of the three definitions, as human interests are not usually directly involved. In deference to the psychological literature, which tends to exclude issues of this kind, I have not considered them.

It is worth clarifying one issue that arises in thinking about situations that involve first order moral norms. There are some moral rules, which nearly everyone will agree are desirable moral rules, that are applicable to an agreed range of situations, like the rules against lying and stealing. Disagreement may well arise as to whether certain mitigating factors would or would not allow us to countenance lying or stealing in a certain situation, but there is little disagreement as to when these rules are relevant. This contrasts with some other rules, which most people will agree are desirable rules in some situations, but will not agree on the range of situations to which they apply, regardless of the influence of mitigating factors. A good example here is the rule that a parent should have authority over their child, which Colby and Kohlberg (1987b) consider to be a moral norm. It is clearly not the case that everyone will agree on the range of situations to which this applies.

Colby and Kohlberg talk about the operation of this moral "norm" in situations where many people would not think it applied. This contrasts with the terminology used by Langford (1991a), that when applied to such situations a rule of this kind is not a norm. It is a norm in some situations, as most people think parents have authority over their children in some, for example life-threatening, situations. But, where the application of the rule is controversial, I will not consider that rule to be a norm for such situations.

On the surface, this is merely a terminological issue that should cause little concern to anyone. However, as Langford (1991a) and Turiel et al. (1991) found that moral reasoning in situations where the relevance of moral norms was doubtful to many interviewees was very different to reasoning about situations to which norms were generally agreed to be relevant, it is important to keep the two senses of "norm" apart. The usage adopted here is one convenient way to do this.

One or two further considerations about the scope of our topic arise from the expectations aroused by the terms "moral development" and "development of moral reasoning". Moral development is obviously something wider than the development of moral reasoning, as it includes moral emotion and behaviour, moral character and personality, as well as moral reasoning.

Texts on moral development, such as Graham (1972) and Rich and DeVitis (1985), often include the Freudian approach. But when we come to discussions of the development of moral reasoning we are likely to hear about ego psychology and cognitive structuralism (i.e. Piaget and Kohlberg), but may not encounter Freud, on the grounds that he was more interested in the emotional or motivational aspects of moral development than in moral reasoning (e.g. Haan, 1977).

I shall include the orthodox Freudian view of development, as well as those of ego psychology and cognitive structuralism, as three broad strands within classical approaches to the development of moral reasoning. There are three main reasons for doing this. The first is that Freud and fairly orthodox Freudians like Erikson, as well as being interested in motivation and emotion, were also interested in ego development. The ego is the part of the personality responsible for rational thought. Their views thus offer a distinctive and interesting approach to the development of the rational aspects of moral reasoning. The second is that in considering "moral reasoning" there seems little reason to restrict ourselves arbitrarily to rational and conscious, as opposed to irrational and unconscious, reasoning processes. Once we begin to think about unconscious and irrational reasoning processes, we are led inevitably to consider Freud's contribution to these topics.

A third reason for including Freud is that when Kohlberg (1958) reviewed work on the development of moral reasoning, as it existed prior to his own contribution to it, he included Freud as a major contributor. This is significant, as it shows that Kohlberg himself, the best known contemporary theorist of the development of moral reasoning, was swayed by the two reasons just given.

STRUCTURE OF THE BOOK

The overall structure of the book is as follows. It begins in Part 1 with a review of the three main theoretical traditions already mentioned. This throws up a major problem with the current state of the field. This is that the dominant approach, that of Kohlberg, involves commitment to theory-laden descriptions of development that comprise a blend of descriptive observations and theoretical interpretation. One of the first tests of a theory in developmental psychology should be that it provides an adequate account of descriptive aspects of development. It is, however, impossible to assess whether Kohlberg's theory passes this kind of test when descriptions of his findings are couched in strongly theory-laden terms. Kohlberg's methods of interview analysis are termed "strongly interpretive" to stress this aspect of them. They make descriptions of development support his theory by a process of circular reasoning: the descriptions assume the theory and then feed back information that supports it.

This leads to discussion in Part 2 of studies that have attempted to provide weakly interpretive descriptions of the development of moral reasoning, as observed in interviews, with a minimum of theoretical presuppositions. It is argued that there is a common underlying method of description in studies of this kind that has undergone significant refinement in recent years. It is also argued that a version of this common underlying method is implicit in the last version of Kohlberg's method of scoring interviews (Colby & Kohlberg, 1987b), though he and his collaborators do not report results in terms of such a method.

Findings from interview studies using weakly interpretive methods provide convincing evidence against Kohlberg's theory. It is argued that current descriptive evidence is, however, consistent with a wide variety of other theoretical interpretations. These include theories derived from classical psychoanalysis and ego psychology. However, other approaches integrating concepts from human ethology, behaviourism, and Jungian and Rankian psychology with aspects of these theories are also possible candidates. Composite approaches of this kind could also include elements from Piaget and Kohlberg, but central features of their theories would need to be removed.

This is followed in Part 3 by consideration of findings from studies using techniques other than the interview. Here again it is argued that commonly agreed descriptive methods exist, which can provide descriptions prior to substantial theoretical interpretation. The same range of theories that can be used to explain findings from interviews is also relevant in dealing with findings from these techniques, although once again we currently have too many explanations and not enough information to decide between them.

Part 4 provides a brief indication of conclusions and directions for future work. It is suggested that, while further descriptive work is needed to confirm and extend existing descriptive findings from weakly interpretive methods applied to interview data, diversification of tactics is also desirable. Thus, diversification of interview styles as well as the use of naturalistic and experimental methods, to provide differential tests of available theories, is indicated.

PART ONE

Theoretical traditions

CHAPTER TWO

Freud and Erikson

SIGMUND FREUD

In Freud's later theory, the adult's moral life consists in large part of a struggle between the id, the ego, and the superego. The id comprises the instinctual strivings of the person, especially those produced by the sexual and aggressive instincts. The superego comprises an internalised parent or parents, who issue moral prohibitions. The ego tries to find ways of satisfying the demands of both the id and the superego, given the constraints imposed by the real external environment. Thus, the id may fantasise immediate gratification for its sexual impulses, but the ego will think about such things as how realistically to obtain a sexual partner and what consequences might follow, while the superego may issue moral prohibitions against certain kinds of sexual behaviour. This picture is complicated by the emergence of the ego ideal, which obtains narcissistic self-gratification from an ideal image of the person, including an image of ideal moral behaviour.

Freudian psychoanalysis is a theory particularly associated with the practice of psychotherapy in the form of psychoanalytic treatment. The aim of therapy in Freud's view is to free the person from irrational fixations and compulsions and to restore rationality to the ego, so that it is able to direct the person towards the rational satisfaction of instincts. This is often associated with attempts to reduce the severity of the demands of the superego, which are usually excessive in neurotic patients. Thus the aim of therapy is to persuade the person to act as a rational being in the absence of irrational tendencies and an excessively severe superego.

The process by which the individual reaches the adult state of conflict between the id, ego, and superego is outlined in Freud's stages of psychosexual development (see especially Freud, 1915). In the oral stage of development, the infant achieves gratification chiefly through sucking with the mouth, joined in the later part of the period by biting. In the anal stage, usually beginning in the second year of life, the infant gains gratification from the expulsion and retention of faeces. In the phallic stage, beginning from 2½ or 3 years of age, gratification is from manipulation of the sexual organs, especially in masturbation. This lasts until about age 5 years and is followed by the latency period, in which the anxiety provoked by fantasies of gratification in the phallic period produces a retreat from sexual feelings, although only a partial one. In adolescence, the increase in sexual libido breaks down this repression, causing earlier fixations and conflicts to be revived. Providing these are satisfactorily resolved, this is followed by a mature genital relationship with an adult sexual partner.

The phallic period is especially important in the formation of the moral personality, as in this period the child conceives sexual desires for the parent of the opposite sex and forms the project of murdering the parent of the same sex in order to displace them. This then leads to fear of extreme reprisals, including for boys castration, from the parent of the same sex. In order to defend itself against this anxiety, the child identifies with the parent of the same sex and shows an exaggerated desire to be like them and to please them. The chief defence mechanism here is reaction formation. Because any thoughts of possessing the parent of the opposite sex by killing the parent of the same sex produce such intense anxiety, these thoughts are rejected with great energy. The opposite idea of cuddling up to the parent of the same sex becomes attractive, as it offers the greatest hope of avoiding the anxiety associated with the earlier fantasies. The result of these various conflicting tendencies is the Oedipal conflict, named after the Greek hero who murdered his father, married his mother, and then suffered terrible retribution at the hands of the gods.

Identification with the same-sex parent leads to the formation of the superego, which issues moral commands. Although it might seem that many misdemeanours that children or adults are tempted to commit, such as stealing, do not have a directly sexual component, Freud thought disobedience to parental commands of any kind was likely to remind the person of the greater disobedience they contemplated during the Oedipal conflict. Any kind of disobedience thus revives the feelings associated with that conflict. As the Oedipus complex is usually repressed during later development, this means that the superego is normally largely unconscious. It also attracts to itself large amounts of aggressive instinctual energy that can no longer find an outlet in fantasised and real attacks on the same-sex parent and are also discouraged when unleashed against other members of the family or those outside it. Instead, aggression is released through the sadistic strictness of the superego, which now directs aggression against the person themself. This unreasonable strictness is often carried through to adulthood, as its source is removed from conscious inspection. It continues to play an important role in the release of aggressive instinctual energy.

The ego also plays a role in moral development through the ego ideal. In his paper *On narcissism* (1914) Freud distinguishes object-libido (love directed towards other people) from ego-libido (love directed towards oneself). The original outside object of love for both sexes, during the oral period, is the mother or other, usually female, carer, who thus forms the child's first love object, as it is she who fulfils the child's lust for oral gratification. But even prior to attachment to the mother, the infant during the oral period also forms a narcissistic love attachment to its own body, which is perceived as an important source of pleasure. Although objectively there would be no pleasure without the mother's nipple or the bottle, the infant takes some time to realise this, at first thinking that its own mouth is solely responsible for the pleasure of feeding. This narcissism expands from the infant's mouth to its body as a whole, just as attachment later expands from the mother's nipple to her body as a whole. The libidinal or sexual energy invested in the infant's own body is called ego-libido, that invested in the mother is called object-libido.

The infant's primitive narcissism leads to the formation of the ego ideal, which is originally the fantasy of the perfect body and later extends to that of being the perfect person. This ideal of a perfect self affords the infant and later the adult a very satisfactory form of gratification, as it is not like an outside love object, such as the mother, who may be in a bad temper or frustrate one's wishes. The pleasures of self-admiration are potentially limitless and ever-present, as we always have our selves with us and the pleasure of self-contemplation, unlike those kinds of pleasure that depend on an external object, is always open to us.

The only blot on the horizon of the infant's self love is the annoying tendency for parents and others to say that it is not the perfect creature it imagines itself to be, but is sometimes naughty, annoying, dirty, and unattractive. This devaluation of the ego may result in a more realistic concept of self and a realisation of the need to turn outwards as well as inwards for satisfaction. But it may also result in vigorous defence of the integrity of the perfect self, resulting in a narcissistic personality that continually rejects any reality testing of its own self-evaluation. The person continues to believe themself to be perfect, and to derive huge enjoyment from contemplating this satisfactory situation.

In both the child and the adult the ego ideal will usually have a strong moral element, as part of the image of an ideal person is, for most people, possessing an ideal morality. Thus most of us have some tendency to think we are morally superior to others, even though we cannot all be right. The energy that powers this kind of moral self-regard, according to Freud, comes from narcissistic libido directed towards the self. While the superego is mainly responsible for telling the child and the adult what not to do, the ego ideal tells us what we should do, if we later want to look back and think how admirable we were.

Freud thought the development of the ego ideal took a rather different course in males and females. In most men and some women the course is from the primary narcissism of the infant to the object choices involved in the later stages of childhood, which are the love objects chosen by the child, especially the mother and later the father for the girl. This is then followed in adolescence by the narcissistic development of the ego ideal, which expands at the same time as the object choices of adolescence are being made, in adolescent love affairs. These object choices of adolescence are a revival and reassignment of the earlier loves of childhood.

However, in a substantial number of women and a lesser number of men the onset of puberty brings with it no significant revival of the object choices taken before the latency period, but a substantial revival of the primary narcissism of the infant. This is associated with pride in the body and the maturing sexual organs, and in these cases the ego ideal is grafted onto a revived narcissism, rather than onto object choices. In such cases, the ego ideal will usually take less account of social ideals received from outside and will thus contain a reduced moral component. In women who take this route, the development of object choices may occur later through having a child, which is experienced as the detachment of part of the body. This can lead to the emergence of a more social and thus more moral ego ideal, though Freud thought that because of the general character of female development women are less inclined to a strict morality than men.

The various agencies we have met so far are not just reservoirs or way-stations for instinctual energy. They also engage in distinctive kinds of reasoning, which are applied both to non-moral and to moral topics. The id thinks through the primary process, which functions chiefly by fantasising the desired object of gratification. The elaboration of such gratification fantasies, which in childhood take the forms of play, daydreams, actual dreams, and masturbation fantasies, takes place not by rational processes but by irrational ones ruled largely by principles of association. Thus things associated with the desired object will be fantasised with it. The primary process also works along paths of association to evade the internal censor that tries to block unacceptable thoughts from consciousness. Thus, certain kinds of sexual gratification may be forbidden and cause anxiety, so the original forbidden objects are replaced by objects associated with them. For instance, in one of the dreams described in *The interpretation of dreams* (1901), the unacceptable idea of having intercourse with a girl is replaced, in one of Freud's dreams, by the image of the girl having an injection, which is a disguised symbol for sexual intercourse.

The ego, on the other hand, uses the secondary process, which involves the use of rational and realistic thinking to go about achieving desired aims in the real world. It also operates defence mechanisms in an effort to reduce anxiety, which otherwise threatens to overwhelm it, when confronted with the problems of meeting the conflicting demands of the id and the superego. The defences of identification and reaction formation have already been mentioned. Some other important defences are repression (forgetting unpleasant thoughts or incidents), projection (attributing one's own unacceptable thoughts and feelings to others), rationalisation (finding a rational reason for saying or doing something irrational) and regression (often involving the return to an earlier and more pleasant period of development).

The superego, because it is partly unconscious, tends to think in terms of the primary process. Thus, it is often guided by associations rather than rational considerations, and may decide that objects and actions associated with those forbidden in childhood are also forbidden. This explains why both neurotics and normal individuals often feel they must not do something, although there appears no rational reason for this.

In *Group psychology and the analysis of the ego* (1922), Freud argues that the two main things that hold groups together, and enable them to form communities, are identification with group leaders, who are treated as surrogate parents to be identified with, and the libidinal ties between group members. Thus, the impulse to help other members of a group to which one belongs comes in large part from the investment of libido in other group members and the desire to please the leader. Libidinal relations with other group members involve two mechanisms that produce helping and tenderness towards others: investment in the expectation of reciprocity, and sublimation of sexual energy.

To understand this, it is worth considering what Freud thinks happens in the formation of outside love objects. In *Instincts and their vicissitudes* (1915), he distinguished between the source, pressure, aim, and object of instincts. The source of an instinct is the physiological process that builds up a need for satisfaction; the pressure is the amount of this need; the aim is the process that will result in the satisfaction of the instinct, such as eating or sexual intercourse; the object is the thing that is needed to assist satisfaction, such as food or a sexual partner. Instincts also generate energy that can be used to procure satisfaction. The energy of the sexual instinct is called the libido and this is pictured as being like fluid in a reservoir, that builds up and creates pressure for release.

The first object of the sexual instinct is the infant's own body, as the infant does not see the need for outside objects to assist in satisfying its needs, imagining that its mouth and later its body are the only means needed to achieve the pleasures of feeding and oral gratification. Later, objects in the outside world, especially people, are also seen to be necessary if frustration is to be avoided, and these are said to be "invested with" or "cathected by" libidinal energy. This investment is not in the objects or people themselves, but in their mental representations. The investment is a kind of shorthand that tells the person they can afford to expend a certain amount of energy in obtaining or retaining the object or person. This is necessary as the time and energy of an individual are limited and they must budget these to ensure that their needs are met.

We can picture the process of investment as much like the thinking of a financier who has a certain amount of money to invest and must decide where it will be most profitably placed. Freud thought that in a similar way the infant may decide, for instance, that it should invest more time and energy in pleasing and staying close to its mother, than in pleasing and staying close to a stranger, as the mother will feed it and the stranger will not. At around 8 months most infants experience a need to be close to the mother or other major attachment figure, and develop a marked fear of strangers. The desire to be close to the mother reflects the infant's libidinal investment in her. According to Freud, the fear of strangers is an attempt to defend against the distress that infants, who have formed the attachment bond, experience on seeing a human figure and then realising that it is not the mother, as this suggests they may have been deserted.

The development of libidinal investment is connected with the reality principle. This operates so that "A momentary pleasure, uncertain in its results, is given up, but only in order to gain in the new way an assured pleasure coming later" (Freud, 1911, p. 223). This replaces the pleasure principle, that causes the young infant to fantasise pleasure without encouraging any realistic attempts to gain control over the sources of that pleasure. The operation of the reality principle means that much of the desire of the child and teenager, to cooperate with and help others, comes from the rational calculation that one must help others in order to receive satisfaction of one's own needs in return. This is what writers like Piaget and Kohlberg refer to as reciprocity; but they thought that the notion of reciprocity developed relatively late, whereas Freud thought that it began in infancy and was the basis for the first attachments. The child is attached to the mother because it expects that she will provide it with gratification. This is the reason that the infant tries to please and help the mother, providing the origin of one of its main moral impulses, that of helping others.

Another source of cooperativeness is the sublimation of sexual attraction. Freud saw sexual attraction to the same-sex parent, to the opposite-sex parent, and to siblings of both sexes, as playing a key role in infancy and childhood. As direct expression of this in behaviour is suppressed and awareness of it is repressed, the libido is redirected to the sublimated forms of sexual activity represented by helping and tenderness to others (Freud, 1933).

In *Civilisation and its discontents* (1929) Freud also introduces the notion of the cultural ideal to explain the dynamics of moral emotions and strivings. This comprises the cultural ideals of a community, particularly as found in its religion and its heroes and heroines, and is the form of ego ideal that a community offers to its members. With typical awareness of the complexity of human emotions, Freud argues that while such ideals function partly to assist the narcissistic self-regard of the individual, they also serve to channel other emotions, particularly those generated by the rearousal of childhood conflicts.

The urge to participate in the cultural ideal develops, in part, from the libidinal ties that bind the individual to members of their own group and society. Stories about the lives of the ethical and religious teachers of the society are particularly important here, as they provide an opportunity for the individual to identify with these people in satisfying and binding ways. It is always easier to identify with an individual than with an idea.

Such stories often involve the suffering and death of the teacher at the hands of the majority in their society. This allows the individual to project Oedipal and other childhood fantasies onto the story. The story of the suffering and death of Jesus is, on the surface, anomalous here. We can assume that some of the central ideas of Christianity make a particular appeal to men, but the Oedipal fantasy in boys involves killing the father, whereas Christianity is based on the death of the son.

In *Moses and monotheism* (1939), Freud suggests that the reason Christianity celebrates the death of the son and not the father is that it is a secondary religion that is built on the more direct celebration of the overthrow of paternal authority found in Judaism, particularly in such stories as the rebellion of Adam and Eve against God and of the Israelites against Pharaoh. Christianity reacted against such fantasies with guilt, and instead offered up its saviour to the father, as an act of atonement for having rebelled against paternal authority. In Christianity, Christ atones for the original sin of disobedience to God's will by the sacrifice of the son.

A religion of guilt, such as Christianity, is particularly appropriate for highly civilised nations in which direct aggression is discouraged in daily life, as aggression can be rerouted through the superego to be experienced as an overwhelming sense of guilt. This has two useful results. It allows aggressive energies that could destroy civilised life to be released, and even, in the masochistic pleasure that results from self-martyrdom, to be enjoyed. It also encourages a controlled and "moral" approach to life, which is essential in a civilised society.

Although Freud (1939) does not explicitly mention it, Christianity also offers the role of the Virgin Mary, who is generally depicted as renouncing herself and suffering in the service of others. This is an appropriate role for women who wish to atone for the guilt induced by the fantasy of mother murder, at the same time gratifying general aggressive impulses channelled into masochism, in addition to the masochistic impulses that are natural to women. Women, Freud believed, are naturally masochistic, as the sexual act is, from biological necessity, a kind of attack by the man on the woman, and in longing for pain a woman longs for this biological attack in a substitute form (Freud, 1925, 1931).

The way in which the positive injunctions of the ego-ideal can become charged with the negative and hostile emotions of the aggressive superego, particularly in highly civilised societies, is also seen in Freud's (1929) comments on the Christian moral command to "Love thy neighbour as thyself". This novel and demanding precept is, he thinks, yet another avenue offered to the sadistic superego of the highly refined person as an outlet for their aggressive tendencies. To demand that we give up such a highly pleasurable activity as aggression is, to Freud's way of thinking, tantamount to a form of sadism. The normal ebb and flow of the libidinal economy involves the enjoyable experience of loving those who are members of our own group, be it family, tribe, or nation, and the perhaps even greater enjoyment of hating those who are outsiders. This provides for the gratification of both the sexual and the aggressive instincts. The Christian law of love defies this natural economy and tries, ineffectively in most people, to get us to love everyone.

In evaluating Freud's contribution to the study of moral reasoning and emotion we can begin with his so-called hydraulic model of instincts. According to Freud (1915, 1933), both the sexual and the aggressive instincts possess a kind of reservoir of energy, that is continually filling and demanding to be emptied, before it becomes uncomfortably full: a kind of psychological counterpart to the bladder. This view of instincts can be criticised on two scores. First, it may be approximately true for drives like hunger and thirst, which Freud grouped with the more narrowly defined sexual instincts, but it is quite probably not true for sexual instincts narrowly conceived. For instance, persons who spend periods in isolation without sexual activity often report a diminution in the sex drive, rather than an increase. Second, there is little evidence that aggression is a drive that builds up like hunger or thirst, and more that it is usually either a reaction to frustration or the aggression of another, or an instrumental attempt to achieve an object (Atkinson & Raynor, 1978; Petri, 1991; Weiner, 1992).

However, even if we agree to these points, this does not make a great deal of difference to the application of Freud's theory to the development of children in modern societies, especially in the West, as outside sexual stimulation, and the frustration that everyone experiences in life, mean that the drives involved in sex and aggression are continually being aroused, even though this comes from outside rather than from inside. The point at issue here is of some significance to social theorists, because if Freud is right there is no hope of ever diminishing these drives if we want to, whereas if the revisionist view just outlined is accepted, then society might be arranged so these things were stimulated less. However, this issue has little direct bearing on our view of moral development in contemporary industrial societies.

Freud's view of libidinal investment can likewise be challenged. The process of libidinal investment in others begins with the infant's bond to the mother or other significant caretaker. The infant is supposed to bond chiefly with the person who suckles them or offers the bottle. But studies of the actual process of bonding in infants show that they some-times form strong bonds not with the person who feeds them, but with another person with whom they are better able to communicate (Schaffer, 1971, 1984). As most infants communicate well with the person who feeds them, this suggests communication has an importance that is independent of feeding, and may even be more important than feeding.

This and other observations have led some theorists to conclude that communication may trigger a biological bonding process, similar to that responsible for imprinting in some birds (e.g. Bowlby, 1984; Schaffer, 1984). Imprinting is the process that leads birds like ducklings to follow any object that moves during a critical period in the first few days of life, and then to continue following the imprinted object for a period after this (see especially Hess, 1973; McFarland, 1993; Sluckin, 1972). It is not necessary to feed or otherwise reward such birds to trigger this process, which seems to have evolved to encourage the young to stay close to the parents to help them survive. It is quite plausible to think that similar evolutionary pressures have produced analogous mechanisms in humans.

If attachment is indeed founded on a biological mechanism of this kind, this implies that the child's awareness of reciprocity is not needed to form the bond with the caregiver. However, this does not mean that there is no awareness of reciprocity. As we shall see in later chapters, there is positive evidence that quite young children are aware of reciprocity in relationships. In addition, it may be that infants sometimes bond with those with whom they communicate well, but who do not feed them, because they desire reciprocal assistance from the adult in matters other than feeding; a view that is compatible with some of the views of the ego psychologists outlined in the next chapter.

Although Freud's theory can be criticised on these and other grounds, it is strong in several respects. The first is that it systematised the application of the notion of defence mechanisms to the explanation of moral phenomena, which earlier thinkers, like La Rochefoucauld and Nietzsche, had deployed in an unsystematic way. It would be true to say that nowadays few clinical psychologists could function without the notion of defence mechanisms. For most psychologists, whether experimentally inclined or not, the issue is not whether such mechanisms exist, but which are most important, when they are operating and what precisely they are defending against (see especially Dixon, 1981; Fisher & Greenberg, 1976, 1978; Kline, 1981; Masling, 1983–6; Robinson, 1993).

The last of these issues is among the most potent. Thus, defence mechanisms operate to defend against unacceptable impulses, but Freud presents only one possible version of what these are. For him, morality is a subtle amalgam of defences against the overt display of sex and aggression, designed to allow covert expression of at least some of these impulses. Nietzsche, by contrast, thought that adult morality was a disguised expression of the will to power, an idea later followed through in relation to children in a modified form by Adler (1917, 1927, 1954), Ausubel (1952), and Ausubel, Sullivan, and Ives (1980). The way in which alternative theories of motivation lead to rival interpretations of the development of moral reasoning of this kind is dealt with in more detail in the next chapter.

The second strength of Freud's account is that it offers an explanation for the expansion of the scope of social concern shown by the child in its development. Children begin life with a rather narrow range of concern for those around them, limited to the immediate family. This later broadens to concern for the peer group and those in a somewhat wider circle; and then in adult life is, in nation states, also directed to members of one's own nation, though it does on occasion extend wider than this.

Theorists long before Freud had noticed this expanding circle of concern, notably the utilitarian philosophers and their psychological allies, during the eighteenth and nineteenth centuries (see especially Lyons, 1965, 1991; Mill, 1861; Plamenatz, 1966; Quinton, 1989; Sidgwick, 1922; Stephen, 1900). It is, moreover, significant that they had quite a different explanation for it from Freud. Most of them thought that it was mainly produced by an expansion in the scope of sympathy, which is the tendency to catch emotions from other people just by seeing or knowing what they are feeling, regardless of our relationship with them. In *Group psychology and the analysis of the ego*, Freud (1922) explicitly rejects this as an explanation, preferring his own view involving identification and libidinal relations. However, his arguments against the sympathy theory are not particularly convincing, and he seems to have rejected it chiefly because it did not fit in well with his own view that all motivation involves reduction in biological tension.

What is most appealing about Freud's view of the expansion of concern is that it offers an awareness of the complexity of the motivational dynamics that could be involved here. Although this complexity has seemed to some to be overplayed, for many others, especially the ego psychologists dealt with in the next chapter, the subtle operation of defence mechanisms during development, taken together with the assumption that actions are often motivated by several motives, seemed to open a door to the less obvious aspects of developmental processes.

The third notable success in Freud's theory was his description of what I shall call the self-other-self cycle in moral development. The infant begins its moral Odyssey as a self-centred being. During childhood and early adolescence, outside social controls become the focus for moral personality, with moral rules and prescriptions derived first from the parents and then from the peer group and school. This is followed in the adult by a partial return of the moral focus to the self, that results from attempts to live up to the moral component of the ego ideal. In many individuals, this results in some withdrawal of libido from the outside world and its reinvestment in narcissistic contemplation of the ideal moral self.

The self-other-self cycle, as a descriptive phenomenon, was no more an original observation by Freud than the expansion of concern. It was one of the main foci of the influential theory of moral development of

James Mark Baldwin (1897, 1906–11) and the main outlines of it go back at least to Kant (1785, 1788). Nor does it require anything more than educated common sense to see that in many individuals something like this occurs in development. Freud's contribution was, however, particularly important, as he showed how the phenomenon could be integrated within his enormously influential general approach to personality development. His ideas about this aspect of the development of the ego ideal were taken up and extended by the ego psychologists.

ERIK ERIKSON

Erikson, in his widely read books *Childhood and society* (1950, fifth edition 1977) and *Identity, youth and crisis* (1968), outlined a series of "psychosocial stages" that were intended to complement Freud's psychosexual stages. The psychosocial stages describe ego development within the framework of fairly orthodox Freudian theory. They are significant because they flesh out some aspects of the development of morality that were neglected by Freud. Erikson's ego, like that of Freud, uses defence mechanisms to cope with the conflicting demands of the id and the superego, as well as rationality to cope with reality. Erikson assumes the substantial truth of Freud's account of the formation of the superego, through the Oedipal conflict and identification with the parents.

Erikson's ego passes through eight stages in its development. Each involves a fundamental conflict that must be resolved if the child is to pass to the next. The first is basic trust versus basic mistrust. This conflict is experienced most sharply in the infant's anxiety about separation from the mother, who is its chief source of comfort and gratification. The second stage involves the conflict between autonomy, on the one hand, and shame and doubt on the other. This is seen at its most critical in conflicts over toilet training, in which the infant must either establish its own control over bowel movements, or submit to the shame and doubt that come from experiencing the reactions of others to uncontrolled movements.

The third stage is initiative versus guilt, which in effect corresponds to the Oedipal stage. The main conflict is between the pleasure of self-manipulation found in masturbation and the guilt that arises from Oedipal masturbation fantasies, as these involve attacks on the same-sex parent. The fourth stage is industry versus inferiority. This corresponds to Freud's latency period, except that Erikson emphasises that in this period the gratification of instinctual impulses is repressed, to make way for greater concentration on building the ego; this occurs mainly at school in Western societies, where the child learns the skills needed to earn a living in adult life. In many non-Western societies, the child will learn these skills by direct apprenticeship rather than at school.

The next stage is identity versus role confusion, which corresponds to Freud's period of adolescent sexuality. Here, although he bows in the direction of Freud's emphasis on coping with the rising sexual libido, Erikson is rather less Freudian than in his previous stages. He stresses the adolescent search for identity, which particularly involves the quest for an occupational identity: the adolescent's reply to the common question from adults "What are you going to be when you grow up?". The main function of adolescent love, he thinks, is not so much to provide an outlet for rising libido, as to provide an intimate forum for the exploration of ego identity. This stage is also one of moral transition (Erikson, 1950, p.263):

> The adolescent mind is essentially a mind of the moratorium, a psychosocial stage between childhood and adulthood, and between the morality learned by the child, and the ethics to be developed by the adult. It is an ideological mind—and, indeed, it is the ideological outlook of a society that speaks most clearly to the adolescent who is eager to be affirmed by his peers, and is ready to be confirmed by rituals, creeds, and programs which at the same time define what is evil, uncanny, and inimical.

The sixth stage is intimacy versus isolation. This corresponds to Freud's final stage of genital relations, in which he emphasised the importance of sexual gratification involving sexual intercourse leading to orgasm, freed from substantial interference by pregenital sexuality. Thus—although Freud thought that much love play is based on traces of the earlier oral stage (e.g. kissing), of oral aggression (e.g. teasing), and of the anal stage (e.g. anal gratification), and that the presence of elements of these things in love play is quite consistent with full genitality—when such interfering factors as guilt from the Oedipal stage prevent satisfactory genital relations, there is a failure of gratification.

However, Erikson's emphasis is on Freud's famous formula for adult normality; the normal adult should be able "to love and to work". To stress genital relations alone, Erikson thinks, is to leave out half of what Freud thought was important. To put this another way, an adult may be able to achieve a good sex life, but if they cannot earn a living, or otherwise provide for their physical and social needs, they are going to be in considerable difficulties, in most cases, in adapting to the demands of life. The young adult, if they have successfully emerged from the previous stage, has chosen a career or work role, but they still have to balance a career and its demand for competitive striving with sexual and emotional intimacy. The main danger here is that the two areas of, on the one hand, love and family and, on the other, career and work, become confused and the competition and assertion needed at work interfere with the love and intimacy of home.

The failure to maintain this balance can lead either to inability to enter one or both the roles of family/intimacy and work, or to their later breakdown. However, Erikson's formulation gives more emphasis to the failure of intimate than of work relations, as he sees the main danger in this period as being that of isolation from intimate relations, rather than of isolation from work relations. The separation of adult areas of duty is linked with the formation of an adult ethical sense, which specifies what duties are required in the various spheres of life in which adults engage. Thus there are important differences between the ethical outlooks required at home and at work in Western societies, with the former stressing the rightness of solidarity and affection, and the latter that of assertiveness and competition.

The seventh stage is generativity versus stagnation. Generativity is primarily concern with establishing and guiding the next generation. According to Erikson (1950) this begins from the expansion of ego-interests that results from libidinal investment in the person's own children. This is linked to "belief in the species", to which the children are seen as a new and valuable addition. Unless this widening of concerns is established, the danger is of stagnation and regression to earlier stages of development.

Erikson's seventh stage restores to his account something that we noted in Freud and missed in Erikson's earlier stages, namely the widening of libidinal investments to include people other than the individual, their family, and their adolescent love choices. Erikson is unusual, and rather controversial, in seeing this broadening of libidinal investments as taking place primarily in adulthood. Freud (1922) mentions schools as one kind of human group in which such broadening of investments occurs, and he implies that libido is already quite widely distributed in the teens. It seems strange for Erikson to imply that we must wait until adulthood to find the expansion Freud and others ascribe to the earlier period.

The seventh stage is also linked to a certain kind of ethical outlook, which is that of "generative succession", particularly the outlook of institutions like the family and educational establishments, that are concerned with the rearing of the next generation. Conscious that there are institutions in most societies that appear on the surface to have ethical outlooks that are indifferent to, or even hostile to, the care of the young, Erikson discusses monasticism. Here we have a movement, found in many disparate societies, that usually teaches its adherents that the production of children, and the resulting involvement in a family, are a barrier to spiritual advancement. However, Erikson explains that monasticism usually encourages care for the creatures of the world, including human beings, and that this constitutes a version of the ethics of generative succession. It is notable that the outlook of military institutions is not discussed; it would be more difficult to relate the ethics of generative succession to some versions of the military outlook. Although he had earlier discussed the assertiveness and aggression found at work in the sixth stage, the role of these motives in the outlooks that develop in the seventh is neglected; however they will surely still be present.

Erikson's interpretation of adult ethical systems of belief, as examples of the outlook of generative succession, is a good example of the role of interpretation in his thinking. Thus everyone knows that many adult ethical systems place considerable emphasis on some kind of care for human interests and welfare. Erikson's theory suggests that the main route to the formation of such concern is through the attachment that people have to their children. Concern for the welfare of others is renamed concern for "generative succession". The new name encourages us to think that there is a particular, and even exclusive, connection between care for children and concern for people in general, although little evidence for this is given.

We can also note in Erikson's view of adult ethics a reflection of his general tendency to stress the Freudian sexual libido and to shy away from the Freudian aggressive or death instincts. Thus ethics of love and caring are emphasised, but Freud's own insistence on the dark side of adult ethics, in our ability to justify and enjoy war and aggression, are downplayed.

The final, eighth, stage is ego integrity versus despair. This is the stage of middle age and has considerable similarities with what other writers term the midlife crisis. The positive achievement of this stage is the acceptance of one's own life cycle, as a worthwhile contribution to the continuation of one's culture. The negative possibility is that one's own life will be seen as a failure, and this will lead to fear of death and dissatisfaction with life.

In conclusion, Erikson's theory successfully fills out some of the lacunae in Freud's writings. However, his view of adult ethics seems in some ways less profound than that of Freud, who showed greater awareness of the role of aggression in morality and moralising than

Erikson. We also miss the account of the development of the ego ideal, which was important to Freud and the ego psychologists.

CONCLUSIONS

The Freudian view of the development of moral reasoning has had greater impact in recent years on general psychological discussion than on formal empirical studies in the area. Studies rarely adopt this as their point of departure, although both Sayers (1987) and Kitwood (1990) have suggested a revival of interest in this kind of study is overdue. Discussion of moral development and reasoning by psychoanalysts using case studies and general clinical experience continues in specialised journals (e.g. Coles, 1981; Deigh, 1984; Finkelstein, 1991; Kaufman, 1983; Marcus & Wineman, 1985). The psychoanalytic view of moral development also continues to draw attention from philosophers (e.g. Wallwork, 1991).

Much of the current interest in the psychoanalytic view of moral development comes from feminists, who are more interested in general cultural and political comment than in formal empirical studies (Chodorov, 1978, 1989; Feldstein & Roof, 1989; Grosz, 1989, 1990; Iragaray, 1985; Kofman, 1985; Mitchell, 1974; Mitchell & Rose, 1982; Slipp, 1993; Whitford, 1991). Most feminists have felt the need to correct Freud's male bias with more attention to female development, and a less jaundiced view of female moral capacities than that offered by Freud.

To expand on what was said earlier about this, Freud felt that libidinal investment in fellow members of social groups played a lesser role, and narcissism a correspondingly greater role, in the moral psychology of females, compared to males (Freud, 1922). He also argued that in the female Oedipal conflict there is less fear of castration, as the girl feels herself already castrated, and correspondingly greater fear of loss of love. This weakens the strictness of the internal parent that the girl introjects through identification, and thus weakens the conscience and general moral sense of women (Freud, 1925).

The process of revising these aspects of Freud's view of female psychology began relatively early in the history of psychoanalysis, with the work of Horney (1924, 1926), and has been continued by more recent authors. It will not be covered in detail here, as the focus in this book is mainly on formal, especially interview, studies of moral reasoning, and the psychoanalytic tradition has not focused on studies of this kind. The approach to interview studies, which will be advocated in later chapters, suggests that differences in the moral reasoning of males and females that can be reliably evidenced by interview and questionnaire studies tend to be in the content of beliefs rather than in the method of justifying such beliefs. This raises a number of explanatory issues addressed in Chapter 8.

It is worth adding that neither interview nor questionnaire studies appear to support Freud's idea that women are less afflicted by pangs of conscience, or less conventionally moral, than men. They do, however, offer some support for other Freudian ideas, especially the early origin of the notion of reciprocity in moral exchange.

CHAPTER THREE

Ego psychology

Today, the contributions of ego psychology are often seen as the main alternative to the approach to the development of moral reasoning suggested by Kohlberg, particularly the work of Loevinger (1970, 1976, 1983, 1993) and Haan (1977, 1986, 1991). Kohlberg (1984) suggests that Loevinger is in fact talking about ego development, rather than moral reasoning, in her writings; but as they clearly deal with material that by definition comes within the scope of moral reasoning, at least as defined in the broader sense, and as Loevinger herself views them in this way, they will be treated as belonging to the topic here.

Ego psychology was a school that originally developed in the United States in the 1920s and 1930s as a revisionist movement within Freudian psychoanalysis, particularly under the inspiration of the writings of Karen Horney. The main tenets of the school were: that motives, particularly the aggressive motives, have weaker roots in our biological makeup than Freud thought; that socially formed motives, as distinct from biological instincts, are more important than Freud thought; and that the ego is more powerful and the id weaker than Freud thought. Orthodox Freudians and others have alleged that the main reason for this change in emphasis was unwillingness to offend the prejudices of American public opinion (Gay, 1988; Hale, 1971). Although this way of viewing the problem certainly succeeds in presenting Freudian theory in an attractively romantic light, it does beg the question of whether or not American public opinion was right. This need not detain us unduly here, as my main aim at this point will be to describe rather than evaluate the views of the ego psychologists.

GARDNER AND LOIS MURPHY

Murphy, Murphy, and Newcomb (1937), in a massive synthesis of research in social psychology that adopts a predominantly developmental perspective, argue that development takes place in two important ways: the development of values, and the development of the self. Values are fixations that set us to try to gain objects that meet needs. Needs, such as hunger and thirst, are biologically given, but the objects that we learn to satisfy them with are not. The baby learns that certain kinds of food and drink will satisfy its hunger and thirst. Although this might seem to lead to a theory that is just as biological as that of Freud, one of the biological needs stressed by the Murphys is the need for arousal, which can be satisfied by an almost infinite variety of objects and activities, many of which are socially determined. Arousal can be produced by any activity that encourages the person to be active, whether mentally or physically. Thus although needs are biological in the Murphys' theory, the objects to which they are directed and the values that arise in relation to objects are frequently not.

Much of the fixation of values in the child comes about through conditioning. The association between the use of an object and the sight and feel of the object give it value, and this value comes to be fixed in it. One particularly important kind of value is that which is held towards human beings, either towards the child's own self or towards other people. The learning of values of this kind is conditioned by a particularly powerful mechanism, which the authors call primitive identification. This is close to the eighteenth- and nineteenth-century utilitarians' concept of sympathy. Thus Murphy et al. (1937, p.209) state:

> Just as the disgust or mirth of the indifferent chimpanzee sends a wild contagion of mirth or disgust through the group which has not seen the original cause of the emotion, so the child assimilates the feelings of those about him by a process which, on its objective side, is the circular response, but which has its all-important subjective aspect in the fact of primitive identification.

The circular response referred to here is the tendency for exciting or arousing actions to be repeated in order to re-experience the excitement they produce, a term also used by Piaget (1952, original French publication 1936) in a similar sense.

One of the results of primitive identification, or contagion of emotions, is that, if other people react to the child with positive emotions, the child catches these emotions back and thus acquires a positive view of itself through conditioning. This can often result in a cycle of contagious emotion, with the child looking happy, the adult catching the positive emotion back from the child, and then further reinforcing the child's own positive state with positive feelings. The corresponding negative cycle is unfortunately also often seen. Attitudes towards others are also caught in this way: thus, if the child meets a relative that the mother doesn't like in the mother's presence, they will catch the negative emotion towards this relative from the mother.

The importance that the Murphys attach to sympathy, or primitive identification, means that they accord socially acquired motives considerably more prominence than did Freud, as the value of objects and thus their motivational significance will be caught from others. This has particular application to the development of aggression, a topic on which their views differ significantly from those of Freud.

In the first year of life, the child experiences an enormous amount of admiration and a generally permissive attitude in disciplinary matters, at least in Western societies. These reactions are produced by the novelty of the baby for the parents, by its inability to be a nuisance by moving around, and by its obvious helplessness. These reactions from others produce the infant's inflated view of its worth, power, and importance by the contagion of emotions.

From around 1 year of age the child is able to move about, and this produces a change in parental attitude, which becomes more controlling and less positive. This provokes conflict with the child, whose inflated ego is now devalued by repeated experiences of punishment, restraint, and contagion from negative emotional reactions by the parents. Thus the aggression often seen during the "terrible twos" is not, as Freud would have it, a result of Oedipal strivings or of a reservoir of aggressive instinctual energy, but rather of changes in the reactions of the parents and in the infant's capacity for locomotion and manipulation of objects.

This conflict abates somewhat after 3 years, but a new one is brewing, as the child is ready to extend its activities and experience, but is usually prevented by modern living conditions, such as danger from cars and strangers, from doing so. This means that adult interference and negative emotional reactions continue, producing simmering aggression and hostility in the child, up until the time it goes to school at around the age of 5 years.

From 5 to about 12 years this is followed by ambivalence towards adults. The first part of this period is marked by teasing and outbreaks of sadism, which are often outlets for anger created by the new and unwelcome restrictions imposed by the school. In the second part of the period, gangs appear that have a cooperative attitude within the group, but whose members often show a hostile or sadistic attitude towards other children, adults, or society at large. These tendencies are attributed in part to the displacement and projection of anger, which is in reality directed against the parents.

The period from 12 to 20 years is termed one of overt rebellion, in which the smouldering and concealed hostility to adults comes out into the open. The adolescent's developing social abilities and rising social status provide the courage to openly defy and denounce adult authority, often leading to a sense of moral and intellectual superiority towards adults. These feelings are reinforced by contagion from the peer group, with whom the adolescent now spends most time.

Finally, after the age of 20 there is an assumption of the attitudes to authority and aggression prescribed by adult society and its various institutions, such as those of work and marriage. The content of these will depend on the culture into which the adolescent has been inducted.

A further cross-cultural element is introduced by the authors' comments on the supposed cultural universality of aggression and conflict with the parents, in childhood and adolescence. They mention favourably Margaret Mead's (1929) claim that in some non-Western cultures these sources of conflict are reduced. They point to the fact that Western society demands a particularly high level of restraint on young children by their parents, and adults generally, because: they must be protected from things like cars and strangers; must not use the many chaos-producing devices of the average Western household to destroy its high degree of order and cleanliness; and must go to school to engage in demanding and constraining activities. Although the quality of Mead's fieldwork and many of her conclusions have come under sustained criticism in recent years (see especially Freeman, 1984), there can be little doubt that these things do produce a heightened degree of frustration and annoyance for Western children. Mead may have exaggerated the Utopian nature of childhood in some tribal societies, but her view that childhood in Western societies involves greater constraint than that in the less constrained of tribal societies is almost undeniable.

In orthodox Freudian theory a crucial experience for the formation of the moral personality is the Oedipal conflict, as this internalises certain irrational attitudes to authority and moral constraint, especially the exaggerated guilt that results from the fantasy of parent-murder. The Murphys also see the formation of a moral personality as partly a process of activating irrational defences, though they place less emphasis on the Oedipal conflict. Thus the hostility to outgroups that begins in childhood and persists into adulthood, involves the displacement and projection of hostility away from the parents, and other annoying authority figures who can strike back, onto weak outgroups who cannot. Such projection is often accompanied by moral rationalisations and the demonisation of outgroups.

Although this idea was later to achieve a particularly influential form in Adorno et al.'s book *The authoritarian personality* (1950), it was clearly presented by Freud in *Group psychology and the analysis of the ego* (1922) and was extensively deployed by another relatively orthodox Freudian, Wilhelm Reich, in his book *The mass psychology of fascism* (1933). However, for Freud, Adorno, and Reich, the development of authoritarianism is bound up with the resolution of the Oedipus complex, with the aggression involved originating in sexual rivalry. For the Murphys, it functions to channel displaced aggression, originating in the more mundane struggle between the child and its parents, over their denial of the child's desire to explore and manipulate the environment.

Development consists not only of learning to cope with aggression and hostility, but also of positive identification and friendship. Once the infant has formed a definite idea of a self over and against other selves, identification with the experience of others begins almost at once. This is initially based on the mechanism of primitive identification. Freud's psychoanalytic identification, in its dominant form, is a defensive reaction to fear of aggression by another person; it may also be a defence against fear of the loss of a love object. The Murphys, by contrast, think that the further development of identification is based on the motivational mechanism of "adience", taken from Holt (1931).

The principle of adience states that "all stimulation will cause the organism to do things which will give it more of the stimulus" (Holt, 1931, p.102). This is closely connected with circular reactions, but whereas the idea of a circular reaction is a purely descriptive one, that of adience is designed to explain why circular reactions occur. This explanation is effected through the suggestion that "Once thoroughly aroused, the individual maintains his orientation to that which arouses him, and does things which will bring him more stimulation of the same sort" (*ibid.*). This is in effect an early, undeveloped version of the main principle of arousal theory, that was later popularised by Hebb (1949) and Berlyne (1960). This states that moderate arousal, which consists of arousal of the central nervous system, however achieved, is inherently rewarding and will be sought for its own sake. This is distinct from the main Freudian motivational principle, which is that arousal, usually termed tension, is unpleasant and its relief gives pleasure. Later versions of arousal theory encompassed this Freudian view as a special case, as they held that moderate arousal is rewarding, but over-arousal is aversive. Both Holt (1931) and the Murphys in 1937 held what is in effect the polar opposite of the Freudian principle, in assuming that all arousal is rewarding, and failing to note the undoubted truth that excessive excitement or arousal is often unpleasant and avoided.

Early identification occurs through the infant's inability to distinguish its own self from that of others. This means that the infant identifies with those around it, especially the mother, spontaneously, not as a result of a defence mechanism. This identification-through-confusion leads the child to copy the behaviour and feelings of others. Because a prime source of reward comes from doing things that are arousing and then repeating them, actions and emotions that are imitated because of primitive identification are then repeated, as their initial enactment is arousing and thus rewarding. This leads to a positive valuation of the person imitated and the tendency to imitate them in future, which is termed developed as distinct from primitive identification.

Early identification with the mother means that early interests tend to tilt towards the feminine, whatever the sex of the infant. Perhaps in conscious reaction against Freudian penis envy, Murphy et al. claim that womb envy among boys is more common than penis envy among girls. This is because both sexes desire to copy the baby-making activities of the mother (Murphy et al., p.510). Although early identification is particularly strong, due to the inability of the infant to separate its own ego from those of others, both primitive and developed identification remain important throughout life. Thus behaviour is copied from the parents, the school, and the media.

Identification also develops from love and admiration for an individual into identification with the roles offered by social groups. The child tries to find roles at school, and in the peer group, that will be acceptable to the group and also fulfil its needs. To do this, it must find a balance between aggression and cooperation.

The child will at first take its moral standards from the parents, as they condition it through reward, punishment, and the contagion of social emotion; later, it must adapt to the moral standards of the peer group and the school. In considering how this occurs, the authors first turn to the work of Piaget (1932) on the development of moral reasoning. Although they find this revealing, they consider that studies by Lerner (1937a, b) have thrown new light on Piaget's conclusions. Piaget's work is discussed in detail in the next chapter, and for the moment we need only note that he thought that young children's moral reasoning, up to the age of 11 years, is dominated first by egocentrism and then by unilateral respect for parental and adult authority. This changes to a morality of mutual cooperation, respect, and agreement among equals, patterned on the cooperation and respect found within the peer group, during early adolescence.

The Murphys argue, using findings from both Piaget and Lerner, that the idea of a generalised moral attitude and method of reasoning, found in Piaget's concepts of early egocentrism (self-centredness) and heteronomy (domination by the moral influence of others), is inappropriate for young children. The young child, they argue, is sociocentric, that is to say it adopts the moral standards of whatever group it happens to be in at a given time. As development proceeds, the limited range of identifications found in younger children broadens. Ultimately, this wider range of moralities and identifications, with which the adolescent must cope, leads to an attempt to build a consistent moral code that is not dependent on the surrounding environment, but is felt as belonging to the self and is applied to the varying social situations encountered.

Infants and preschool children are capable of considerable sympathy with the pleasures and sufferings of others, they argue. Young children also learn the positive identifications and objects of fear and hatred of the groups to which they belong. One informal, but touching, argument, given against the idea that the young child is either entirely heteronomous or entirely egocentric in its moral attitudes, is that young children will often take the side of insects, against adults who want to exterminate them. This cannot be based on things heard from adults, as, at least in 1937, adults were almost all against insects; nor is it straightforwardly in the child's interests. This attitude is rather, they think, based on the ability of the young child to take the point of view of the insects, and feel that they do not like being exterminated. This is a good example of the operation of primitive identification or sympathy.

More formal evidence for sociocentrism comes from a study in which Lerner (1937b) questioned children about where more lies are told: in the child's own city, in another city, in the child's own school, or in another school. Children younger than 11 years tend to give replies that favour their own social group, rather than that of others. Older children give more "relativistic" replies, that take account of the particular kinds of lies and situations involved, and show a reduced tendency to favour the child's own group.

It is argued that Piaget's (1932) claim, that children in the period 7–11 years tend to give replies that show they take their morality from adults or older children, is telling us only part of the truth about the development of moral reasoning, which is that one source of the young child's moral reasoning is parents and older children. This, however, leaves out the importance of identification with the peer group and other social groups, as well as of personal experience. Although this point is relatively undeveloped in their text, and even in Lerner (1937a, b), it is an important one, as one of the most worrying things about the analyses of interview data conducted by Piaget (1932) is his tendency to select aspects of his transcripts that suit his theory, and reject the rest. One of the virtues of the less interpretive and selective methods of interview analysis described in the second part of this book, is that they enable us to see whether allegations like that made by Murphy et al. (1937), and later elaborated by Murphy (1947), about the theoretically loaded methods of analysis practised by Piaget, have any substance to them. In this particular case, the answer is that they do, as young children frequently rely on their own opinions and those of equals, as well as those of adults.

The process that leads from submission to the external moral demands and promptings of particular groups, to the dominance of internal standards, occurs through the development of the ego. Freud has already introduced us to the idea that through narcissism the ego ideal can become a source of gratification. True to their general theoretical outlook, the Murphys give a somewhat greater role to conditioning in this process than did Freud. As the ego, in the shape of the self-image, is the source of many satisfactions, so by association it comes to be considered as an object of value itself. External objects of positive value may or may not be attainable, but our own self, on the contrary, is always with us and always attainable. The issue is not whether it can be attained, but rather whether it is worth having. Am I a good son or daughter, a good student, or good friend? Can I admire myself for these positive qualities, which include a large moral component, or do I have to live all the time with a negative, degraded view of myself?

The nature of the highly desirable self is altered during development by two forces. The first is the influence of travel and the media, in promoting more general ideals of self-respect, particularly that of being a good citizen of one's country. Discussions of general moral principles with others also offer the ideal of being a good person, in an abstract sense, that is, someone who abides by general moral principles.

Gratifications obtained from the ego ideal, including those obtained by admiring one's own highly moral qualities, however imaginary these may be, are particularly influenced by fantasy. For although it is possible to fantasise that we possess highly desirable objects in the external world, it is in many ways easier to believe fantasies about what we are, as they are less amenable to reality testing. Adolescents are particularly prone to this kind of self-gratification, often involving an element of self-delusion. They fantasise a glorious future, that may or may not come to pass. In extreme cases of narcissistic personality disorder, the person turns away entirely from attempts to gain satisfaction from the outside world to fantasies about the ideal self. This often, particularly in adolescence, incorporates a moral ideal associated with religious or political convictions.

In his 1947 book *Personality*, Gardner Murphy elaborates the same basic theory of development as in the earlier book. Somewhat more attention is given, however, to competing views of the development of moral reasoning. On the one hand, we are offered Lerner's adaptation of Piaget, as in the earlier book, but this is now joined by two alternative views. The first is that of Westermarck (1939), who identified three stages in moral development. In the first, actions are judged by whether they aid or injure the child. Next, through a process of generalisation, classes of actions or people are identified that may aid or injure the social group to which the child belongs. Finally, the quality of being beneficial or injurious to people in general is abstracted, and this leads to abstract conceptions of morality. We are also recommended to consider the Freudian view of moral development.

In attempting to reconcile these three views, Murphy argues (1947, p.388) that it is mistaken to try to select one as the best: "... within the same individual in a stress situation the Piaget type, the Westermarck type and the Freudian type of attitudes appear furtively and fluidly as he looks to anchors to which to secure the need to defend himself". Although, as in the earlier book, the implications of this are not thoroughly worked out, he once again cautions us against the tendency to work solely within one theoretical tradition, a warning that is, if anything, even more relevant now than when it was first given.

In their later writings, Murphy and Murphy incorporated the more recent approach to arousal theory of Hebb (1949), Harlow (1953) and Berlyne (1960) into their theory (Murphy & Murphy, 1966; Murphy, 1968). In other respects, their overall approach to the development of moral reasoning remained relatively unchanged (Murphy & Kovach, 1972, p.411). Although the general idea of reducing the role of sexual instincts and increasing that of arousal-based motivation has been continued within ego psychology by other writers such as Kohut (1971, 1977, 1978–91), they have not concentrated on the development of moral reasoning, and will not be covered here.

HARRY STACK SULLIVAN

Sullivan was the founder of a distinct strand of ego psychology, which led to the work of Loevinger, among other notable psychologists. Sullivan's (1953) view of human nature emphasises two aspects of motivation: euphoria and tension. Euphoria is defined as a state of utter well-being, in which there is a complete absence of tension, as in deep sleep. Tension is the opposite, its most extreme manifestation being terror. Sullivan's view of motivation is thus closer to Freud than to the Murphys and other arousal theorists, in that the most pleasant state, and the one that is most sought, is complete relaxation, rather than the moderate arousal of most later arousal theorists.

Unwanted tension is often induced by unsatisfied needs, such as those experienced in hunger, thirst, or sexual arousal. In the infant, the tension induced by the first two of these needs calls out a corresponding tension in the carer, and this leads to caring and nurturance, which are experienced by the infant as tenderness. Sullivan uses the term empathy to mean much the same as earlier writers had meant by sympathy. The empathy that produces these caring actions in the carer is something that the Murphys, like the utilitarians, had emphasised, though Freud had emphatically rejected it. The association of tenderness in the carer, with need-satisfaction in the infant, produces a derived need for tenderness in the infant.

Besides the tension arising from bodily needs, the infant also experiences unpleasant tension as a result of empathising with others who are themselves feeling anxiety, either on account of the infant or for some other reason. If the carer is anxious, the infant picks this up as a result of empathy and becomes anxious too. The absence of anxiety in the carer leads to interpersonal security.

The beginnings of self-esteem emerge in later infancy, when the carer begins to shape the infant's behaviour using the reward of offering tenderness, and the discouragement of showing anxiety, and thus producing this state in the infant. This leads the infant to form three preliminary versions of the self, which are three different kinds of feeling attached to its conception and experience of its own body. The "good-me" results from experiences of tenderness; the "bad-me" from those of moderate anxiety produced by empathy with anxiety in the carer; the "not-me" is a third area of the self normally only accessed in dreams or unusual states of consciousness, in which terrifying aspects of experience are projected onto an alternative self or doppelganger. This last results from states of terror, associated with real or fantasised situations of extreme physical danger.

The aim of the self-system is to maximise euphoric and pleasant experiences and thus the duration of the "good-me", and to minimise bad and unpleasant experiences and thus the duration of the "bad-me". The initial task of the self-system is to organise relations with the carer to ensure this. Much of this relationship is mediated by gestures and language. One of the results of language learning is that it encourages fusion of the "good-me" with the "bad-me" into a unified self-concept, as the infant learns that its own name, and personal pronouns applied to it, refer to a single entity. A similar process also occurs in "personification" of other people, as words like "mama" encourage a unified conception of the mother, replacing fractured images of the bad mother and the good mother.

The later course of ego development, and of moral reasoning, is seen in rather similar descriptive terms to those used by the Murphys, although we miss their encyclopaedic reference to the literature on descriptive aspects of development and the wealth of detail they include. There is somewhat more emphasis on the emergence of strong lustful feelings in adolescence, and the need to achieve satisfactory genital relationships to channel these. This is a natural reflection of Sullivan's tendency to take a more Freudian and biological view of motivation, emphasising the biological sex drive in adolescence, as against the Murphys' tendency to stress the nonsexual aspects of adolescent adjustment.

Sullivan (1953), in discussing late adolescence and adulthood, also emphasises the need for fully mature adults to develop intimacy with one or more people, often a spouse or partner. As this comes in a book that was printed from lectures given in 1946–47, it in some degree anticipates the idea of the adult stage of intimacy versus isolation suggested by Erikson (1950), though he too had been thinking about this issue for some time before that date.

In theoretical terms, the picture of social development drawn by Sullivan stresses the initial social bond with the mother or other carer, formed as a result of the physical care given to the infant, and the mother's or carer's satisfaction of its biological needs. In moral development, this leads in later infancy and early childhood to bonds with the immediate family circle, formed for rather similar reasons, and a tendency to wish to help those within this circle because of these bonds. At the same time, actions disapproved of by the family circle will be felt as wrong, because they lead to the anxiety that performing them will produce displeasure in family members.

Positive friendship bonds are later formed with members of the peer group. Although the basis for the helping and care involved in these is not discussed explicitly, it is a reasonable deduction from the general nature of the theory that these are a combination of Freudian mechanisms: namely, expected reciprocity in the gratification of needs, sublimated libido, and identification with group leaders, together with the influence of empathy or sympathy.

Sullivan's views provide a revealing contrast with those of Freud and the Murphys, as they offer a third mix of explanatory interpretations for very similar descriptive trends in moral development. The same basic phenomena are explained, but this time in terms that are midway between the largely biological view of Freud and the substantial social element introduced by the Murphys' emphasis on sympathy. Sullivan appeals to sympathy, but to a lesser extent than the Murphys.

JANE LOEVINGER

Loevinger (1970, 1976, 1983, 1993) bases her work on the development of moral reasoning jointly on the foundations she believes were laid by Piaget (1932) and Sullivan (1953). Her aims are to describe a sequence of stages in ego development consistent with the views of Sullivan, and to devise a method of assessing these in children and adults. She explicitly states that, for her, the study of ego development, and that of the development of moral reasoning, have such a large degree of overlap that the two cannot be separated. She distinguishes six stages in ego development.

In the first stage, the infant constructs a stable world of objects and distinguishes its own self from the surrounding world. In the second stage, it learns to use the word "No" to assert itself. The infant is still impulsive, and its impulses are only controlled by reward and punishment from the caregivers, and the natural consequences of actions. It sees punishment as retaliatory and immanent in people and things. Good people are those who help the infant; bad people are those who don't help it, or mean it harm.

The third stage is that of self-protection. The tendency to refer the goodness or badness of actions to their consequences for the pleasure and welfare of the self is still prominent. This is linked to the notion of life as a zero-sum game in which anything I gain is something you lose, and there is little understanding that in many situations cooperation can lead both people to win. There is greater understanding of other people's motives, and how to manipulate them through understanding their motives, than in the previous stage. The child understands the notions of moral blame or fault, but tends to assign these to other people, or factors beyond its control, on every possible occasion. This lasts from late infancy until the time of first school.

During the first years at school, the child becomes socialised into the peer group and learns the attitude of conformity typical of the fourth stage. It first conforms with authority and then with its peers. There is a right way for people who occupy given social roles, like boys and girls, teachers and students, to do things, and social roles are rigidly stereotyped. Rules are accepted because they are prescribed by groups as part of socially accepted codes of behaviour; social acceptability is highly prized and social disapproval much feared. Many adults have failed to progress beyond this stage.

The fifth stage is marked by conscientiousness, which begins to develop in some individuals during early adolescence, but is not found in a majority until the first two years of college (18–19 years). Guilt is chiefly felt when the person has hurt someone else, rather than when they have broken a moral rule. Moral rules have exceptions and hold only in certain situations, while long-term goals and moral ideals become important, and what ought to be is clearly separated from what is. The moral worth of individuals is often interpreted in terms of their long-term psychological development. Thinking becomes more reflective and involves self-awareness and self-criticism. It is realised that in many situations there is no absolute right or wrong, but rather shades of grey, and that it is necessary to strike a balance between the beneficial and the harmful results of actions. Moral issues are separated from conventional rules and aesthetic preferences, and moral achievement is assessed by the extent to which one lives up to one's own inner moral standards, rather than being primarily a matter of what is socially approved.

The sixth stage is that of moral autonomy. This is marked by the awareness that even when the individual has become financially and physically independent of their parents, they remain emotionally dependent. The intense moralism that is often involved in living up to the internal moral standards that are important at the previous stage, is tempered by the realisation that it is difficult to get along in relationships with others if you expect too much from them. During the transition to the autonomous stage, inner conflicts of motivation are often seen as the responsibility of the outside world. Thus, a woman may believe that the conflict she feels, as a result of conflicting demands made on her by her children, could be overcome, if only outside agencies, such as social workers or counsellors, would step in and solve the problem for her. In the fully autonomous stage, the individual realises that conflict is inherent in the human condition, and takes responsibility for solving such conflicts for himself or herself, rather than projecting blame for them onto the outside world. It is also recognised that not all conflicts are soluble. Loevinger estimates that no more than 1% of any social group will succeed in achieving this final stage, in a fully resolved form.

The main instrument used for measuring this stage sequence is the Washington University Sentence Completion Test. This consists of sentence stems that the individual is asked to complete. The instructions are open-ended, the main ones being "You see that these are incomplete sentences. Please finish each one." The manual for form 9-62 (a form for women) is the only detailed description of the scoring method included in Loevinger (1970), which is her main publication on detailed scoring methods, but this is extremely detailed and explicit. Examples of sentence stems offered in this form are: 1. Raising a family ... ; 2. Most men think that women ... ; 3. When they avoided me ... ; 4. If my mother ...; 32. If I can't get what I want ... ; 33. Usually she felt that sex ... ; 34. For a woman a career is ... ; 35. My conscience bothers me if ... ; 36. A woman should always ... .

The purpose of these stems is to offer an opportunity for the subject to project their most prominent methods of dealing with social interactions into their replies. The scoring technique aims to classify the manifest meaning of the reply given into categories corresponding to the stages already described, rather than to classify either the surface details of wording or interpretations of underlying meaning. Thus, every stage comprises certain kinds of reply that are assigned to the stage, which for convenience can be called the descriptive categories underlying it. In this, it differs markedly from the aims of the methods used by Kohlberg, which interpret underlying meaning. In this respect, the aims of the scoring methods of Loevinger are close to the weakly interpretive methods of describing interview results covered in Part 2, although they are used to assess stem completions and not interviews. However, as we shall see, there is one significant difference; findings are reported in terms of stages, rather than in terms of the descriptive categories used to assign replies to stages. This is a disadvantage of the method, as it means that information about the descriptive categories is lost. The implications of this are discussed in Chapter 9.

Loevinger's stems are intended to assess the individual's predominant methods of dealing with social interactions generally, rather than just their predominant methods of dealing with situations involving moral issues, even in the broadest meaning of the term. Thus some of the stems listed earlier invite projections about moral issues in a broad sense, particularly 35 and 36. The others could all result in projections about moral issues, but they could also result in projections about other aspects of social adaptation. Thus a woman who gives, in response to "Most men think that women ... ", the reply "are wonderful" is giving a perfectly sensible reply, just as is one who says "are unbearable", but these replies are only indirectly moral. This is reflected in the descriptions of the six stages, which describe both moral development and the wider development of ego functioning. From the standpoint of Loevinger's theory this is not just desirable, but essential, as moral development is seen, as with Freud and the other ego theorists, as an integral part of the development of the personality as a whole. However, from the standpoint of someone like Kohlberg, who wants to describe moral development separately, before relating it to that of other aspects of the personality, this tactic would be questionable.

Loevinger (1979, 1983, 1985a, 1985b, 1987, 1993) has reviewed evidence about her theory of stages in ego development derived from studies using her instruments. As the instruments have undergone a continuous process of development over the years there is some problem in comparing findings from the various versions, but as she remarks in her 1970 book, this is an inevitable hazard for any instrument that undergoes improvement, as a result of feedback from earlier findings.

The internal and inter-rater reliabilities of the instruments were found to be satisfactory. Cross-sectional studies during early and mid-adolescence have shown that there are consistent gains in mean stage scores with age over this period. However, it is not a necessary deduction from the theory that gains in stage scores will always take place as a result of increasing age. True to the Freudian roots of her theory, she conjectures that, in both individuals and groups, regression to an earlier stage may be seen. Not only has regression been observed in longitudinal studies of individuals, but among college students it is also sometimes found in the mean level of groups. Thus Loevinger (1985a) reported a slight, but persistent, lowering of average level of ego development in a longitudinal study of females during their stay at an American liberal arts university in the 1970s, although this only acted to eliminate their previous superiority to males. Such findings were not encountered at a technological institute with students of a similar age. Such regressions are a result of the stresses of development in late adolescence, whose features are considered in more detail later in this chapter in connection with the work of Perry (1970).

It could be objected that, by allowing for stage regression to occur, theories like those of Loevinger and Perry become untestable, as it does not matter whether stage scores increase or decrease with age: the theory will still be verified. However, this flies in the face of the almost universally acknowledged fact that regression in emotional development does occur quite frequently in children. It is very likely that this will be accompanied by regression in moral reasoning, as conceived by ego psychologists. In addition, the tendency for there to be a generally orderly advance in stage scores during childhood and early- and mid-adolescence, even though we can allow for some regressions, presents us with a definite expectation about the form of development that can be tested. This prediction has been verified. Given the difficulty of achieving further advance in development during late adolescence and adulthood suggested by the theory, it is also predictable that regression will be more common in these periods, as developmental achievements are more fragile. Such regression is sometimes observed to occur (Loevinger, 1985a). Thus, although existing studies only provide a partial confirmation of expectations from Loevinger's theory, findings so far do support the theory. It also seems to derive some confirmation from everyday experience and clinical practice.

One weakness of Loevinger's work, which has already been mentioned, is the practice of reporting results in terms of stages rather than raw descriptive categories. This makes it hard to know whether the age trends in the frequency of the descriptive categories support the theory in the way that trends in stage scores do. Thus, it is possible that age trends for some categories do not follow those predicted for the stages to which they belong, although it is a prediction of the theory that they should do so. Another difficulty is that her method concentrates on stem completion, rather than interview findings, or the naturalistic study of moral discourse. This is a weakness, as interviews in particular offer a more flexible and in-depth method of investigating moral reasoning. For these reasons, interviews are considered by most students of the field to be a more central method of investigation than stem completion. Interviews are able to indicate the degree of integration in a person's reasoning, which stem completion cannot do, as it asks for only a single response to each stem. Stem completion also constrains replies to those particular aspects of a topic suggested by the stem, whereas interviews are less constraining. The naturalistic study of moral discourse also has these advantages over the stem completion method.

This second weakness is somewhat compounded by the lack of any satisfactory explanation of why her findings from stem completion studies, and those from investigations using interviews, have produced such different pictures. Loevinger (1987) has made a full-scale attempt to provide such an explanation, but as we shall see in Chapter 6 this contains insuperable difficulties. Some of the work presented in Parts 2 and 3 throws light on the reasons that findings from the two methods have been so divergent.

W.G. PERRY

Perry's work is most widely known through the single study described in Perry (1970), but, as this is one of the best-known studies in the ego psychology tradition, it is well worth consideration. Perry takes a more eclectic theoretical view of ego psychology than Loevinger, and he is also somewhat less explicit about his theoretical assumptions.

Perry's study involved interviewing 31 Harvard undergraduates at the end of each of their four years at the university for one hour, beginning from 1954. Interviewees were approached in a recruiting letter that stated the investigators' interest in how the student's year had gone and how they felt about it. The main interview instruction was "Why don't you start with whatever stands out for you about the year." Although the interview was mainly sustained by nondirective prompting from the interviewer, occasional further questions of a more substantive nature, on the general topic already indicated, were used.

Comments on the techniques of scoring interviews used will be given more appropriately in Chapter 8; this discussion will provide a short digest of conclusions from the study. The investigator identified nine positions that interviewees adopted, on the nature and sources of the knowledge they acquired in their studies, and on the nature and sources of morality and values. Opinions on epistemological and moral issues were claimed to be closely linked and were found to be roughly sequential, in the sense to be outlined shortly. They were grouped into three overall levels, each containing three positions, as follows.

The first level involves the notion that there are absolute standards of knowledge and value. Position 1: Right answers to all questions concerning knowledge exist that are known to authority. Knowledge and goodness are absolute, and are to be attained by hard work and obedience. Position 2: It is perceived that there is more diversity of opinion among adults and authorities, than can be accounted for by the first view. This is explained by incompetence on the part of authorities, or on the view that authorities have declined to give the right answer, although it exists, so that students can discover it for themselves. Position 3: The discrepancies noted in the previous position are now accounted for on the grounds that in some areas authorities have not yet discovered the right answers, but it is thought that they will be found eventually.

The second level involves the idea that all knowledge and values are relative. Position 4: (a) Legitimate uncertainty is extensive in designated areas (e.g. artistic taste, sexual morality), although in other areas (e.g. science) authority knows what is right and best; (b) to this may be added the notion that authority only appears to know what is right, in its designated realms, because this serves its interests. Position 5: All knowledge and values are relative to the context and interests of the participants, and there is no such thing as a right answer or an absolute moral code. Position 6: Complete relativism is felt to be unsatisfactory, and the person sees the need for a personal commitment to beliefs and values, as distinct from unquestioning belief in their certainty, although such commitment is not yet made.

The third level involves personal commitment to beliefs and values. Position 7: There is personal commitment in some area. Position 8: Exploration of the implications of the commitment that has been made, including the subjective and stylistic implications of responsibility.

Position 9: The affirmation of identity among multiple responsibilities, and awareness of the developmental nature of commitment to this identity, which now encompasses most or all, as distinct from one or a few, areas of life and activity.

Interviewees generally showed forward movement through the positions over time, though there were many instances of marking time or regression. Progress through the sequence is pictured as a struggle to overcome the contradictions experienced, as a result of the conflicts between the ego and the external world and within the ego itself. The main reason for claiming that the positions represent a developmental progression, is that later ones depend on integrating knowledge and outlooks contained in earlier ones. The inter-rater reliability of the scoring method was found to be excellent.

Some students were found to regress in their development through this sequence, as they found the process of assuming personal responsibility for their views too painful, preferring to return to the more comfortable reliance on authority of the initial positions. Perry also came to the interesting conclusion that some students operated defence mechanisms other than regression to escape from the difficulties of development. Such escape took two main forms; dissociation and encapsulation. In the former, the person defends against intellectual and value conflicts by becoming detached, both emotionally and intellectually, thus denying that such conflicts impinge on them. In the latter, the various activities that the student engages in, such as different kinds of study, are encapsulated or compartmentalised and sealed off from questions of value. This is very similar to the stance of the "course negotiating" student, familiar from studies of learning and study styles, who is prepared to appear to be whatever the lecturer or teacher wants, without having any personal commitment to the outlook espoused by the teacher or the course (see Broadbent, 1989; Entwistle, 1985; Hudson, 1968).

This is a particularly important study, both for the richness and generality of the developmental issues raised and because it is the only well-known study within the ego psychology tradition to have used interview methods. The main weakness of the study is that scoring categories were used that assume we will find a fairly coherent outlook expressed by interviewees, when they often appear to exhibit considerable confusion and lack of integration in the replies cited. This and other difficulties with the scoring methods will be discussed further in Chapter 8.

HARVEY, HUNT, AND SCHRODER

Although this approach has not been widely applied to the study of moral reasoning (Johnston, 1989 is a rare exception), it is worth brief mention as it offers a general approach to the relations between the role of the ego in personality functioning and conceptual thinking in general. Harvey, Hunt, and Schroder (1961) argued that conceptual integration in any given domain may pass through four levels, provided that the individual has the motivation and learning environment to undertake the intellectual work involved. Their book gave rise to a substantial tradition of studies attempting to assess the motivational and environmental conditions required for passage to higher levels of conceptual integration (for reviews see Hunsberger et al., 1992; Pratt, Hunsberger, Pancer, & Roth, 1992; Rowley, Ross, & Harvey, 1992; Schroder, Driver, & Streufert, 1967; Suedfeld, 1985; Suedfeld & Tetlock, 1977; Tetlock, 1986). A widely used method of analysing the conceptual complexity of written texts and interviews within this tradition is the adaptation of the scoring method of Schroder et al. (1967) suggested by Suedfeld and Tetlock (1977). Evidence has been obtained using this and other measures that conceptual complexity is reduced by external social threat, such as that of war, and increased in areas that are both of high interest and present the individual with conceptual conflict. Comment on the methods of text and interview analysis used by this tradition is deferred until Chapter 8.

NORMA HAAN

Haan is another contemporary author who has attempted to use the tradition of theorising about ego development, which began with Freud, to throw light on the development of moral reasoning. She believes that both classical psychoanalysis and Loevinger erroneously regarded the ego as a state or a thing, rather than a process. She wishes, on the contrary, to consider the ego as a process and her approach thus stresses the notion of defence mechanisms to an even greater extent than that of Loevinger. In the orthodox Freudian view of the ego, codified by Anna Freud (1968), defence mechanisms play a key role. Thus, it is quite logical for Haan (1977) to argue that the development of the ego is largely the development of the processes involved in such mechanisms.

One of the leading ideas, to emerge from her empirical studies of defence mechanisms, is that there is considerable stability over time in the dominant defences used by individual children and adolescents

(Haan, 1977). In addition, the main factor to emerge from factor analyses of her empirical findings, from both children and adolescents, was "coping", giving rise to the idea that, at all periods of development, the difference between individuals who cope with developmental tasks and those who do not is the most significant. Thus, her work in this respect emphasises continuity during development, rather than qualitative change.

She also distinguishes the notion of "interpersonal moral development", from "structural moral development"; and argues that her own work focuses on the former aspect of moral reasoning, whereas Kohlberg has focused on the latter. Haan (1977, 1986) distinguishes five levels of interpersonal morality. These levels were found useful as a means of classifying the moral reasoning of teenagers from 12–17 years, in a number of types of discussion and simulation games, involving moral issues. The levels initially appeared to form sequential stages in development, later stages showing increasing complexity and depth in reasoning concerning interpersonal moral balances. However, Haan (1991) reports that more concerted attempts to test the sequentiality of these stages proved so disappointing that she has abandoned them. In particular, she finds evidence both from her own studies, and from reviewing the studies of others, that quite young children are able to operate at advanced levels, which negates the idea that the levels are developmentally ordered.

Although Haan's levels have turned out not to be developmental, her work has played the following valuable preliminary and corrective roles: a preliminary role in claiming to identify a particular kind of interpersonal moral reasoning; and a corrective role in showing that young children are more sophisticated in their moral reasoning than claimed by some other workers, particularly those within the Piagetian and Kohlbergian traditions.

Interpersonal moral reasoning is particularly prominent in the reasoning involved in face-to-face moral exchanges. To elicit this kind of reasoning Haan feels it is better to have subjects in a face-to-face encounter, than to present them with stories about other people, as did Piaget and Kohlberg (see Chapters 4 and 5). She also prefers to have groups of established friends discussing issues in the absence of an experimenter, to enhance the level of personal involvement and reduce the inhibitions of participants. Thus, one of her studies involved presenting a group of 10 teenagers who knew one another with an audiotaped voice that said it was the voice of a computer called Humanus (Haan, 1977). It told them they were the last surviving people on earth, following what was implied to be a nuclear disaster. Humanus posed a number of questions for them to resolve, including: 1. Which 10 items would they want to have with them? 2. How will they regulate their new society? 3. Whether or not they will let a survivor in.

This kind of discussion is likely to be, in part, about moral issues in the broader sense defined in the introduction, and in part, about non-moral issues. Haan focuses chiefly on the former. However, her conclusion that the kind of moral reasoning elicited by her discussion procedure is really substantially different from that elicited by Kohlbergian and other kinds of moral interview procedures, is not adequately substantiated. To show this, we would need to apply a common scoring procedure to transcripts from interviews and from Haan's preferred form of discussion group. She attempts to establish her claim by showing that her discussions scored by her own scoring method, and Kohlbergian interviews scored by Kohlberg's method, yield different findings. This difference, however, is just as likely to be due to the different scoring procedures used, as to the different questions posed and interpersonal atmosphere created.

Studies in which common scoring methods have been applied to Kohlbergian, and other kinds of interviews, are reviewed in Chapters 7 and 8, and tend to the conclusion that quite wide variations in interview procedures influence quantitative rather than qualitative aspects of findings. Studies of this kind focusing on Haan's discussion technique might establish her point in the future, but for the present it seems best left open.

To appreciate Haan's (1991) claim that young children exhibit sophisticated kinds of interpersonal reasoning it will help to review her levels of reasoning. The levels are as follows (Haan, 1977, 1986). At Level 1 the young child has no separate view of itself and is merged with its caretakers. At Level 2 it is aware of its separation from others, and forms a preliminary conception of moral exchange, in which it uses its own current state as a model for what to expect from others. Thus, if the child is in a state where it is demanding its own way, regardless of the interests of others, it will expect others to behave in the same way, and will not be outraged if they do so. On the other hand, if the child intends to keep faith with others and consider their interests, then it is deeply hurt and angered if others do not keep faith with the exchange expected. The child's retribution against others who fail to live up to their moral exchanges with it is based on the morality of taking an eye for an eye.

At Level 3, the child has ceased to view itself as an individual who makes exchanges with others and now thinks of itself as part of a human collectivity or group. The group is a harmonious one in which everyone cooperates for the greater good, but this notion of harmonious cooperation is stereotyped, and the child finds it hard to fit cases of bad faith in moral exchange into it.

At Level 4, the child has the expectation that everyone must be subjected to the same requirements for moral exchange, and that everyone should have the same duties and the same rights. It recognises that people often enter moral exchanges in bad faith and, for this reason, wants the rules for exchange to be very clear and well codified, and backed by clear sanctions against any who break them. It is willing to suffer these sanctions itself. This leads to an emphasis on clarity, rather than sensitivity, in human relationships.

At Level 5, the emphases of Levels 3 and 4 are successfully integrated. There is now a more diffuse and flexible attitude, rather than a rigidly legalistic and rule-bound one. It is realised that we must trust others to keep their moral bargains, as there is no alternative to trust; there is no other meaningful solution to living together in society. Individuals must, however, still take responsibility for distinguishing instances of good faith from those of bad faith, and the maintenance of the moral balance is everybody's business all the time. The person can see themself as others see them and this leads to a realistic, detached, and even humorous view of the self. Ideal interpersonal morality is seen as one of reciprocity, in which everyone genuinely tries to give as much as they get back from exchanges.

The finding by Haan (1991) that young children are able to perform at Level 5, when they are thinking about a simple and concrete situation, is quite at variance with the views of Piaget and Kohlberg; they argue, as we shall see, that young children are incapable of understanding the notion of reciprocity in moral reasoning. Within the tradition of ego psychology it is not so revolutionary, as it accords with Freud's claim that young children think about morality in terms of reciprocal exchange. It is also in accord with the findings from weakly interpretive methods of interview analysis reviewed in Chapters 7 and 8.

One peculiarity of Haan's method of analysing discussions of moral issues needs to be mentioned: her scoring method is neither mainly descriptive, like the methods reviewed in Chapter 7, nor strongly interpretive, like those of Piaget and Kohlberg. Instead, it focuses on certain aspects of moral reasoning involved in moral exchange and provides a descriptive view of these. However, many statements that are made, both in involved discussions and in interviews, cannot be accommodated within her scoring method and are left out. This is a serious disadvantage, as these are not reported on. Thus, the picture of moral reasoning gained by using this method, although valuable when considered in conjunction with other methods, can by itself give a rather one-sided view of such reasoning.

Another difficulty is that Haan (1977, 1991) argues that her own involved discussion groups and Kohlberg's interviews differ, with the former enabling us to study moral exchange in a personally involved setting, the latter the logical structure of moral reasoning, especially the role of logical deduction in such reasoning. However, her proposed distinction between these two kinds of reasoning is misleading, as it is wrong to see Kohlberg's work as being primarily about the deduction of one moral proposition from another. In fact, although there was interest in this in Kohlberg's early work, it was progressively reduced in the later work, where it ended by playing a very minor role (see Chapter 5). However, there are genuine differences between the kinds of reasoning elicited by Kohlberg and Haan, discussed in Chapter 6.

CONCLUSIONS

The tradition of ego psychology has suffered from fragmentation and lack of coordination between its different strands. It has also lacked a satisfactory method of interview analysis, which is a serious defect, as interviews are a central method for investigating moral reasoning. Even their strongest supporters would only claim Perry's (1970) methods as suitable for college students, but as we shall see later they have additional limitations. On the positive side, ego psychology has continued to offer appealing general theoretical principles to account for the descriptive trends in development known to Freud and other earlier writers from informal observation. It has also continued to question the key assumptions of the dominant Kohlbergian tradition in ways that, as we shall see later, can also be justified by formal interview studies.

CHAPTER FOUR

Piaget

This chapter and the following one deal with the work of two theorists from the tradition of cognitive structuralism: Piaget and Kohlberg. This tends to combine the following elements: belief in development through stages that are unified by cognitive structures; belief that development is relatively spontaneous, coming from within the individual, rather than imposed from outside; commitment to the use of interview methods as a key tool of investigation; strongly interpretive reporting of findings, that is to say, reports of findings are provided in an already-interpreted form, rather than being uninterpreted summaries of what is said.

Piaget's own work on the development of moral reasoning was largely undertaken in the 1920s and after 1931 he did not return to work in the area again (see Piaget, 1932, for the English translation). Thus, his work on this topic reflects his earlier ideas in both theory and methodology. Notwithstanding this, it had great influence on later workers.

THE DEFINITION OF MORAL REASONING

Piaget's definition of moral reasoning is implied in the following statement (Piaget, 1932, p.1): "All morality consists in a system of rules, and the essence of all morality is to be sought for in the respect which the individual acquires for these rules." By "rules" Piaget understands mainly moral norms, that is, generally accepted moral rules, and the rules of games, which are conventional rules. As explained in the introduction, Piaget avoids dealing with decisions that influence human welfare about situations to which no generally accepted first order moral rule applies, such as political decisions and those about contested areas of sexual morality, despite the fact that second order norms usually apply to such situations. This is because he implicitly restricts his understanding of the idea of moral rules to first order norms, like those against lying and cheating, and the rules of games. For reasons explained in the introduction, the rules of games are usually considered to be conventional, rather than moral (Turiel, 1983; Turiel et al., 1991).

GENERAL BELIEFS ABOUT THE INTERPRETATION OF EVIDENCE

At the outset of *The moral judgement of the child* (1932), Piaget provides a brief discussion of his methodological stance and refers the reader to an earlier work on another topic for fuller details of his "clinical method", which is his method of conducting interviews with children and interpreting them. In the work referred to (Piaget, 1929, p.7), we learn that the clinical method is modelled on the psychiatric interview and has something in common with the methods of depth psychology. We also learn (1929, p.8): "It is true that in the nature of things we shall be compelled to schematise our cases, not by summarising them (which would be to misrepresent them), but by taking from reports of conversation only those passages which have a direct interest." Later, (p.9) he says of his interview technique " ... at the same time he (the investigator) must constantly be alert for something definitive." Thus, the aim of the excerpts from interviews with children, which are liberally included in *The moral judgement of the child*, is to cite parts of the interviews that are of theoretical interest, rather than to give an idea of what children may say in total. One reason for this is that Piaget thinks that some of the things children say are merely repeating what they have heard others say, whereas the parts of the interview he is interested in are those that reflect what the child has thought out for itself.

THE STAGES OF DEVELOPMENT

The first topic studied in *The moral judgement of the child* is the development of children's understanding of, and attitudes towards, the rules of marbles. Piaget's first interest is in children's understanding of the rules. The first stage he identifies here is one in which rules are scarcely acted on at all and the child has little conception of what a rule is. This persists up to the period from about 4–7 years (all ages given are intended to be approximate only), in which rules are used, but only in an egocentric way and not cooperatively. Thus children play marbles alongside one another, but do not cooperate in accepting common rules.

In the third stage (about 7–10 years), children desire to cooperate in playing marbles and succeed in practice, as they copy the child who seems to know most about how to play. Although most of the children at this stage have a rather inadequate grasp of the rules of any particular game played with marbles, they have a desire to play according to common rules and thus they look to the best-informed child, often one who is somewhat older, to help them out on detailed points of procedure about which they are unsure. But when interviewed alone they cannot give a consistent and detailed account of the rules of the various games they play. In the fourth stage, from 11 years onwards, children show an interest in systematic codification of games played with marbles and are usually able to give a systematic account of the rules of a particular game when not advised by another child, and even when not playing.

To find out about children's attitudes to marbles, Piaget asked three questions: Can rules be changed? Have rules always been the same as they are today? How did rules begin? Beginning at the start of the second stage of development (about 4 years), the child replies to these questions in a way that implies the rules are immutable and eternal. In the third stage, this is joined by the idea that they are laid down by authority, particularly that of older children. This persists until the second half of the third stage. From this point, at about 9 years, and extending throughout the fourth stage, this attitude changes. Now rules are changeable and result from mutual agreement among equals, and if the players agree to a change in the rules, it is thought one could be made.

The remainder of *The moral judgement of the child* uses further evidence drawn from clinical interviews, especially about lying, stealing, and appropriate punishments for misdemeanours, to argue that the four stages described for understanding the rules of marbles are general stages of moral development. Furthermore, these correspond to the general stages of intellectual development specified by Piaget's general theory. Thus, stages one and two in moral development correspond to the preconceptual and preoperational periods. In the first of these, up to about 4 years, it is held that the child has difficulty in internalising the mental operations underlying rules at all. In the second, from about 4–7 years, it is held that the child can internalise such operations, but they are not reversible. This accounts for children being able to form the idea of common moral rules, even though they cannot abide by them consistently.

The third stage in moral reasoning (7–11 years) corresponds to the stage of concrete operational reasoning. Here, concrete operations in the external world can be internalised in a reversible form, which accounts for the ability to overcome the egocentrism of the preoperational period and play cooperatively with some understanding of the rules of marbles, or of other joint social practices, so long as these are embedded in actual practice. This gives the child's thought the concrete support it requires at this stage. The fourth stage in moral reasoning (11 years onwards) corresponds to formal operational reasoning, in which the child acquires the ability to deal with the rules of marbles in the absence of the marbles themselves and other concrete aspects of play. Other rules, such as those about lying and stealing, can now also be conceived in a general abstract form removed from practical situations of use.

The infant, according to Piaget, suffers from severe cognitive egocentrism, finding it difficult to adopt any perspective other than its own. The process by which this egocentrism is gradually reduced is also reflected in the stage sequence. In the first stage, the child is dominated by egocentrism, resulting in a radical inability to cooperate with others in the use of moral rules. In the second stage, egocentrism diminishes and the notion of cooperating with others takes hold, but the rules needed for joint cooperation are only dimly apprehended. This is followed by the third stage, in which egocentrism passes into its opposite, namely subservient respect for the views of authority as represented by older children and adults. Finally, in the fourth stage, balance is restored between authority and the self, in autonomous cooperation, and the adolescent now sees moral rules as established by mutual agreement, and believes they are based on cooperation to achieve mutual benefit and respect.

The way in which the main stage sequence ties in with attitudes to rules is occasionally unclear. Thus, we have already seen how Piaget says that the change, from the idea that rules are eternal and laid down by authority in the game of marbles, to the idea they are mutable agreements among equals, takes place in the second half of the third stage. This means that this change is not neatly tied into the general stage sequence. However, although this is clearly stated in relation to the game of marbles, at other points he seems to lose sight of this and the general sequence is presented as governing attitudes to rules, as well as the understanding of rules.

The solution here possibly lies in the Piagetian notion of *decalage*, or "uncoupling". In later versions of Piaget's general theory he uses the idea that structural developments that occur in one area sometimes take some time to be reflected in another. If we apply this to moral reasoning, it could be that attitudes to rules are more advanced in thinking about conventional rules like those of marbles, than in thinking about other, more narrowly moral, rules. However, the idea of *decalage* was not very well developed in Piaget's thinking when he wrote on moral reasoning, and he does not deploy it systematically. Thus, commentators have often been guided by what he says in his general theoretical statements about the connection between attitudes to rules and understanding rules, and have assumed that there is a close connection in the development of these two areas (Langford & Claydon, 1989; MacRae, 1954; Pittel & Mendelsohn, 1966; Tomlinson, 1980). There are grounds, in his detailed descriptions, for thinking that his own evidence indicated a rather looser connection than this implies.

Piaget also introduces the term "moral realism" to describe the young child's attitude to moral rules, such as those against stealing and lying. This means, first, that rules are thought of as imposed by adults; second, that they must be applied in a literal and rigid way; third, that a person's intention is irrelevant to obedience to rules. Only the first and third claims are the subject of studies based on interviews.

To establish attitudes to rules, Piaget asked children why people should not tell lies. He claims (1932, p.164) that "the reason most universally invoked and that which comes first chronologically is that you mustn't tell lies because 'you get punished'." This is followed by illustrative examples from children between 6 and 9 years. He also claims that the more likely lying is to be detected and punished, the worse the act of lying has been for younger children. For these reasons, younger children think lying to other children is not bad, but lying to adults is bad. Older children, on the other hand, from 7 to 11 years, in the third stage, are more likely to say that it is as wrong to deceive children as adults. It is significant that although the attitude of older children to lying is said to be based on reciprocity, that is the expectation of receiving consideration in return for considering others, no examples are given of any actual explanations by older children stating the principle of reciprocity. It will be argued in Part 2 that such explanations are in fact quite infrequent, and do not follow the age trends that Piaget claims.

The ability to take account of the intention and motives of the actor, in considering the moral character of their actions, is also said to improve with age, a claim for which there is far more direct evidence, although the age ranges cited have been thrown into doubt by later work. Piaget told children stories in which a moral rule is broken either by accident, in order to do something for someone else, or in order to do something selfish. Up to about 9 years, children tended to judge the badness of an action by the magnitude of the infringement. Thus, someone who breaks 15 cups is worse than someone who breaks one, regardless of intentions. From 9 years on there is greater use of the actor's motive to determine rightness, and people who break rules by accident are not to be blamed.

These findings seem to indicate that the shift to the use of intentionality as a criterion in moral judgement occurs in the middle of the third stage. However, in his general theoretical statements Piaget says that this change actually takes place at the start of the third stage. Commentators have again tended to take his general theoretical statements rather than his detailed reports of data as definitive (Langford and Claydon, 1989; MacRae, 1954; Pittel & Mendelsohn, 1966; Tomlinson, 1980). Once again, it could be that *decalage* is involved here, or that there is something wrong with the theory.

Piaget adopts the odd tactic of using his studies of the basis for rules, and of intentions and motives, to throw light mainly on the nature of heteronomous morality (morality taken from the views and authority of adults) and moral realism, both early forms of moral reasoning (1932, p.195). He then moves on to studies of the idea of justice, to throw light on the nature of autonomous or cooperative morality, which are later forms of reasoning. His arguments and use of data would have been more convincing here had he tried to demonstrate that, in attitudes to rules, in use of intentionality and motives, and in justice, children go from heteronomous/realistic to cooperative/autonomous reasoning. It is odd to study early forms of reasoning in two areas and then contrast these with advanced forms in a different area.

The consideration of justice begins with a study in which children are asked to choose between various alternative punishments for an offence. Some children give replies that are severe and "expiatory", others are less severe and base their thinking on "reciprocity". In the latter, the punishment is designed to do to the wrongdoer what they have done to the victim. Thus, if they hurt someone else they should be paid back with equal hurt. The proportion of reciprocity punishments rises gradually from 28% in 6–7-year-olds to 78% in 11–12-year-olds.

These findings about reciprocity in punishments can be compared with the view, noted in the previous chapter, that the notion of reciprocity begins as early as 5 years in many children. This was based on the work of Haan (1991) and also derives support from weakly interpretive interview methods. Although Piaget cites his findings as favouring his view that reciprocity is typical of the fourth stage, it is more usual to locate the start of a stage at the point where 50% of children give an appropriate reply. On this basis, the predominance of reciprocity begins around 8 years, according to his own data, rather than the 11 years required by his theory.

This is still not as early as some other authors claim. One probable reason for this is that reciprocity is being used in somewhat different senses by Piaget, in this instance, and by the other investigators mentioned. Thus those who think that reciprocity has an earlier origin tend to think of it as indicated by explanations from interviewees that moral rules, moral decisions, or moral exchanges should enable all participants to be better off. Exacting a penalty to match the harm done by a wrongdoer to others, Piaget's indicator of reciprocity in this case, is one manifestation of this attitude in reply to questions asking for appropriate penalties for a misdemeanour, but it is not the only one that is possible. Thus, some children may reason that the interests of all participants will be better served by having a punishment that does not precisely match the amount of harm done to the victim of the misdemeanour. Even inflicting more harm than was done to the victim can be justified on this basis, as it may deter the offender from harming others in future.

In addition, the love that many young children have for draconian penalties may stem in part from the enjoyment they take in recommending permitted acts of aggression against others, uninhibited by the older child's guilt at such enjoyment of their misfortunes. This suggestion is supported by the fact that they often recommend much stronger punishments than an adult would, indicating that they are not taking their morality from adults so much as from their own inclinations.

This second possibility certainly indicates immaturity in the young child's thinking and is also a departure from the principle of reciprocity. It may be that the topic of punishment brings out the beast in young children. It is not that they are unaware of the principle of reciprocity and unable to apply it in many situations, especially where using it as an argument will help them to achieve their aims, but in some circumstances they allow its influence to be overruled by the desire to enjoy the contemplation of strong punishment.

A further study of justice involved telling children stories, in which an adult gives an order to a child that involves unequal treatment of that child in relation to others. This puts the child's desire to accord with authority in conflict with its desire for equality of treatment. Younger children once again tend to think that authority is right and should be obeyed in such situations. This is followed by a period, roughly coinciding with the second stage, in which the action of the adult is condemned as being unfair, but the child is recommended to obey the adult's order, showing residual respect for adult authority. Finally, both moral judgement and recommended action are based on the criterion of fairness. Replies based mainly on equality and fairness become preponderant at around 7–8 years, with slight variations due to the particular story used, thus placing this change at the transition from the second to the third stage. This finding is in flagrant contradiction to Piaget's claim that children in the third stage take their morality from adults, and supports the view that young children are more morally mature and less influenced by authority than his theory suggests.

DETAILED CONSIDERATION OF
INTERPRETIVE METHODS

There are two aspects to Piaget's interpretation of interview findings: how the statements selected for reporting are identified; and the meanings given to the statements that are selected in the light of theory. It is often difficult in reading *The moral judgement of the child* to know just how the excerpts of interviews with children, which are used to illustrate the four stages of development, were selected. We know that they were selected in the light of theoretical considerations, but the details of how this selectivity operated are usually hidden from us. However, some passages provide intermittent insights into how the selectivity operates, particularly some in which Piaget comments on his study of the idea of lying (Piaget, 1932, pp. 135–194). In this, he asked, among other things, why we should not tell lies. He writes (p.167):

> In point of fact the older children of 10–11 generally invoke against lying reasons which amount to this: that truthfulness is necessary to reciprocity and mutual agreement. Among the alleged motives there will be found, it is true, a whole set of phrases inspired by adult talk: "We mustn't tell lies because it's of no use" (Arl, 10). "We must speak the truth ... our conscience tells us to" (Hoff, 11). But along with these commendable but too often meaningless formulae we can observe a reaction which seems to be, if not altogether spontaneous, at least founded on experience. The reaction in question implies that truthfulness is necessary because deceiving others destroys mutual trust. One is struck by the fact, in this connection, that while younger children had regarded a lie as the worse for being unbelievable, the older ones, on the contrary, condemn a lie in so far as it succeeds.

This provides a good example of one kind of strongly interpretive tactic in using interview replies, which is selectivity in reporting. Here certain replies, those that emphasise reciprocal trust, are held to represent the noteworthy and reportable part of what is said. This kind of reply appears noteworthy to Piaget in children who are in or approaching the fourth stage of moral development, as it accords well with his theory that at the fourth stage (about 11 years onwards) adolescents believe in a morality of agreement among equals for mutual benefit. On the other hand, two other kinds of justification (and in fact there are more) are ruled out as being the meaningless product of copying adults.

The uncommitted observer is bound to wonder about this kind of selectivity. It is true that the interviewer is often struck, in this kind of interview, by the tendency for some replies to be given in a very fluent way, as if the child is repeating a previously prepared reply, perhaps borrowed from others; whereas other replies seem to be deeply thought out. However, even this raises a problem for the distinction Piaget wants to draw, as many of the fluent replies could be those the child had thought out for itself on previous occasions.

But Piaget makes no use of evidence about the fluency or degree of hesitation found in replies. Instead, he relies entirely on their content to find out if they are spontaneous or copied from others. However, the idea that you should not lie in order to maintain trust between people seems just as likely to be one that children will hear from adults and older children, as the other kinds of reply mentioned; and so his claim that this is a peculiarly spontaneous kind of reply is weak.

It is noticeable that in all his studies Piaget cites almost no examples of children or adolescents who actually explain the key principle of reciprocity, as applied to moral rules, despite the fact that it is this principle that is held to regulate the thinking of adolescents and adults. In reporting advanced replies to questions about attitudes to the game of marbles, for instance, he emphasises those that say rules are formed by agreement and can be and have been changed. A few replies in which rules are said to be present to avoid quarrels are also given. No mention is made of mutual benefit to be derived from the rules, possibly because the rules of marbles are conventional rather than strictly moral rules. However, in dealing with children's replies to the question "Why should people not tell lies?", which is the best opportunity given in the entire book for children to explain the principle of reciprocity, no replies stating the principle are cited. As already mentioned, this kind of reply appears from later studies to be unusual, but is given equally by older and younger children. Piaget's best evidence on the topic of reciprocity comes from his study of reciprocity in the magnitude of punishments. But, as we have seen, this did not produce direct explanations of the general principle of reciprocity, and insofar as it did throw light on the topic it did not support his theory.

We turn now to the second aspect of interpretation, which is the inferences that are made about the underlying meaning of the statements identified as being of significance. In Piaget's version of strongly interpretive methodology, interpretation by selection is more important, and the interpretation of underlying meaning less important, in establishing the link between theory and interview evidence. In Kohlberg's work, which is the topic of the next chapter, this emphasis is reversed. However, Piaget does make use of some interpretations of underlying meaning, and it is important to understand how these take place.

Of particular interest here are Kohlberg's (1963) comments on Piaget's interpretive methods, in relation to replies mentioning punishment, as these provide us with an opportunity to see rival interpretations of underlying meaning at work. Kohlberg writes (1963, p.20):

> In the Piaget view, the child is oriented to punishment only because punishment is a cue to what is disapproved by adults or by the "sacred World-Order". In contrast to Piaget's interpretation, it has seemed to us simpler to start with the assumption that the Type 1 (i.e. what was later called Stage 1) definition of wrong in terms of punishment reflects a realistic-hedonistic desire to avoid punishment, rather than a deep reverence for the adult "World-Order".

Thus, if a child says "It is wrong to lie because you get punished", this is interpreted by Piaget as indicating respect for adult authority, which is partly established by punishment. In reading Piaget it is easy to think of this as a natural interpretation of statements of this kind, but Kohlberg's rival interpretation shows us quite clearly how another can be given, which is that the child has mentioned punishment because it wants to avoid it. In this interpretation, the reason for mentioning punishment is that the child seeks to maximise its own pleasure and minimise its own pain in all situations. It interprets the request to say why lying is wrong to mean "Say why lying is an action that contradicts the principle of maximising your pleasure and minimising your pain". The answer to this question is "Because you get punished".

One of the main themes of the present book is that the process of making strong interpretations of this kind ought to be separated from the initial categorisation of interview evidence. Piaget is somewhat at fault in failing to make clear the difference between the expressed meaning of what the child says here, which is only that lying is wrong because you get punished, and his interpretation of this meaning.

However, his way of reporting his interviews does not fundamentally obscure the nature of what is said by providing strong interpretations, because statements that express the same surface meaning tend to be discussed together. The reader can thus reinterpret them if desired. He was, on the other hand, considerably at fault in failing to report aspects of his interviews that did not fit in with his theory, as this means that anyone who has a rival theory cannot have access to the findings in an undigested form to see if their theory can also explain the data.

OTHER CRITICISMS OF PIAGET

Three other broad areas of criticism of the Piagetian view of the development of moral reasoning can be mentioned. The first is the strong focus on the rules of marbles. This is of concern to anyone who thinks, as in fact most of those who have attempted to define morality and moral reasoning have thought, that these should be excluded. To most investigators, moral rules should have some inherent bearing on human welfare or some inherent value, which conventional rules do not. Piaget assures us that attitudes to the rules of marbles are similar to attitudes to more central moral rules like those against lying and stealing, but the importance given to the rules of marbles remains disquieting and some of his own evidence, as already mentioned, tends to suggest there is a difference. These doubts were later amply confirmed by the work summarised in Turiel (1983) and Turiel et al. (1991).

The concentration on the rules of marbles raises a further difficulty. This is because these are conventional rules of a rather complex variety, as they relate to relatively complex games. Most children can grasp and apply the rules of snakes and ladders, ludo, and other simple board games by the age of 5 years. This throws doubt on the claim that consistent use of rules during the actual practice of a game does not appear until around 7 years. Most children also appear able to grasp the practical use of the rules prohibiting lying and stealing by 5 years, a point that Piaget skirts around in his discussions. Piaget's claim that children in the period from 5–7 years cannot grasp and use simple rules was an early target of critics of his general theory, and this criticism has often been repeated and evidence produced to refute it by later commentators (Bullock, 1985a, b; Driver, Guesne, & Tiberghien, 1985; Deutsche, 1937; Huang and Lee, 1945; Isaacs, 1930; Langford, 1987a). Two of the most telling points, made by critics in all periods, have been that this claim is simply contrary to everyday experience of children and depends too much on complex systems of rules, ignoring simple rules.

In adolescence, focus on the rules of marbles may, on the contrary, lead to an overoptimistic view of the adolescent's moral capacities and attitudes. It is plausible to think that adolescents will view the rules of marbles as a product of agreement earlier than non-conventional moral rules, like those prohibiting lying and stealing. After all, both children and adults do often vary the rules of games by mutual agreement, whereas we do not usually consider varying the rules prohibiting lying and stealing. The suggestion that conventional rules are judged as the product of agreement earlier than moral norms has been amply confirmed by later work, summarised by Turiel et al. (1991). This issue is discussed further in Chapter 8.

Piaget's general tendency to overestimate the abilities of adolescents has often been mentioned by commentators (Brainerd, 1978; Langford, 1987b; Shayer, 1980, 1990, 1992a, 1992b, 1993). Piaget himself in part recognised this difficulty with his early work in later formulations of his theory of formal operations (see especially Piaget, 1972).

The second kind of criticism of Piaget has arisen from attempts to replicate his (1932) findings. One problem here is the sheer difficulty of trying to replicate claims based on the selective use of interview material, where the nature of what has been left out is not specified. However, some of his claims about what we can expect children to say at different ages, in response to particular questions, have been found sufficiently well-specified to be tested by others (Langford & D'Cruz, 1989; Lickona, 1976; MacRae, 1954; Pittel & Mendelsohn, 1966; Tomlinson, 1980). We can usefully consider how three of Piaget's most important claims have fared: his view of the child's understanding of moral rules; his view of developmental progress in the use of intentionality in making moral judgements; and his view of the connection between the development of understanding moral rules and the development of attitudes to such rules.

Criticisms of Piaget's view of the development of understanding moral rules have already been mentioned in dealing with his concentration on the game of marbles. In general, he seems to have underestimated the ability of children in the 5–7-year age range to understand simple rules.

There have been a large number of studies focusing on Piaget's claim that intentionality is increasingly used as a criterion for making moral judgements in the 7–9-year age range (for reviews see Ferguson & Rule, 1982; Karniol, 1978; Keasey, 1978; Lickona, 1976; Shultz, Wright, & Schieffer, 1986). It appears that Piaget was again unduly pessimistic in his assessment of young children here, with a majority of 5-year-olds being able to use intentionality in this way when questioned in an appropriate manner.

Studies of the claimed links between the level of understanding of rules and attitudes to them (including justifications for them) have not tended to support Piaget's conclusions (for reviews see Langford, 1992b; Lickona, 1976; MacRae, 1954; Pittel & Mendelsohn, 1966; Tomlinson, 1980). In view of the doubts already expressed about Piaget's view of the development of understanding of moral rules, and about his interpretation of his own data on the connection between such understanding and attitudes to the rules, this conclusion is not surprising.

The third area in which Piaget's work is limited is in its treatment of the period from 13 years to adulthood. His interviews concentrated on children and adolescents below 13 years. Kohlberg was later to show that there is a complex process of development that occurs between this age and adulthood, that was not investigated in detail by Piaget (see especially Kohlberg, 1958, 1984).

CONCLUSIONS

Although some writers have expressed continued support for the Piagetian view of the development of moral reasoning in recent years (e.g. Gibbs, 1979; Siegal, 1980), the difficulties just outlined have led to a substantial decline in its popularity. Gibbs (1979) suggested that the approach could be remedied by adding a treatment of advanced moral reasoning to Piaget's existing four stages, but he failed to address the other deficiencies of the approach. Langford (1991b) has also pointed to significant problems in Gibbs' treatment of advanced moral reasoning. Most researchers currently working within the cognitive structuralist framework in this area adopt Kohlberg's rather than Piaget's view of the topic.

CHAPTER FIVE

Kohlberg

The most influential work on the development of moral reasoning in the past three decades has been that of Lawrence Kohlberg. Like Piaget, Kohlberg was committed to the general outlook known as cognitive structuralism. Thus one of his primary interests was in how the spontaneous development of the individual might lead them to pass through an ordered sequence of stages in moral reasoning. However, both his methods of investigating this development and the sequence of stages he proposed were rather different from those of Piaget.

It is convenient to divide Kohlberg's work into two periods. The earlier of these extended from 1955 to 1974. In 1955 Kohlberg began work on the PhD thesis that developed many of the methods and most of the theory used in his early publications (Kohlberg, 1958). The year 1974 saw the publication of two influential articles that were highly critical of the ability of results from the early methods to support the theory (Kurtines & Greif, 1974; Simpson, 1974). He was later to say that these, together with his own reservations about the early work, led in 1975 to his first work on revisions to methods and theory (Kohlberg, 1984). This was to culminate in the last product of the second period, which was the two-volume magnum opus Colby and Kohlberg (1987a, b).

It is convenient to divide consideration of Kohlberg's work during each of the two periods into four aspects: his definition of moral reasoning; his theory of stages; his methods for diagnosing the stage or stages found in the reasoning of an individual; and empirical evidence for the existence of stages. All four of these aspects of the theory and methods changed somewhat over the years.

DEFINITION OF MORAL REASONING

Kohlberg's definition of moral reasoning altered over the years in ways already outlined in the introduction. It was argued there that it was the early definition that was responsible for the dilemmas that were the focus for Kohlberg's work throughout his career. The later definitions, emphasising his evolving conception of the idea of justice, did not produce any change in the content of his dilemmas and tend to assume acceptance of his theory. For these reasons, this discussion will concentrate on providing more detail about the earlier definition.

Kohlberg there laid considerable stress on the notion of generally accepted moral rules or norms in defining the topic of moral reasoning, and, as noted in the introduction, he implicitly confines these to first order moral norms. The fullest discussion he ever wrote of this comes in the section of Kohlberg (1958) in which he discusses the distinction between moral and non-moral acts. Moral acts are always preceded by moral reasoning.

The first point of interest here is the claim (1958, p.12) that "Moral judgments tend to be considered as objective by their makers, i.e. to be agreed to independently of differences in personality and interest." The rules that say we should not steal, cheat, or lie are given as typical examples of moral rules having this objective and universal quality. Moral reasoning is above all reasoning about such rules, which in practice Kohlberg, like Piaget, restricts to first order norms. As previously noted, his emphasis on this kind of generally agreed moral rule significantly restricts the scope of his definition of moral reasoning; there are many cases where people hold strong views on issues affecting human interests, that they are inclined to say are moral views, that do not involve rules of this kind. Thus the statements "Capitalism is a morally repugnant system", "The Soviet Union was an evil empire", and "It is wrong to have sex before marriage" are all of this kind.

Many of Kohlberg's own interviews involve dilemmas that mean that in one sense the judgements of interviewees are uncertain. Thus, a situation may be presented in which a person either has to steal something or allow another person to die. Many interviewees are uncertain about how to resolve such dilemmas. In the quotation given earlier, Kohlberg seems to be thinking more about judgements made about the rules taken individually than about what happens when rules conflict with one another, as they do in dilemmas. Thus, the interviewee is often certain of their commitment to the rules taken individually, but uncertain about how to resolve conflicts between them.

A second definitional point made by Kohlberg (1958, p.9) is that:

> Moral judgments are viewed by the judge as taking priority over other value judgments. Moral action involves a willingness to overcome opposition or disinclination to perform an act and usually involves some conflict.

This involves us in a definition of the field that would not be accepted by all. It is, after all, a quite natural and common way of talking to say "My moral duty was immediately clear to me", implying that no "opposition or disinclination" was involved. This aspect of Kohlberg's definition was of key importance in determining the kinds of evidence he used to support his views, by influencing the interviews he used. As already mentioned, nearly all Kohlberg's interviews present situations in which there is a moral conflict, because one or more moral rules suggest doing one thing and one or more suggest doing another. Thus, in his most famous moral dilemma story, a man considers whether to steal a drug needed to save his wife's life; a drug that he has no money to pay for. Here, one understanding of the story involves the rule that we ought not to steal coming into conflict with the rule that we ought to preserve human life. Other views of the story involve similar conflicts.

A third definitional point is that "Moral judgments tend towards a high degree of generality, consistency and inclusiveness" (Kohlberg, 1958, p.12). If taken literally, this could be seen as an attempt to make an important element in his theory true by definition. Several recent authors have claimed, with some reason, that most of the replies that children and younger adolescents give to Kohlberg's own interviews are piecemeal and uncoordinated (see Chapter 7). We would naturally, on the surface, think of such replies as constituting "moral reasoning" in Kohlberg's sense, as they are given in reply to questions about first order norms under challenge. However a strict application of the criterion just mentioned would rule them out. Taken literally this criterion would license an investigator to take, say, 5% of highly general and consistent replies made by an interviewee, and say that these reflect their moral reasoning, and the other 95% should be ignored. Thus the theory that moral reasoning is general and consistent is "proved" correct by application of a definition. As we shall see, a tendency to do this certainly exists in the earlier work, reported in Kohlberg (1958, 1963). This tendency is considerably reduced in the later writings of Kohlberg's early period, and drops out almost entirely in the second period (see Kohlberg, 1964, 1969, 1974).

One further point about Kohlberg's later terminology is worth adding. This is that although the term "norm" in his writings is easy for readers to interpret in the social psychological sense of a moral rule that is in fact generally recognised in a given society, there are signs that Kohlberg sometimes wants to use this term in the Kantian sense of a moral rule that can be taken as a universal law, regardless of whether this fact is recognised by everyone (see especially Kohlberg, Levine, & Hewer, 1983). To add to our perplexity, we sometimes are in doubt as to whether the norms he deals with fall under either heading. Thus, occasionally the "norms" involved in the dilemmas certainly do not come under the first heading and he fails to provide specific arguments as to why they fall under the second.

At crucial points he is even vaguer. Kohlberg et al. (1983, p.75) say, in defending the universal nature of the norms studied, that "the moral norms and elements [listed in a particular table] are norms and elements that have been used by moral reasoners in all the cultures we have studied." This is confusing for two reasons. If the appeal is to the empirical universality of the norms, then we would need to hear that the norms had been used by nearly everyone in all the cultures studied. This is not just loose phrasing, as it would not be an empirical fact that all the norms involved would meet this second condition (see Chapter 1). Furthermore, the way the norms are listed makes it quite unclear what they are, with such items as "Erotic love and sex" being included. As we shall see later, reference to the dilemmas claimed to embody this and some other norms does not suggest they are empirical norms.

Despite the vague edges to Kohlberg's definitions, both of norms and of "justice", it is clear that the dilemmas he chose to concentrate on chiefly embody conflicts between first order norms, that are both universalisable moral rules in the Kantian sense and are at least candidates for rules that are accepted by most people in most societies. It will be assumed here that he was chiefly interested in dilemmas embodying conflicts between norms of this kind and that the slight admixture of other kinds of rules in his dilemmas did not significantly influence his results, at the level of first approximation for which we will be aiming.

THE EARLY PERIOD

The method of interview analysis

Kohlberg's early methods for studying moral judgement and reasoning involved giving subjects dilemma stories, of the kind just mentioned, and then asking what the person should do and why; a number of other probe questions were also used in the interview that followed presentation of the dilemma. The subject's replies to all interview questions were included in the analysis.

In considering this procedure, one point should be emphasised, which is not explicitly mentioned in any of Kohlberg's earlier writings, but is contained in the outline of his research career given in Kohlberg (1984). This is that, in devising this method, he was particularly influenced by projective tests, such as the *Thematic Apperception Test*, a widely used research instrument. In this test, the subject is shown a picture of a group of characters and asked to tell a story about what they might be saying and doing. This offers them an opportunity to project their own preoccupations onto the characters.

The model of a projective test determined two of the most important features of Kohlberg's methods throughout his career. First of all, the great majority of the moral dilemmas presented to subjects involve individuals like the man and his wife, in the story of the drug, rather than groups of individuals. The interviewee is encouraged to identify with the main protagonist in the story and it is assumed that, in saying what the main protagonist ought to have done and why, they are revealing what they think they themselves ought to have done and why. This is important, as having individuals as the main protagonists in most of the stories (though not all) may well have determined some of the features of the replies obtained (this point is developed further in Chapter 8). Thus, even if we accept all the elements of Kohlberg's definition of moral reasoning previously outlined, we still face the decision of whether to ask questions that pose dilemmas for groups or for individuals. That most dilemmas are asked about individuals is determined chiefly by the desire to offer the subject an opportunity to project their preoccupations onto one of the individuals in the situation presented.

When the interviewee says something about the main protagonist in the dilemma story, this is generally assumed to refer to themself. This leads on to one of the focal issues that divides the Kohlbergian method of interview analysis, with its strong interpretation of replies, from weakly interpretive methods.

Children at Kohlberg's first stage, predominant up to the age of about 10 years, are held to react to moral dilemma stories through a fundamentally egocentric approach to morality, in which they see what is right as what will avoid punishment for them and promote their own interests, with little desire to promote the interests of others in the situation, and still less to promote those of people in general. They manifest this in two ways in particular: by saying that the main story protagonist ought to act to avoid punishment; and by saying that the interests of the main protagonist should be promoted. It is an inference that in saying these things the child is being egocentric, as they might, especially in the second instance, be demonstrating their capacity to empathise with the interests of the main protagonist in the story, who is not the interviewee, but someone else. They could be manifesting concern for another person rather than an egocentric view, but this is not how Kohlberg interprets such replies, as he assumes interviewees are projecting themselves into the role of the main protagonist. This is an issue we will return to later.

An example of one of the nine dilemma stories used by Kohlberg (1958, p.356) will help to give a more concrete idea of his interview procedures. His first dilemma runs as follows:

> Joe was a 14-year-old boy who wanted to go to camp very much. His father promised him he could go if he saved up the money for it for himself. So Joe worked hard at his paper route and saved up the $40 it cost to go, and a little more besides. But just before camp was going to start, his father changed his mind about letting him go. His father's friends had decided to go on a special fishing trip and Joe's father was short the money it would cost him to go with them. So he told Joe to give him the money he had saved from the paper route. Joe didn't want to give up going to camp, so he thought of refusing to give his father the money. Should Joe refuse to give his father the money or should he give it to him? Why? [This "Why?" is repeated until the interviewee can give no more replies.]

Then follow two lists of probe questions that are to be used, depending on the kind of initial judgement made about whether Joe should give up the money. For example, if it is said that Joe should give up the money, a list of probes follows drawing attention to the circumstance that a moral rule, involved in the initial part of the story, is that we should not break our promises. The first probe here is "Would a loyal son have to loan his father the money or is it up to Joe?". Then follows a second part of the story which suggests that, in order to go to the camp, Joe lied about how much money he made, giving only part to his father and using the balance to go to the camp. The subject is asked if this was wrong or justified and this is followed by a further list of probe questions.

Kohlberg's method of analysing interview transcripts was strongly influenced by the "ideal types" of the German sociologist Max Weber (Kohlberg, 1958, p.80):

The ideal typological method involves observing a great mass of more or less qualitative material and seeking for joint presence of various elements which have some "understandable" relationship to each another. Thus it involves simultaneous willingness to select out and stress empirical consistencies which can be coherently interpreted and willingness to revise and reform principles of observation and interpretation as new empirical patterns seem to emerge.

He later (p.88) adds:

When we attempted to construct empirically a developmental type, we selected from a great deal of qualitative material certain age-related characteristics which seemed to cluster somewhat independently of age and to have some understandable coherent relationships to each other. Construction of the type proceeded in terms of the construction of other types, such that there was some plausible basis for moving developmentally from one type to the next.

The methods used in interview analysis are thus interpretive and selective. Although it is not stated in the quotations on methodology, interpretation of the underlying meaning of statements often takes place to assign them a role within the types. Sections of transcript that are coherent and unified by some principle are preferred; selection is also done with a view to forming a developmental theory that will arrange different types of interview in a developmental sequence. Not only does this kind of selection operate quite strongly to encourage the investigator to focus on particular parts of a particular interview, but certain individuals, who manifest the ideal types thus isolated, are selected for emphasis and those who do not manifest these types are de-emphasised, at least in the initial phase of analysis.

The theory of stages and the assignment of individuals to stages

As a result of these procedures six ideal types or "stages" of moral reasoning are isolated. These are arranged into three levels. In the version of the theory presented in Kohlberg (1958), the developmental import of the theory resides entirely in the three levels. The two "stages" found within each level are said to represent alternative attitudes present within the level, and are thought to be influenced more by individual than by developmental differences. Thus in more conventional terminology only the levels constitute developmental stages, with individual differences manifested within each stage being specified by the types within it. Kohlberg's (1958) types were labelled 0–5, but the labelling of 1–6 of Kohlberg (1963) will be used here, to point up the continuity between these and the later stages that grew out of them, only slightly modified. These are as follows (Kohlberg, 1958, p.343):

Level 1: Value resides in external quasi-physical happenings, in bad acts, or in quasi-physical needs rather than in persons and standards. Type 1: Obedience and punishment orientation. Egocentric deference to superior power or prestige, or a trouble-avoiding act. Objective responsibility. Type 2: Naively egoistic orientation. Right action is that instrumentally satisfying the self's needs and occasionally other's. Relativism of value which is unshared. Naive egalitarianism and orientation to barter and exchange.

Level 2: Moral value resides in performing good or right roles, in maintaining the conventional order and the expectancies of others. Type 3: Good boy orientation. Orientation to approval and to pleasing and helping others. Conformity to stereotypical images of majority or natural role behavior, and judgment by intentions. Duty and true self-interest always coincide. Assumes authorities are always good. Type 4: Authority and social order maintaining orientation. Orientation to "doing duty" and to showing respect for authority and maintaining the given social order for its own sake. Regard for earned expectations of others.

Level 3: Moral value resides in conformity by the self to shared or shareable standards, rights or duties. Type 5: Contractual legalistic orientation. Recognition of an arbitrary element or starting point in rules or expectations for the sake of agreement. Duty defined in terms of contract, general avoidance of violation of the will or rights of others, and majority will and welfare. Type 6: Conscience or principle orientation. Orientation not only to actually ordained social rules but to principles of choice involving appeal to logical universality and consistency. Orientation to conscience as a directing agent and to mutual respect and trust.

The procedure by which we get from interview transcripts to the assignment of an interviewee to a type or types can be appreciated from some samples that Kohlberg gives of replies that he says are clearly examples of the various types. For convenience, replies to questions from the first part of the first interview have been chosen. Thus a reply at Type 1 is:

(Q: Should Joe refuse to give his father the money?) Well if he wanted to go to camp bad and his father said that he couldn't go; well, he promised him in the first place and that if he saved enough money he could go. I think that his father should have saved his own money. His father should have saved up enough money and then they both would have had enough money to go. (Q: Should he give it or refuse?) Give it to him. Well you should be nice to your parents and do what they say. (Q: Would it be wrong for him to refuse?) Yes. Well, he wanted to go to camp and his father said he couldn't and he wanted to go on a fishing trip and if he refused to give his father the money, he could have taken away most of his privileges, and stuff too. (Q: Does Joe have a right to refuse?) Yeah, he has the right. Well, his father said that he could go to camp if he saved up enough money and his father changed his mind and wants to go on a fishing trip; while Joe will be sad because he wanted to go and his father wouldn't let him. (Q: Does his father have the right to tell him to give him the money?) Yes, he has the right. Well, his father—he does stuff for Joe and Joe should do something for his father. (Q: Was it wrong for the father to break his promise to his son?) Yes. (Q: What harm would it do?) Well, he promised Joe that he would let him go, and he said—he changed his mind. (Q: Worse for father to break promise or son to?) I think a father to break his promise to his son. Well, his father is older than his son and if he broke the promise, well he'd be excused the first time but he could do it over and over and then he wouldn't be excused. But the boy, he might do it a lot of times and then they'd excuse him. But his father's older than him and he should know better than the boy (Kohlberg, 1958, p.406).

The most obvious thing that marks this out as belonging to Type 1 is the use of punishment to justify a moral judgement. It is wrong for Joe to refuse to give the money to his father because he might get punished. However, as mentioned in the previous chapter, to get from this to the particular interpretation of such comments about punishment that Kohlberg gives in his definitions of the first two types, we have to add something further. The subject might think that punishment is simply a mark of something being wrong; you can tell what is wrong by looking at what is punished. But Kohlberg wants to go beyond this to say that the subject identifies with Joe in the story, and his reason for mentioning punishment is that he looks on moral situations from an egocentric point of view. His mention of punishment is really because he personally wants to avoid punishment. Not only does this particular subject not say this explicitly, but hardly any subjects in this interview ever say this explicitly. This example thus illustrates a key feature of Kohlbergian interview interpretation: a considerable amount of surplus meaning is added to what is actually said in order to interpret it.

We can next consider a second primary feature of Types 1 and 2, which is that the individual is said to define morality by the egocentric pursuit of self-interest. At Type 1 there should be little attention to the interests of others. At Type 2, attention to others' interests is seen, but only in the expectation of receiving something back from them (reciprocity). This raises a problem in assigning this particular transcript, as some attention is paid to the father's interests. However, not all replies in a transcript are assumed to be at the same stage; there may be a spread of stages in the replies. In this case, the mention of Joe's father's interests seems to belong at Type 2, as it mentions reciprocal consideration: " ... his father he does stuff for Joe and Joe should do something for his father." In such cases, Kohlberg argues, Joe is really only considering his father's interests because he is expecting his father to do something for him in return. This is one interpretation of what the interviewee says, but it is not the only interpretation. The more literal reading of this statement is that the interviewee is thinking in terms of reciprocity, but beginning from the viewpoint of the father rather than from that of Joe. What is actually said is that Joe's father can expect Joe to do something for him in return for what he has done for Joe. It is typical of Kohlberg's interpretive methods that this is reinterpreted to mean that the interviewee is egocentric, when on the surface they give evidence here of not being so.

In addition, the proportion of the transcripts given as typical of Types 1 and 2 that is actually taken up with comments about punishment, or about Joe's interests, is relatively small. Although some of Kohlberg's methodological remarks have prepared us for the idea that the remainder of these interviews might be ignored as consisting of stereotyped or conventional replies, or for other reasons, it turns out that these remarks apply chiefly to the way that the main characteristics of types are identified. Such main characteristics do not have to be numerically preponderant in the interview replies so long as they are theoretically important. But minor features of a type are not thrown away; in the actual scoring of transcripts most of the subject's remarks are scored, but many of them belong to features of the types that are not explicitly mentioned in their overall definitions, given earlier.

The bridge between the overall definitions of the types and minor features of the types is provided in Kohlberg (1958) by an appendix (B), giving a summary of characteristics of the moral types, and another (C), giving "global rating guides". Both appendices are based on eight aspects of moral reasoning: value, choice, sanction, negative standard or rules, self-image and role, authority, content, and justice. Any reply by an interviewee that falls under one of these headings can be assigned to one of six types, corresponding to the six ideal types identified in the overall theory. The summary of characteristics gives a general definition of what we would need to find in a reply to assign it to a type. The global rating guides provide specific instructions about what we can expect to find, in the way of replies belonging to a type, for each particular dilemma story. We can best appreciate the eight aspects of moral reasoning by looking at how some of them are applied to the first dilemma story about Joe.

Value refers to the way in which moral value is given to human actions and their results. In Type 1 a bad person is one who will be punished and will suffer; a good person is one who has power and possessions to do what they want and to prosper. In Type 2 "ends are individual and private, not shared except through bargaining and exchange" (Kohlberg, 1958, p.378). Thus, for the story about Joe, Type 1 means "No orientation to assessing the purposes involved. Going to camp is not a purpose but a permitted gratification, e.g. 'he can go another year instead'. Saving money is not an identified-with purpose. No evaluation of father." Type 2 means "Orientation to purpose of going to camp and to holding onto own money. No evaluation of father." (p.384)

Choice refers to the way in which moral choices are taken. At Type 1 the interviewee sees the main problem in solving the moral dilemma presented in the story as being to guess what the interviewer, as a superior authority, thinks is the right answer. At Type 2 "There is no basis on which to take one person's perspective as opposed to another's except one's own natural identification of the self or its interests with one person or another" (p.378). Once again, there is a very considerable role for interpretation here. Interviewees do not often tell us explicitly that they have guessed their replies and it is hard to know when they might be guessing. It is also hard to know when someone is simply identifying their own interests with those of a character in the story, or when they are genuinely concerned about that person's interests as the interests of another person. Although we can usually assume that the interviewee identifies with the main protagonist, and that consideration of anyone else's interests will count as a desire to consider the perspective of another, the quotation shows that we cannot always be sure who is being identified with, and that sometimes this is assumed to be someone other than the main character. It is not always clear how identifications of this sort are established by the scorer.

Sanction refers chiefly to the use of punishment as a criterion for moral value, which has already been discussed. *Standard, rule or law* refers to whether or not a moral rule or law is invoked and what attitude is taken to it. At Type 1 moral rules are not accorded value; instead value is established by authorities. At Type 2 (Kohlberg, 1958, p.378):

> Different groups may have different conventions with no overall or moral basis for coordination. Rules are not oriented to some general "right", but are either simply customary or instrumental to the ends of the individuals making them ... "Individual rights" means that the self and its property are the self's own possessions to dispose of as it pleases.

Once again, the application of these criteria involves interpretation of what appears on the surface, as children in the age range 5–10 years, who are supposed to be predominantly at Types 1 and 2, will standardly mention rules like "You should not lie, steal, cheat, or murder" as justifications in moral dilemma interviews. In the sample of Type 1 already given, in reply to the question about what harm it would do for the father to break his promise to Joe, the interviewee says "Well, he promised Joe that he would let him go ... " This would appear to be an appeal to the rule that we should keep our promises. Such a rule is not here or in most interviews said directly to be a product of authorities, nor is it said to be the particular convention or convenience of a particular group. When subjects scoring in the first two types mention moral rules as justifications Kohlberg interprets this to mean that such rules are the products of authorities or particular groups, even though they do not say this and in fact their appeals to such rules are couched in much the same terms as those of adolescents and adults. Interviewees of all ages generally mention the rule without further comment.

In turning to the global rating guide for the first dilemma story, to find out how we penetrate beneath the surface of the interview, to reach the conclusion that young children have the attitudes to moral rules mentioned, we encounter a difficulty that reappears throughout the evolution of Kohlberg's scoring methods. This is that the particular scoring of this dilemma on this aspect does not seem to follow directly from the definition of what we should expect at Types 1 and 2 in relation to this aspect in general. Instead, we are told that this aspect should be scored in relation to rules about property only, neglecting the more obvious rules about promises and lying that are the more apparent topics of this dilemma. Thus, Type 1 involves "Little sense of ownership rights" (this is all that is said); Type 2 involves "Simple fact that boy earned, it's his money" (Kohlberg, 1958, p.384).

The example given of a Type 1 interview can certainly be assessed as showing little sense of ownership rights, as they are not mentioned. However, in interpreting why they are not mentioned we are also inclined to ask why the interviewee should mention ownership rights in an interview where these are not explicitly dealt with. In fact, it is tempting to speculate that one reason that younger interviewees do not mention property rights is precisely that they are not explicitly mentioned. Older interviewees will be more inclined to include aspects of the situation that are not mentioned, but have to be inferred or drawn out of what is said. This is, as we will see later, a recurrent suspicion in trying to understand some of the age trends in replies discussed by Kohlberg. He tends to assume that, because in his interviews some kinds of reply are characteristic of older rather than of younger children, these replies demonstrate characteristics of the thinking of older children in general. But they may only show what older children are likely to say in reply to a particular interview. If we asked the questions in another, more direct, way, younger children might say the same thing.

Enough examples should now have been given to appreciate the general nature of Kohlberg's first scoring method, as applied to the first two types. To summarise, the aim is to focus on particular aspects of the interview in two ways. The first kind of focusing, as we move from interview transcript to analysis in terms of types, is to select from the transcript what bears on the eight aspects of reasoning. This results in the transcript of replies to a single dilemma story being given a type score on each aspect. It is not assumed that the transcript will score in the same type for each aspect; nor do different transcripts for different dilemmas from the same interviewee have to have the same scores. Instead, the type scores originating from the global ratings will show a spread. Younger subjects will generally have a lower average type score, and older ones a higher average type score, but within individuals there is considerable variation.

The second kind of focusing occurs when the type scores for individuals and for groups are reported with the general descriptions of stages attached to them. This kind of focusing is very important in understanding the history of Kohlberg's reception by the research community, as the only readily available account of how the earlier scoring methods actually worked in detail is that found in Kohlberg (1958), which was an unpublished PhD thesis. When Kohlberg began to publish reports of his early research in journals and books in the 1960s and 1970s, these reports omitted the detailed descriptions of how to get from transcripts to type scoring, which were simply too voluminous to include (e.g. Kohlberg, 1963, 1964, 1969, 1974). Thus even the very attentive reader of Kohlberg's published reports learned only that the general characteristics of types (or stages as they were later known) were as stated in the general descriptions of these things. Small samples of how the particular aspects were scored appeared in print, but it would be true to say that these tended to show the scoring method in the best light possible (e.g. the extended sample in Kohlberg, 1969). The way in which the general descriptions of stages emphasised some of the aspects of replies found in transcripts, rather than others, was hidden from most readers, as there are many things that interviewees say that are not directly dealt with in the theoretical descriptions of types. These have to be interpreted as belonging within the types, even though on the surface they sometimes do not. Even the statements that are most central to a type require some interpretation to make them accord with its general description, but, as we move away from these central kinds of reply, the interpretations become more indirect and in some cases even appear arbitrary.

This is not to say that Kohlberg hid the fact that he was highly selective in his reporting; on the contrary he explained this point fully and clearly. The difficulty was rather, and this continued in his later scoring methods, that most readers were not fully aware of how the process of selectivity actually worked. It was not clear which replies could count as belonging to a type or stage that were not covered by general statements about the nature of that stage. The general descriptions of stages focus only on their central features, but many replies are assigned on the basis that they belong to the minor characteristics of a stage. Often these minor characteristics are tied into the stages in obscure and dubious ways, but this is hidden from the reader of Kohlberg's published papers.

Having appreciated the general nature of the early methods, we now pass on to a brief consideration of how the remaining types (3–6) are scored and some examples of them. The main focus here will be on understanding how the central features of these types are interpreted, and how some of the difficulties in doing this, which we encountered earlier, are tackled. We can begin by looking at an example of a Type 3 interview, that Kohlberg (1958, pp.433–4) gives as typical of this type, given in response to the first dilemma story. (Note that some of the probes are not given according to the general instructions. This looseness in interview procedure was considerably tightened in later work.)

> I think that Joe worked very hard to get to that camp, and since his father's short of money for maybe other purposes—I don't think it said why he was short of money did it? If he was short of money and he needed to put a payment on his house, that Joe should sacrifice a little for his father and give him the money. And his father will most likely repay him in some other respect. (Q: Would it be wrong for him to refuse? Does he have the right to?) I don't think it would, after all he worked for the money. He made it himself. Now if his father gave it to him, he shouldn't refuse, because it's his father's money anyway. If his father needs that money very desperately to make a payment on his house or car, he should sacrifice it. And then again since he worked for it, maybe he should want that money to go to camp with it. If I was him, I would sacrifice it, and give it to my father ... (Q: The father has spent money on Joe. Doesn't that give him the right?) Yeah, I think that Joe should think on both sides. Of his fun, and of what his father has done for him, and then maybe he could decide which one he would want—to give his money to his father first or for himself. (Q: Was it wrong for the father to break his promise to his son?) I think it was. (Q: What harm would it do?) The son doesn't trust him as much; he doesn't have as much respect for him. As if he would keep his promise, he would have more respect for him, and when he grows up he thinks his father's an Indian giver or something. (Q: Is it worse for the father to break his promise or the son to?) Son breaking promise to his father. Because his father probably respects his son, too, to a certain extent. He brought him up and—so that he should keep his promise, and he brought him up the way that he should keep his promises and brought him up good.

The Type 3 orientation is called "Good Boy Orientation" (later changed to "Good Boy, Nice Girl Orientation") and is said to be mainly based on "orientation to approval and helping others". It is not hard to see this as one orientation in the reply. The interviewee at first says that Joe should do as his father asks. On the presumption that the interviewee identifies with Joe, this certainly represents deference to another person's wishes and the desire to help.

There is also a less obvious indication of a Type 3 consideration of interests in this reply. Reference to the global rating guide, under choice, tells us that a prime feature of replies that say Joe should give his father the money, which are to be assigned to Stage 3, is "Tends to say that 'boy doesn't have to give the money, but I would.'" This appears to be stated, if somewhat ambiguously, at the end of the reply to the second question. However, this aspect of the reply, as with many such minor aspects, is poorly tied into the concept of the type as a whole. This kind of reply implies that the subject's identification with Joe is incomplete, and they are able to step outside it to comment on their own view. There is no particular theoretical reason for linking this break from identification to Type 3, but for reasons that are not made clear this link is made. Thus although we have only minor difficulty in linking what is actually said about Joe helping his father to Type 3, as outlined in the global rating guide, we have substantial difficulty in relating what is said about replies on this topic in the global rating guide to the general theory.

Once more we begin to suspect that certain kinds of reply are placed in a developmental level because they tend to be given by children and adolescents at a certain point in development, rather than because the theory can explain why they appear at that point. Kohlberg had originally promised to include in his scoring only aspects of the interviews that were theoretically comprehensible and manifested developmental trends, but he seems repeatedly to succumb to the temptation to include aspects that manifest developmental trends, even though these are not comprehensible in terms of his theory.

There are other elements in this reply that would probably have to be scored at other types. This is quite in accord with the theory, but an example will help to round out our understanding of this transcript. We have already learned that the desire to help others, in order to receive consideration in return, belongs to Type 2. The present transcript says "I think that Joe should think on both sides. Of his fun and of what his father has done for him … " An earlier one says "Well, his father—he does stuff for Joe and Joe should do something for his father." Neither statement is completely explicit in saying that Joe should do something for his father, so he can expect his father to do something for him in return. But if the latter can be interpreted as conveying this idea, then the former should be as well.

Next, we can consider an example of Type 5—contractual legalistic obligation. A typical reply to the first part of the first dilemma scored predominantly at this type is as follows:

(Q: Should Joe refuse?) I think that since he earned the money, he has a right to use it himself. (Q: Does his father have a right to ask him for the money?) I don't think he has a right to tell him to give him the money, but Joe might be a nice son, and he could say that Dad wants the money more than he does, and he might give it to him. (Q: His father broke his promise. Was this wrong?) I think wrong, but maybe if something different came up, but under condition I don't think he should have changed his mind just because he wanted to go someplace. (Q: Which was worse, the son breaking his promise or the father?) The father breaking promise—head of family setting example (Kohlberg, 1958, p.446).

The emphasis in this series of replies is obviously on the legal right that Joe has to money he has earned. Nor is it particularly surprising that this kind of reply should be more common in the late teens than earlier. Although Kohlberg, like Piaget, promises to look mainly at spontaneous features of moral development, it is arguable that this kind of reply is chiefly determined by the tendency for older adolescents to earn money and have it regarded as their own private property in the manner of an adult, to dispose of as they wish. Younger adolescents and children possess and earn money, but they tend not to be granted the absolute right to dispose of it as they wish within the (adult) law. It could also be that age trends in replies mentioning the legal aspects of ownership are, as mentioned earlier, produced partly by the circumstance that ownership of the money is not explicitly mentioned in the interview, and thus must be drawn out of what is said. Older interviewees are better able to infer inexplicit aspects of the situation, as well as being more likely to think in legalistic terms.

The trend for replies based on legal aspects of ownership to become prominent in late adolescence is not much in doubt, but it is possible to put a rather different construction on this than Kohlberg does. His explanation emphasises spontaneous development in the structure of thinking that moves the individual into a new period of thought, enabling kinds of thinking that were not possible before to be undertaken. The alternative view given earlier suggests that this trend may owe more to changes in the social environment and expectations of the adolescent, combined with the ability to draw the inexplicit from the explicit. Legal forms of thought may be available to younger adolescents; what is new in older adolescents may be the willingness and ability to introduce them when their bearing on a situation is not initially made explicit.

The examples that Kohlberg (1958) gives of Type 6 are unsatisfactory realisations of its definition. This is because the definition of Type 6 implies an ability, on the part of the interviewee, to integrate their replies using general principles, and none of the cited transcripts shows this. Colby and Kohlberg (1987a) admit that this is the case and conclude that genuine instances of Stage 6, the later counterpart of Type 6, are rare.

Later developments in the early period

In the period from 1958 to 1974 Kohlberg's theory and method of scoring interview transcripts developed in a number of directions (see especially Kurtines & Greif, 1974). On the level of theory, there was an increasing desire to reframe the descriptions of types of moral reasoning, so that they would become sequential stages. In the original theory it was only argued that Level 1 (Types 1 and 2) preceded Level 2 (Types 3 and 4), which preceded Level 3 (Types 5 and 6). By 1974 it was clear that Kohlberg hoped to show something stronger, namely that Stages 1–6, only slightly redefined from the original types, appeared in numerical order (see especially Kohlberg, 1969).

Techniques for scoring interview transcripts also developed in two significant ways: by the expansion of the eight aspects of moral reasoning scored from the interviews to 30; and by the addition of the "detailed method" of scoring to the original "global method". The expansion of the list of aspects scored provided a more detailed analysis of transcripts, with a broader range of aspects considered. So many aspects are now scored, that most replies are considered by the scorer.

The global method was applied in this period in two ways. In the first, the rater considered both the various aspects present in a transcript, and the most prominent types within each aspect (Kohlberg, 1958, p.91). The rater then reported on the overall weighting that they felt should be accorded to each stage in the light of this global consideration, taking account of the emphasis the interviewee attached to each aspect and to types within aspects. Thus, using the new terminology that took over in the 1960s, the profile that arose from a transcript might be Stage 1, 20%; Stage 2, 40%; Stage 3, 25%; Stage 4, 15%. Alternatively, in some studies only the modal stage would be reported. Thus in this case, as Stage 2 is the most frequent, this subject would be reported as being at Stage 2.

This method of scoring was good for exploratory work, but, as the use of Kohlberg's methods spread, there was a demand for something that required less personal judgement by the rater, that might also achieve greater reliability. Although Kohlberg (1958) had reported a fairly satisfactory inter-rater reliability study using the global method and other reliability studies using it were also fairly successful (Kurtines & Greif, 1974), there was the hope that even better results could be achieved with a method requiring less judgement on the part of the rater.

In the detailed method of scoring, each transcript was first divided into "thought-content units", which are segments of transcript expressing a single justifying idea. These were then, in the later versions of the method, assigned to one of the 30 general aspects of morality described by Kohlberg (1963). Each of the 30 aspects, like the original eight aspects, carries with it a 6-stage scale that describes not only what can be expected in this aspect at each stage in general, but also what can be expected in particular on each of the dilemma stories. Thus each thought unit scored is, by this means, assigned to a stage. The subject's profile of stage scores is the proportion of their replies at each stage, expressed as a percentage. For instance, if they give 10 thought units in their replies and three are at Stage 1, four at Stage 2 and three at Stage 3, then their profile is 30% at Stage 1, 40% at Stage 2 and 30% at Stage 3. Alternatively, in some studies only the modal or the average stage score is reported.

The detailed method represents a further shift away from the selectivity in transcript scoring that had been advocated and practised by Piaget (1932) and Kohlberg (1958). Instead of only scoring those parts of the transcript that fall under one of the original eight aspects, the rater now has to score nearly every unit of the transcript, as nearly every unit will fall under some aspect. Furthermore, in reporting the results of their scoring, they give equal weight to every unit. Thus, from one point of view, the method has become more descriptive. In fact, on the surface it has become almost entirely descriptive, as each unit appears to be assigned to a descriptive category using a definition, and to be given equal weighting in arriving at summary statistics.

However, the method does not provide an uninterpreted description for two reasons. First of all, the process by which descriptive features of replies are mapped onto stages continues to involve a mix of strong, and sometimes debatable, interpretations and ad hoc decisions. Second, the procedure of mapping types of reply onto stages, and publishing only information on the frequency of replies at stages, prevents readers of research reports from having access to information about the frequency of detailed types of reply. This is a significant difficulty, as the theory makes predictions about the developmental trends that should apply to these detailed types of reply, but information about this is not available. As we shall see later, when it has been made available by weakly interpretive methods of scoring, such information has been found to disconfirm the theory, even for some of the most central and theoretically significant types of reply.

Surprisingly, the hoped-for improvement in inter-rater reliability with the detailed method was not greatly in evidence in the studies surveyed by Kurtines and Greif (1974). However, the method possibly made the training required by raters rather shorter and less arduous, than for the global method. In general, quantitative and qualitative differences between findings from studies scored using the detailed and global methods appear to have been slight.

Kohlberg's main interest was developmental, and the aim of much of the work reported in the 1960s was to deepen understanding of the developmental aspects of his levels and stages. The central developmental finding from the methods used up to 1974 was that replies at lower stages are more common in younger interviewees, whereas as age increases replies at higher stages become more common. Thus, in a study reported by Kohlberg (1969), about 38% of replies in moral dilemma interviews, with a sample of 10-year-old American subjects, were at Stage 1, 30% at Stage 2, 22% at Stage 3, and 10% at Stage 4. Responses at Stages 5 and 6 were virtually absent at this age. By age 16 years, about 10% of replies were at Stage 1, 13% at Stage 2, 20% at Stage 3, 25% at Stage 4, and 27% at Stage 5. Thus, between 10 and 16 years of age, we go from finding that the most common replies are at Stages 1 and 2, to finding that they are at Stages 4 and 5.

Somewhat similar results are reported for Taiwanese and Mexican adolescents, although here we find a greater proportion of replies at Stage 1 at 10 years (approaching 50%), whereas the most common stages at 16 years are 3 and 4, with Stage 5 replies still quite infrequent (Kohlberg, 1969). These cross-cultural differences are explained on the grounds that American society and life provide greater general stimulation for the essentially spontaneous developments represented by the developmental sequence of stages. An alternative view would be that as Stage 5 reflects an emphasis on legal rights, the cross-cultural differences between 16-year-olds are, at least partly, due to the circumstance that the more traditional societies of Mexico and Taiwan place less emphasis on a legal rights view of adult life, and thus place less pressure on adolescents to adopt this.

In general, findings of this kind, which are typical of cross-sectional studies from this period, are quite encouraging from the point of view of Kohlberg's developmental theory. However they were not entirely convincing for three reasons.

First, some critics felt that the dilemma stories used were not properly representative of moral reasoning in general, as they were rather male-oriented and used some issues peculiar to American culture (Kurtines & Greif, 1974; Simpson, 1974). Another difficulty in this area, which was not much commented on by critics at the time, but has assumed greater significance in recent years, is that the dilemma stories used by Kohlberg are, for reasons already outlined, particularly concrete realisations of his definition of moral reasoning, focusing on stories about individuals. This may have influenced important aspects of his findings.

Second, the cross-sectional studies failed to demonstrate convincingly sequential progression through stages by individuals in a manner that satisfied Kohlberg, whose expectations in this area had altered considerably from the early theory. There were two aspects to this problem of sequential passage through the stages. The first was that, when Kohlberg and Kramer (1969) published a longitudinal study of individuals, they found that there was a significant number of cases in which college students regressed, from scoring predominantly at Stages 4 and 5, to scoring predominantly at Stage 2. This kind of finding would not have created much consternation for Loevinger or Perry, for reasons we have seen, but Kohlberg's version of cognitive structuralism claimed that regression on this scale was unlikely, as it took individuals back to a much earlier structural level. Permanent regression in cognitive structure should not occur on this dramatic scale. It is accepted by cognitive structuralists that substantial structural regression may occur under the temporary influence of stress, but Kohlberg did not believe that the degree of stress that these students experienced at the time of their interviews could account for their return to such an early level.

The second aspect of the sequentiality problem was that Kohlberg's version of cognitive structuralism suggested that an individual should either be at a single stage, or at two neighbouring stages, being in transition from one to the next. This follows from the following notions: cognitive structures act to integrate all aspects of an individual's thinking once they are well established; transition to a succeeding stage cannot take place until the previous one is well established. However studies like that of Kohlberg (1969) showed that individuals often scored at three or four neighbouring stages. Kohlberg could have taken the easy way out here, simply relaxing his theory to accommodate this finding, but he preferred to try to show that it was a result of defects in the scoring method. He hoped that, when properly scored, transcripts would produce findings in accord with his strong version of cognitive structuralism.

The third general area of difficulty with the early work was not adequately recognised by Kohlberg, but was stressed by some of his critics (e.g. Peters, 1975; Wilson, 1973). These doubted that stage scores measured what they were claimed to measure. This problem was perceived to arise, in part, from the way in which strong interpretation was applied to the interviewee's statements to infer implied meanings that are not explicitly stated. Some critics were also unhappy about other aspects of the methods used in assigning replies to stages, especially the ad hoc assignment of minor features of the stages using the 30 aspects (Peters, 1975; Trainer, 1977).

It is important to stress that aspects of the first problem, the representativeness of the dilemmas, and most of the difficulties in showing sequential passage through stages, were fully recognised by Kohlberg and those of his critics whom he heeded (especially Kurtines & Greif, 1974; Simpson, 1974). The third problem was emphasised by other critics (notably Crittenden, 1978; Peters, 1975; Trainer, 1977; Wilson, 1973) but was not heeded by Kohlberg and little was done to remedy it. This is a key point in understanding reactions to the second phase of Kohlberg's work, as those who reacted favourably to his efforts to remedy the first two problems were often puzzled by the continuing negative reactions of those whose worries extended to the third score. Kohlberg himself worked assiduously to maintain the view that criticism was largely on the first two grounds or on general philosophical grounds. Thus, in his lengthy set-piece response to critics in 1983 he selects those who concentrate on these points, and then shows how he has acted to disarm them, with little attention to critics who emphasise the third problem (Kohlberg et al., 1983).

THE LATER PERIOD

Kohlberg's later work, as already mentioned, was mainly aimed at solving the first two of the three problems just outlined. The first area of criticism of the early work to be taken up was that the dilemma stories were in some way not representative of moral reasoning in general. This took two prominent forms among critics: that the protagonists and issues involved in the dilemmas are predominantly male-oriented, and this was responsible for the tendency for females to respond with slightly lower average stage scores than males (Gilligan, 1977; Holstein, 1972; Kohlberg & Kramer, 1969; Kurtines & Greif, 1974; Magowan & Lee, 1970); and that some of the situations involved in the dilemmas are peculiar to Western culture, and this makes them unsuited to the kind of cross-cultural research in non-Western cultures that Kohlberg and his collaborators undertook with them (see especially Simpson, 1974).

Kohlberg et al. (1983) set out detailed replies to these points. The defensive strategy here is that the critics are largely mistaken on these two points and Kohlberg's continued use of the slightly modified versions of the original dilemmas was sound. On the first point they admit that there is some male bias in the stories, but argue, quite reasonably, that although the situations presented may be sightly unfair to females, the average differences in scores between males and females reported tend to be slight; in some much-cited studies they are probably not even statistically promising, let alone significant.

On the second point, they also admit some validity, but point out that in several of the cross-cultural studies the dilemmas offered were altered so as to be culturally relevant to non-Western subjects. For instance, it is central to the story about a man who must decide whether to steal a drug for his dying wife, that drugs can be manufactured and sold for profit by a drug company; this could be incomprehensible to people in traditional societies. However, in most of the studies of non-Western societies undertaken with this story, it was changed so that the man had to decide whether to steal food he could not afford for his dying wife, a notion that, it is argued, was familiar to the interviewees.

A further difficulty associated with possible differences in reasoning about different dilemma stories was raised by Kurtines and Greif (1974). This was that the entire original set of stories took a long time to administer and up to 1974 most researchers had been using a reduced selection of dilemmas, but the selection used was haphazard, and thus probably resulted in unknown and uncontrolled variation in findings. On the other hand, it was quite open to Kohlberg and his supporters to feel that the general similarity in findings from different studies, despite the fact that they used rather varied selections of the stories, showed that the various stories produced rather similar results. Nonetheless, this criticism undoubtedly sensitised Kohlberg to the need for further attention to this issue during the later period, resulting in standard subsets of the dilemmas being devised and included in Colby and Kohlberg (1987b).

In retrospect, early critics of Kohlberg's dilemma stories may have missed a more important criticism than those that were actually made about the content of the stories (though Wilson, 1973 implies it at points). This is that the desire to use stories with individual protagonists, with whom subjects could identify, produced ones that were mainly about individuals, whose decisions were explicitly stated to affect only a small number of people. Younger interviewees may not be able to break out of the set created by these stories to discuss wider human interests, which are at stake but can only be drawn out of the stories by implication. This problem is considered again in Chapter 8.

Most of the later work was designed to address the second of the three problems with the early work mentioned earlier: sequential passage through the stages. Two areas received particular attention: the description of the stages; and the method of scoring replies to assign them to stages.

The later description of stages

The later description of the stages was first published in Kohlberg (1976) and appears unchanged in Colby and Kohlberg (1987a). Each stage description involves three elements: what is right; reasons for doing right; and a sociomoral perspective.

Level 1: Preconventional. Stage 1 (Heteronomous morality). It is right to avoid breaking rules backed by punishment, to manifest obedience for its own sake, and to avoid physical damage to persons or property. The reason this is right is that it avoids punishment and is in accord with the superior power of authorities. This involves an egocentric point of view in which the interests of others are not considered, and it is not recognised that these differ from those of the actor; the person is incapable of entertaining two points of view; actions are considered physically rather than in terms of the psychological interests of others; there is confusion of authority's perspective with one's own.

Also in Level 1 is Stage 2 (Individualism, instrumental purpose, and exchange). It is right to follow rules only when it is in one's immediate interest, to act to meet one's own interests and needs, and to let others do the same. It is right to do what is fair, what is an equal exchange, a deal, or an agreement. These things are right because one should serve one's own needs or interests, in a world where you have to recognise that other people have their interests too. This involves a concrete individualistic perspective, in which you are aware that everybody has their own interests to pursue and that such interests conflict with one another, making right relative in the concrete individualistic sense (i.e. relative to each person's interests).

Level 2: Conventional. This begins with Stage 3 (Mutual inter-personal expectations, relationships, and interpersonal conformity). It is right to live up to what is expected by people close to you or what people generally expect of people in the role of son, daughter, friend, etc. "Being good" is important and this involves having good motives and showing concern for others. It also means keeping mutual relationships, with an emphasis on trust, loyalty, respect, and gratitude. These things are right because the person needs to be a good person, in their own eyes, and those of others. There is belief in the Golden Rule ("Do to others as you would have them do to you"). Also, there is a desire to maintain rules and authority that support stereotypical good behaviour. The sociomoral perspective of this stage is that of an individual in relation-ships with other individuals. The person is aware of shared feelings, agreements, and expectations that take precedence over their own individual interests. The person relates points of view through concrete application of the Golden Rule, in which you put yourself in the other person's shoes. The generalised perspective of the social system as a whole is not yet considered.

Also in Level 2 is Stage 4 (Social system and conscience). Here the person must fulfil the duties to which they have agreed. Laws are upheld except in extreme cases where they conflict with other established social duties. Right is contributing to society, a group, or institution. This is right because the person seeks to keep an institution going as a whole, to avoid the breakdown of the system that would occur if everyone did wrong things. They also seek to obey the imperative of conscience to meet their defined obligations. The sociomoral perspective differentiates the point of view of society from agreements between individuals and the motives of individuals acting within such agreements. The person takes the point of view of the system that defines rules and roles, and considers relations between individuals in terms of their place in the social system.

Level 3: Postconventional or principled. This begins with Stage 5 (Social contract or utility and individual rights). It is right to be aware that people hold a variety of values and opinions and that most values and rules are relative to your own group and may not be held by others. Such relative rules should usually be upheld in the interests of impartiality and because they are part of the social contract. The social contract means that in belonging to society individuals have implicitly agreed or contracted to obey the rules and fulfil the obligations of society, in return for the benefits they get from it and the protection of fundamental rights that it affords. Some nonrelative values such as the rights to life and liberty are included among such fundamental rights and are also upheld as necessary to all societies and supported regardless of majority opinion. These things are right because there is a sense of obligation to the law, because of the social contract and its promotion of the welfare of the members of society and protection of basic rights. This produces a feeling of contractual obligation to the family, to friends, and those who are trusted, as well as to work obligations, which are seen as agreements freely entered into. There is a concern that laws and duties be based on rational calculation of what will promote the greatest good of the greatest number. The sociomoral perspective is termed prior-to-society. This is the perspective of a rational individual who is aware of the existence of values and rights prior to the existence of social attachments and contracts. Such an individual integrates perspectives by formal mechanisms of agreement, contract, objective impartiality, and due process. They consider both the moral and legal points of view. They recognise that these sometimes conflict, as the law sometimes makes people do what is immoral, but they find it difficult to reconcile the two.

Level 3 also includes Stage 6 (Universal ethical principles). To do right is to follow self-chosen ethical principles. Particular laws or social agreements are only valid because they rest on such principles. When there is a conflict between moral principles and what the law says we should do, then the dictates of moral principle are chosen. Moral principles are universal principles of justice and involve equality of human rights and respect for the dignity of human beings as individual persons. These things are right because the individual believes that universal moral principles have a rational foundation and there is a sense of personal moral commitment to them. The sociomoral perspective here is that social arrangements derive their validity from a moral point of view. This perspective is seen as that of any rational individual who recognises the nature of morality or the fact that people must be treated as ends and not as means.

Although Kohlberg's descriptions, paraphrased here, sometimes seem to list points that belong under one heading (e.g. reasons for doing right) under another (e.g. what is right), the overall descriptions of the stages are reasonably clear. It is also clear that the changes between the 1958 descriptions of stages and the new ones are relatively minor, especially if we compare the description of what is held to be right in the 1976 version with the original description, which focuses mainly on what is thought to be right. The chief differences in dealing with what is right are: that there is now less emphasis on respect for authority in the description of the fourth stage; and the fifth stage now mentions that the will of the majority may sometimes be opposed if it violates fundamental moral rights. The main innovations in the new descriptions are the statements about the reasons for doing right and the sociomoral perspective of the stage. However, as much of this material was contained in the discussions that accompanied the stage descriptions in Kohlberg (1958), their inclusion provides a more explicit summary statement of the principles involved in these areas, rather than something fundamentally new. The new theory is a moderate refinement of the old rather than a radical departure.

The revised scoring system

Colby and Kohlberg (1987a, b) describe the final version of the later scoring system, termed standard issue scoring. The basic procedure for standard issue scoring is described as follows (Colby & Kohlberg, 1987a, p.158):

> Standard issue scoring involves (a) breaking down interview material into discrete interview judgments; (b) matching these interview judgments with their conceptual counter-

parts; and (c) assigning stage scores at the issue and global
levels on the basis of the interview judgment–criterion
judgment matches.

The interview judgements mentioned here correspond to the
thought-units of the earlier detailed method. The terminology used is
confusing, as what is really being scored is a justification for a judgement, rather than the judgement itself. Because Kohlberg consistently
uses this terminology in his later writings, I will occasionally have to
follow it, although keeping as far as possible to the less confusing practice of distinguishing between the judgement made about what the story
character should do, and the justification offered for this judgement.

The first thing the scorer must decide is which judgement (in the
narrower sense) the subject has made when asked what the characters
in the story should do. This is called the issue, the term being used here
more in the sense of "result" than of "topic". Thus if the question is
whether Joe should give his father the money, there are two issues, one
that Joe should give the money and one that he should not. The object
of scoring is to score the justifications that the subject gives for one or
other of these judgements.

The next thing the scorer does is to find out what norm the
interviewee is responding to. Each kind of judgement (that is each issue)
will focus the interviewee's attention on between one and four norms.
Thus in the Colby and Kohlberg (1987b) version of the story about Joe,
which remains substantially unaltered from earlier versions, if the
interviewee judges that Joe should not give the money, they may focus
on various moral rules or norms. They may mention that the father has
broken the rule that we should keep our promises; they may mention
that they are upholding the rule that we may dispose of our possessions
as we wish. They may focus on the rule that children should obey their
parents; on the value of the relationship between the father and son; or
on what the promptings of conscience tell the participants. These
various rules or concerns are termed, respectively, the norms of contract,
property, authority, affiliation, and conscience. Other norms involved in
other dilemma stories are the value of life, truth, erotic love, law, civil
rights, religion, and punishment. The term norm is used so that it is
sometimes unclear whether a particular rule or a cluster of related rules
is intended, but this is not a serious problem for the scorer. (Strictly
speaking, religious norms are usually second rather than first order
norms, but their inclusion constitutes only a minor exception to
Kohlberg's general concentration on first order norms, as they play only
a minor role in the dilemmas. Their role in moral reasoning generally
is considered more fully in Chapter 8.)

In the Colby and Kohlberg (1987b) version of the moral dilemma interviews, a fuller list of probe questions is given at the end of the dilemmas than in early versions, designed to focus on some of the norms suggested by the dilemmas. Thus, the probes that follow the story about Joe focus on contract, affiliation, and authority. Probes designed to elicit information about the contract norm ask: "The father promised Joe he could go to camp if he earned the money. Is the fact that the father promised the most important thing in the situation? Why or why not? In general why should a promise be kept? Is it important to keep a promise to someone you don't know well and probably won't see again. Why or why not?" Justifications bearing chiefly on the contract norm may be given in response either to these, or to the more open-ended request to justify the initial judgement as to whether Joe should give his father the money, or to other questions. The scorer has to identify which norm the interviewee has focused on in a reply.

The claim that all justifications for moral judgements in Kohlberg's interviews focus on one or more moral norms is not uncontroversial, as many replies do not mention norms and are not given in response to questions that make it clear which norm is being focused on. This raises two problems: it is often not clear which norm is involved, although the manual always gives a particular norm; it is often not clear that any norm was involved for the interviewee, although the scorer assumes that they were thinking of one.

Beginning with the first difficulty, an interviewee might, for instance, judge that Joe should not give the money to his father and, in response to the initial general request to justify this judgement, say that this is because "Joe really wanted to go to the camp." The 1987b scoring manual interprets this reply as support for the rule that we should be able to dispose of our own property and thus concludes that it is about the norm of property (p.188). However, the interviewee has not mentioned property or the rule about property and neither has the interviewer. Furthermore, the interviewee might have based their reply on the norm of contract, as Joe's father has broken his promise, which would account for the reply just as well as the norm of property.

Turning to the second kind of difficulty, the 1987 system of scoring assumes that first order norms, which is what Kohlberg usually means by norms, are involved in justifications even when they are not mentioned. As nearly every dilemma involves a conflict between at least two opposed first order norms, any judgement will support one or another such norm and thus any justification can and is interpreted as involving such a norm, even when none has been mentioned. This kind of interpretation makes the theory—that all justifications given in the interviews involve a first order moral norm—true by acts of interpretation that may not be accepted by everyone. This kind of interpretation builds an emphasis on first order norms into the method, which some will not be happy to accept.

For instance, someone who prefers to think of judgements about what is best for human interests, rather than about first order moral norms, as fundamental to moral reasoning might prefer to make the reverse kind of interpretation. As human interests are always involved in the stories told to the interviewee, we could say that when the interviewee justifies a reply by appealing to a first order moral norm, and does not mention human interests, they really intended to say that the rule promotes human interests, as these are involved. This kind of argument can be extended to show that all moral judgements involve human interests. I am not suggesting that we ought to make this second kind of interpretation without further reasons for doing so, but the possibility of doing so serves to highlight the effect that Kohlberg's style of interpretation has here, in making this aspect of his theory true by acts of interpretation.

Having identified the norm involved in a reply, the scorer then has to identify the kind of justification for giving value to the norm that is being offered. This is called its moral element, and these are divided into modal elements and value elements. Modal elements focus on upholding the norm. They may do this in five ways:

1. Obedience to the instructions or views of authority;
2. Blame or approval;
3. Retribution or exoneration;
4. Having a right or no right;
5. Having a duty or having no duty.

In the story about Joe, examples would be, respectively:

1. "He should do what his father tells him";
2. "I don't approve of what his father did" (in trying to take money from Joe);
3. "He needs to pay his father back for breaking his trust";
4. "He had no right to take the money";
5. "He is failing in his duty to his son."

Alternatively, elements of justification may focus on the consequences that actions have for the interests of participants. These may be of 12 kinds, which are divided into four groups. The first group is egoistic consequences, that is consequences for the participant whom the interviewee is assumed to identify with. There are two of these:

6.   Acquiring a good or bad reputation;
7.   Gaining a reward or receiving a punishment.

The second group is consequences for individuals or groups, other than the individual the interviewee is assumed to identify with, and thus represents altruistic desires, as against the selfish desires involved in egoistic consequences. There are again two of these:

8.   Good or bad consequences for individuals;
9.   Good or bad consequences for groups.

The third group is ideal or harmony-serving consequences, which are those that promote human interests by promoting social ideals or social harmony. These are:

10.   Upholding a person's character;
11.   Upholding self-respect;
12.   Serving a social ideal or promoting social harmony;
13.   Serving human dignity and autonomy.

Finally, the fourth group of fairness elements involve fairness in the distribution of good and bad consequences to individuals:

14.   Balancing perspectives or role-taking;
15.   Reciprocity (expectation of return benefit from helping others) or positive desert;
16.   Maintaining equity and procedural fairness;
17.   Maintaining social contract or freely agreeing.

The scorer must establish the kind of element of justification that is involved in a reply, which now puts them in possession of the issue, norm, and element of the reply. Armed with these, they turn to the list of criterion judgements provided in the 1987b scorer's manual. For every issue, norm, and element several groups of sample replies, termed "criterion judgements", are listed that are each assigned to a stage. The scorer's task is to find which of these most closely matches the justification given by the interviewee. This will indicate to which stage the reply is to be assigned. Replies are nearly all assigned to stages 1–5 or to intermediate stages 1/2, 2/3, etc. It is admitted that so few individuals give replies at Stage 6 that we can discount this possibility for practical purposes.

Results from the revised scoring system

There is no doubt that the 1987 scoring system makes scoring much easier and less ambiguous than earlier methods. It also achieves results that are more in line with Kohlberg's theoretical expectations than those previously reported using his earlier methods, although substantial difficulties remain. Colby and Kohlberg (1987a) review studies showing that with the new scoring method most individuals score only at one or two adjacent stages, which is in line with the predictions of Kohlberg's version of cognitive structuralism. However, this is only achieved by the introduction of the ad hoc scoring rule that any stage that scores less than 10% of replies can be discounted as error. In view of the rather unambiguous way that replies are assigned to stages this seems a high proportion of replies to attribute to scoring error, and it is not clear what other kinds of error might be involved. Thus we can reasonably conclude that many subjects still show a spread of scores across three or four stages, but this is hidden by an ad hoc scoring rule.

Although this might appear a serious difficulty for those committed to orthodox cognitive structuralism, for many cognitive psychologists it will not present much difficulty, or even create much surprise, and the developmental behaviour of stage scores will continue to be seen as both orderly and interesting. That stage scores show a greater spread than some might anticipate, can be interpreted just to show that development is not quite as neat and tidy as Kohlberg had hoped.

In longitudinal studies with both Americans and various other nationalities, including Taiwanese and Mexicans, it was found that the predominant stage at which an individual scores nearly always either progresses with age or stays the same, seldom regressing to an earlier stage. Thus a second expectation about sequential passage through stages was rather unambiguously confirmed. Reliability studies with the new method also showed somewhat improved inter-rater reliabilities, compared to the pre-1975 methods.

These findings show that the stage scores produced by the new scoring system show a regular and interesting developmental progression. However, as with the old scoring system, what these stage scores measure remains a key issue. They evidently measure some kind of maturity in moral reasoning, but two questions remain. Is the development of this maturity adequately described by Kohlberg's stages? Are the kinds of reply found with Kohlberg's interview questions representative of moral reasoning in general?

The first question continues to be an issue, as the same kinds of strong interpretation of replies that caused some observers to be cautious about the earlier system, are embodied in the new scoring procedure, together with some new and in some ways even stronger forms of interpretation.

These new forms of interpretation, like some of the old ones, are frequently deployed in an arbitrary manner, meaning that a reply is assigned to a particular stage using one kind of interpretation, when had other kinds of interpretation been applied, that appear equally appropriate in terms of the theory, then the reply would have been scored at a different stage. The suspicion is even stronger in the new scoring system, than it had been in the old, that this kind of arbitrary assignment of replies is used chiefly to ensure that replies are assigned to stages in such a way that the stages manifest the desired developmental characteristics, even though the theory cannot explain, in any unambiguous way, why many replies belong in the stages to which they are assigned.

The representativeness of Kohlberg's dilemma interviews continues to be of interest, as other interview techniques have been shown to produce different findings; an issue that will be dealt with more appropriately in Chapter 8. Discussion of the interpretive aspects of Colby's and Kohlberg's (1987b) scoring system now follows.

Interpretation in the new system

One of the problems with the new scoring system is that justifications for assigning criterion judgements to stages are given individually for each criterion judgement in Colby and Kohlberg (1987b). As there are over 900 criterion judgements listed, this means that we have to review a large number of such justifications to find out what kinds of reasons are offered for assigning replies to stages. What follows provides examples of the kinds of interpretation we find in these justifications (for additional consideration see Langford & Claydon, 1989).

Before passing on to these, it is important to emphasise that, despite the detail contained in Colby and Kohlberg (1987a, b), there is no review of the general principles of interpretation used to assign criterion judgements to stages. We are simply given over 900 examples of justifications for the particular stages to which criterion judgements are assigned, and left to work out the principles involved for ourselves. Considering the key importance of the issue of assignment to stages in establishing the validity of the connection between the theory of stages and the scoring method, this is unsatisfactory. Detailed consideration of the justifications offered suggests that one reason that no review of principles of interpretation is offered is that many of the assignments involve the ad hoc use of interpretive principles, which even go beyond those used in the earlier scoring methods, and are difficult to justify. By making it hard for readers to access the principles of justification involved, the authors divert attention from the most controversial aspect of the scoring method.

Justifications for assigning replies to stages often follow the original tactics of interpretation that we found in Kohlberg (1958). We have already encountered an example where, in reply to the story about Joe, the interviewee says that Joe should not give the money to his father because to do so would damage Joe's interests. The 1987b scoring manual assigns a reply of this kind to Stage 2, on the grounds that the interviewee has identified with Joe; and thus in justifying their reply in terms of Joe's interests they are using an egocentric form of justification that, in effect, appeals to their own interests. This kind of interpretation is reasonable enough if we accept the central tactics of interpretation for replies of this kind that were originally used by Kohlberg (1958). If something is said to be in the interests of the main protagonist this is assumed to represent an egocentric reply, as the interviewee is assumed to identify with the main protagonist.

Another kind of interpretation with which we are also already familiar assigns most uses of punishment, as a form of justification, to Stages 1 or 2. Thus, if the interviewee is asked why Joe's father, or people in general, should keep their promises, and replies that this is to avoid punishment, this is scored at Stage 1/2 (intermediate between Stages 1 and 2). It is argued that mention of punishment for anyone in the story, whether this be Joe or his father, represents an egocentric desire to avoid punishment, although this is not explicitly stated by the interviewee. Why Joe's interests represent those of the interviewee, but not those of his father, while both Joe's punishment and that of his father represent the punishment of the interviewee is not explained in either Kohlberg (1958) or Colby and Kohlberg (1987a, b).

It is also common for interviewees to argue that Joe should give his father the money to promote his father's interests. Scoring of this kind of reply to this dilemma has changed considerably between the earlier and later versions of the scoring system. Such a reply can now only be scored in two cases: when it mentions the idea of mutual assistance between the father and son; and when it mentions their relationship. Replies of the first kind are placed at Stage 2, as the idea of mutual assistance is the main key to this stage, whereas replies of the second kind are placed at Stage 3, as this emphasises relationships valued for their own sake. Other kinds of mention of the father's interests, which are quite common, cannot now be scored at all. Thus in dealing with this dilemma the element of interpretation in assigning this kind of reply to a stage has diminished somewhat, compared to earlier versions of the scoring system, and replies are only assigned to stages when they explicitly include mention of aspects relevant to the stage.

However, when we turn to the guidelines for scoring the story about the man who was tempted to steal a drug to save his wife (Dilemma III), we find that here a different procedure is adopted for scoring this kind of reply, which retains a large element of interpretation. Thus "He should steal the drug because his wife needs it or will die without it" is here scored at Stage 2. As this seems to be an example of concern for the welfare of someone other than the main protagonist, it should be interpreted as concern for the welfare of someone other than the interviewee. Such concern can only be shown at Stage 2 if it is due to an expectation of reciprocal favours or consideration in return. But as such reciprocal consideration is not mentioned in this type of reply it must have been read into the reply, but it is not clear on what basis.

The rationale given for this assignment is as follows:

> Breaking rules is justified if doing so is instrumentally necessary because of Heinz's wife's needs. The connection between her desire to live and the rightness of stealing is direct and unmediated. That is, the woman's need to live is used as a sufficient reason, and is not stated in terms of the empathy or concern of a moral person considering her need. (Colby & Kohlberg, 1987b, p.14)

The claim that the interviewee's statement betrays an "instrumental attitude" is another way of saying that the interviewee is expecting something in return. But they have not said they are advising help for the wife in the expectation that this will promote the husband's interests (with whom they identify); this has been inferred. Nor is there any particular reason to conclude that such statements lack "moral concern". When interviewees justify judgements by saying that they aim to help groups of people, this is admitted as a moral concern, but just the same kind of statement about an individual is dismissed as not a moral concern. This is a good example of how Kohlberg continues to read considerable surplus meaning into what is said.

A further example of how mention of human interests is dealt with is that, in the story about the man tempted to steal a drug for his wife, one kind of justification scored at Stage 3 is "because we are all human beings and should be willing to help others" (Colby & Kohlberg, 1987b, p.6). Although promoting the welfare of others is mentioned, in the general stage definitions, as belonging to this stage, on the surface there is nothing in this kind of reply to determine whether the reply belongs at Stage 2, 3, 4, or 5, all of which may involve concern for the welfare of others, though on different bases. Its assignment to Stage 3 is justified as follows: "In this judgment a Stage 3 loving concern for a wife or friend is generalised to all human beings" (Colby & Kohlberg, 1987b, p.20). This involves interpreting a stated concern for the general interest as expressing hidden concern for a wife or friend, although nothing is actually said about the latter. It also invites us to infer that any concern for the interests of a wife or friend can, as desired, be based on the interest in role relationships that characterises Stage 3. As many of the characters in the dilemma stories occupy roles like father, son, wife, and husband, this means that many kinds of reply, mentioning the promotion of human interests in general, can now be interpreted as really involving an interest in roles, even though nothing is actually said about roles.

Again, replies in the drug story that say that the maker of the drug "should be trying to help the wife" would appear on the surface to be urging consideration for the interests of the wife, who represents someone other than the interviewee. But once again this kind of reply is assigned to Stage 3, and once again we have the problem of deciding why this kind of promotion of human interests should be assigned to Stage 3, rather than 2, 4, or 5. The justification given in the manual is "The wrongness of stealing is mitigated by the antisocial character attributes inferable from the druggist's overcharging. Stealing because of the druggist's exploitation and indifference may be seen as a way of indicating one's disappointment with the druggist's failure to demonstrate prosocial virtues" (Colby & Kohlberg, 1987b, p.22). However nothing has actually been said by the interviewee about the drug maker's "exploitation and indifference"; nothing has been said about his social reputation. It is inferred that social reputation was involved in order to place the reply at Stage 3, although nothing was explicitly said on this issue.

If we look again at the implications of these last two examples we can see that the principles of interpretation used seem to go beyond those used in the early work. From the first we gather that, even if general human interests are mentioned, we may assume that the interviewee was really projecting feelings towards individuals, or small close-knit groups like the family, onto humanity in general. On other occasions the reverse tactic is used, with statements about promoting the interests of individuals interpreted as intending the promotion of the interests of groups, or of humanity in general. In effect this means that we can reinterpret the breadth of interests mentioned at will.

The second example implies that even when human interests are mentioned, because those who possess these interests also have social reputations and roles, we can infer that it was these reputations and roles that were really intended, not the interests actually mentioned. The reverse implication is in this case not so commonly used. This principle, which is used repeatedly, licenses us to reinterpret any replies couched in terms of human interests as being really about reputations and roles.

It is important not to overemphasise this new and wider kind of interpretation in the new scoring method. It plays a substantial, but not the major, role in assigning criterion judgements to stages. The main reason that it seems to have been introduced is that in the 1987b scoring manual, unlike those from the early period, the assignment of every kind of reply to stages must be justified. In the earlier manuals there was a considerable amount of ad hoc assignment of replies to stages, as we have already seen, but this did not have to be justified. The broader style of interpretation that appears in the 1987b scoring manual seems chiefly designed to provide a justification for all stage assignments, even where this is hard to give. Taken with the original methods of interpretation, this does not license the assignment of a certain kind of reply, when given for a particular issue in a particular dilemma, to any stage whatsoever. But there is often such a wide range of possible assignments that we are obliged to wonder if the real basis for assignment is not, in many cases, the normal age range and developmental point at which the replies are given in response to a particular dilemma, rather than the theoretical rationale that has been offered.

So far, we have looked at the assignment of two of the most common kinds of reply given: those that mention punishment; and those that mention human interests. Three other kinds of reply are very common in the interviews following Dilemmas I and III: those that mention the opinions of individuals or groups; those that mention the law or legal obligations; and those that mention rules or norms explicitly, but nothing else. A conspicuous example of the first kind is that which mentions the views of authorities, such as parents, teachers, or the police. In general such replies are assigned to Stage 1. Here, the assignment is thoroughly in accord with the theory, as this stage involves respecting the superior power of authorities. There is an element of interpretation here, as authorities might be heeded for reasons other than the mere wish to avoid their displeasure, but Kohlberg views the latter as the subtext of such remarks. Similarly, the assignment of replies that focus on the law predominantly to Stage 5 is as easily justified as it was for the earlier scoring methods; although as before we can give other reasons for the developmental position of this kind of reply than those suggested by Kohlberg.

The scoring of replies that mention rules or norms explicitly, but nothing else, is more perplexing. At first blush, we might expect that first order norms mentioned explicitly would not be scored, as it is claimed that all justifications for moral judgements involve reference to a predominant moral norm. Scoring is supposed to be of the moral element that adds to this reference to the norm, not of the norm as such.

However we are also told that all justifications are to be scored. In this case what are we to do with cases where a justification only mentions a norm? For example, an interviewee may justify saying that Joe should keep the money by arguing "He [the father] should keep his promise" or, more generally, "We should keep our promises." This is introducing the rule that we should keep our promises, which surely should be counted as a norm and not an element of justification. In fact, justifications based on some norms alone, especially those to do with property, are scored and others are not, although the reason for this is not explained.

Hopefully enough has now been said about interpretation in the 1987 scoring procedure to given a flavour of some its strengths and difficulties. The main strengths are its unambiguous assignment of replies to stages and the empirical findings on sequentiality achieved by using it. The main difficulties are in the way the developmental position of replies is explained by the theory of stages. Sometimes this involves strong interpretation that is applied in an unambiguous way consistent with the theory, but which could be challenged by those holding a rival theory. On many other occasions it involves strong interpretation applied in an arbitrary way, adding unstated meaning to the stated meaning of a reply, when another kind of unstated meaning could just as plausibly have been added using the principles of the theory.

These difficulties will be explored in a more systematic way in Chapter 7, dealing with the application of weakly interpretive methods to the Kohlbergian interview. One advantage of these methods is that they enable a systematic survey of such difficulties to be made. A serious defect of the 1987b scoring manual is that it lacks an overview of the principles on which it was constructed. In fact, although more could have been done in this direction, it is a fundamental problem of the method that it is only by stepping outside it, to look at purely descriptive categories of reply, that we can find out how the scoring system achieves its results.

The later treatment of autonomy

We now turn to a further innovation contained in Colby and Kohlberg (1987a, b), which is a revised treatment of the issue of heteronomous versus autonomous morality. This is contained in appendices by Tappan et al. (1987) and Schrader, Tappan, Kohlberg, & Armon (1987). One of the differences between the early versions of the theory and its final 1976 version was, according to Tappan et al. (1987), that, in the early version, as development proceeded moral autonomy increased, whereas in the later version this assumption dropped out. Their basis for this claim is, however, somewhat obscure, as in both theories we can interpret the direction in which autonomy shifts in two ways.

In the first, there seems to be a cyclical movement in which we go from Level 1, in which the main outlook is egocentric, basing morality on the interests and viewpoint of the individual, through Level 2, where it comes chiefly from conformity to the opinions and values of those around the person, and on to Level 3, where it comes from self-chosen moral principles and thus is returned to the individual. This interpretation is based on seeing egocentrism as the most fundamental characteristic of the first level. We can, however, alternatively stress the importance that those at Level 1, particularly in its first stage, attach to authority as giving some support for the idea that the young child is heteronomous. If we take this view, then the overall shift is from heteronomy to autonomy.

The claim that the later theory did not involve stage-related shifts in autonomy really seems to have arisen not from the actual descriptions of the stages published by Kohlberg (1976), but from the gloss that Kohlberg, in that article, put on these descriptions in his commentary on the stage definitions. His aim in doing this was to deal with the problems raised by the apparent regression of some college students to Stage 2. It was now argued by Tappan et al. (1987, p.322) that:

> the college relativists of Kohlberg and Kramer (1969) [i.e. those regressing to Stage 2 by once again locating the basis for morality in their own interests] had not truly shown structurally postconventional reasoning in high school (Stage 5), but had been misscored using the 1958 scoring system. This misscoring was due to a confusion between content and structure. Primarily this confusion centred around content characteristics of autonomous moral reasoning that these high-school-aged subjects had shown in their responses to moral dilemmas.

For this reason it was desired, in 1976, to draw a distinction between the content of moral reasoning and its structure, such that autonomy–heteronomy would be reflected only in the content assessment of replies to an interview, whereas structure would be reflected only in the stage score. To achieve this, each stage was subdivided into a Substage A, in which the content of reasoning showed a heteronomous approach, and a Substage B, in which it showed an autonomous approach. The "college relativists" typically said that they themselves were the origin of moral values, and that what was right was that which was in their interests. This could now be seen as a viewpoint that displayed extreme autonomy in content, but at the same time exhibited advanced elements of structure, as it involved using an overriding principle to organise thinking. This, it will be argued in Chapters 7 and 8, is an essentially correct solution to the problem of the college relativists, but it could not be presented in a consistent form using any of the later versions of Kohlberg's scoring methods, as these failed to provide an index of logical structure that was in any way independent of the content of reasoning. In fact, the 1987b method of scoring has severe problems in providing any index of logical structure at all, as it codes only single justifications, and logical structure is the connection between justifications.

Although the approach just mentioned initially seemed to Kohlberg and his collaborators to offer a plausible solution to the problem of the college relativists, it ran into the difficulty that, when longitudinal studies were scored using a method of scoring based on this idea, empirical results did not confirm it. This appears to have been partly for the reason just given, but the origins of the failure were misdiagnosed, leading Tappan et al. (1987) to seek to define distinct types of heteronomous and autonomous reasoning at each stage, based on a somewhat different theoretical approach to that used earlier. This new method scores those who show predominantly heteronomous morality as being of Type A and those who show predominantly autonomous morality as being of Type B. This is intended to categorise the content of moral reasoning, as distinct from its structure. However, no comparable effort to devise an adequate index of logical structure was undertaken, as it was erroneously believed that the 1987b stage scoring method already provided this.

The distinction between heteronomy and autonomy is now drawn in a more complicated way than it had been previously. Nine ways in which heteronomous individuals may differ from autonomous ones were drawn up from a survey of psychological and philosophical literature on the subject:

1. Freedom. Heteronomous justifications involve reference to authority, law, or tradition, whereas autonomous ones do not.
2. Mutual respect. Heteronomous justifications do not show respect for cooperation between equals in coming to fair and just decisions, whereas autonomous ones do.
3. Reversibility. Heteronomous justifications do not involve looking at a situation from the differing points of view of all those involved, whereas autonomous ones do.
4. Constructivism. Heteronomous justifications involve a sacred, rigid, and inflexible view of rules and laws, whereas autonomous

ones view them as flexible formulations of the human mind designed to further cooperation among equals.

5. Hierarchy. Heteronomous justifications may involve nonmoral and pragmatic considerations in thinking about a dilemma, whereas autonomous ones show clear preference for moral values and prescriptive duties above such considerations.

6. Intrinsicalness. Heteronomous thinking views persons as means to an end, whereas autonomous thinking always views them as ends in themselves.

7. Prescriptivity. Heteronomous thinking reflects an instrumental or hypothetical view of moral duty, whereas autonomous thinking views moral duty as binding regardless of the inclinations of the actor or of pragmatic considerations.

8. Universality. Heteronomous thinking is not explicit or universalised, whereas autonomous thinking is.

9. Choice. Heteronomous individuals are more likely to make dilemma choices that accord with Levels 1 or 2, whereas autonomous individuals will make choices that accord with the postconventional Level 3.

Tappan et al. (1987) hold that a person who is ideally heteronomous will be heteronomous on all nine of these characteristics, whereas a person who is ideally autonomous will be autonomous on all nine.

Using this notion of the distinction between heteronomy and autonomy, Tappan et al. (1987) devised a method of scoring replies to Kohlberg's moral dilemma stories that claimed to score only the heteronomy–autonomy content and not the structural stage of the replies. Guidelines for applying this method are presented based on the notion that for every dilemma a subset of the nine characteristics will be most prominent in replies, and therefore this subset of characteristics is selected as the main basis for scoring with that dilemma. Once all an individual's replies have been scored, the scorer then looks to see whether heteronomous or autonomous replies are the more common. The individual is scored as being either heteronomous or autonomous depending on which kind of reply predominates. Thus the scoring method converts the observed balance between the two kinds of response into an all-or-nothing score, in which the person is held to be either heteronomous or autonomous.

A number of predictions are given about the expected behaviour of such scores. First, as age increases individuals will become more autonomous. This prediction is claimed to return us to the views of Piaget (1932) and Kohlberg (1958), though as already pointed out it is also consistent with one interpretation of Colby and Kohlberg (1987a).

Second, the developmental achievement of autonomy will be stage-like. In a series of interviews, taken longitudinally on the same individual, we will find an initial series of scores at the heteronomous Type A. Ideally there will then be a "one-time shift to moral autonomy", if one occurs at all, with no later regressions to heteronomous Type A scores. However, it is admitted that empirically observed patterns may not be quite as neat as this would imply. Third, it is predicted that children brought up in social environments that stress cooperation and mutual respect will be more likely to progress to autonomous Type B moral reasoning at a relatively early age; social environments emphasising constraint and respect for authority will delay its onset and encourage regression to Type A heteronomous morality when Type B does emerge. Fourth, autonomous individuals will be more moral in their actions than heteronomous individuals.

Reliability studies with this new method were found to be satisfactory. Longitudinal studies using the method on US subjects and other nationalities are reported, which support all the predictions just outlined. Although there were some regressions by those who had progressed from Type A to Type B back to Type A, these only involved from 6–8% of subjects and this was considered to be a suitably low figure, comparable to the degree of regression we would normally find in other cognitive achievements held to have a stage-like character. In addition, it was found that the higher an individual's score on Kohlberg's structural stage sequence the more likely they were to score at the autonomous Type B.

There is no doubt that this work is of interest, but it is not clear that it really validates a stage-transition view of the development of moral autonomy, or precisely what the connection between autonomy and Kohlberg's stages now is. Tappan et al. (1987) admit that what actually happens to the proportion of replies indicating autonomy rather than heteronomy in moral dilemma interviews, as the child gets older, is that it gradually increases. There is no sudden, stage-like shift in this proportion. The fact that the Type A and Type B scores, which they derive from the individual replies, shift in a stage-like manner with age is an almost inevitable result of the way these scores are derived from the raw scores. As the proportion of autonomy-based replies remains below 50% the child continues to score as a Type A subject; as this proportion shifts above 50% they begin to score at Type B. The underlying trend is for a gradual shift from heteronomy to autonomy. This is made to look stage-like by the way the Type A and Type B scores are derived.

The connection with Kohlberg's stage scores is also problematic. It is claimed that Types A and B indicate content, which is independent of logical form, that is supposed to be assessed by Kohlberg's stages.

Criterion 9 in the list of criteria for autonomy explicitly mentions its connection with Kohlberg's stages, with those at Levels 1 and 2 scoring as heteronomous and those at Level 3 as autonomous. Criteria 1–3 are also clearly related to the stages, with those scoring at Stage 1 likely to score as heteronomous, and those scoring above as autonomous. Several of the remaining criteria seem likely to be related to the stages in a less clear-cut fashion. In addition, the claim that Kohlberg's (1976) stage sequence is a content-independent measure of logical structure unrelated to autonomy is inherently implausible, for reasons that have already been mentioned. In view of this, it is hardly surprising that empirical results show that stage scores and autonomy scores, calculated in the new way, correlate. This is, however, contrary to predictions made about the connection between these two kinds of scores by Tappan et al. (1987).

The Type A and Type B distinction of 1987 seems to be based mainly on a sample of those aspects of reasoning that go to make up the stage scores, converted to an either-or categorisation by taking the most frequent type of reply. This kind of assessment would seem to be more useful if the balance between heteronomy and autonomy replies were cited, rather than the either-or type score. Findings using such scores do not help to validate Colby's and Kohlberg's stages as an index of the structure of reasoning, which they clearly are not

CONCLUSIONS

Colby and Kohlberg's (1987a, b) successful demonstration of the sequentiality of stages meant that Kohlberg's work enjoyed a resurgence of popularity immediately following the publication of these books. Few commentators noticed that most interviewees only scored at one or at two adjoining stages with the assistance of the dubious rule that if there are less than 10% of replies at a stage, these are discounted as error. Even once we notice this, the empirical evidence for a slightly weakened form of sequentiality is still impressive. That the theory already commanded substantial support can be seen from the contributions to Modgil and Modgil (1986), a major edited work in which a wide range of contributors were invited to give their views on Kohlberg's theory. A majority was favourable, though a minority was scathing, as had been the case from the early days of the theory.

Increased support for Kohlberg's views following the 1987 publications was probably indicated by contributions to Kurtines's and Gerwitz's (1991) three-volume handbook of moral development research. Despite the first editor having been among the most cogent and notable of the critics in 1974 and the wide range of contributors, the book is overwhelmingly favourable; most contributors give Kohlberg's views almost unqualified endorsement, with minority, though spirited, opposition shown only by Haan, Hoffman, and a few other brave souls.

It has been argued here that this unqualified enthusiasm was mistaken, being based on an almost complete absence, on the part of either Kohlberg or the majority of his critics, of a clear realisation of the role of strong interpretation and arbitrary placement in the assignment of replies to stages, or of the limitations of the interview methods used. There is little doubt that Kohlberg's interviews and scoring methods assess the orderly and sequential development of some kind of moral reasoning. Four key questions remain. Does his scoring method really provide an adequate description of the developmental trends in replies that occur in these interviews? Are there alternative ways of describing these trends? What is the best way to explain such trends? Is it really possible to draw definitive conclusions about moral reasoning in general, as Kohlberg defines it, from his dilemma interviews?

Examination of the writings of Kohlberg and his collaborators has shown that there are serious problems, in responding to the first three of these questions, in a way that is unambiguously favourable to Kohlberg's enterprise. The findings from weakly interpretive studies reviewed in the next three chapters will reinforce these doubts. They will also add to them considerable doubts about the validity of the Kohlbergian interview as a general index of moral reasoning.

PART TWO

Interview findings in the light of weakly interpretive methods

CHAPTER SIX

The problem outlined

COMPARTMENTALISATION AND THE DEFINITION OF THE TOPIC

The first part of this book outlined three significant theoretical traditions in the study of the development of moral reasoning. There are two common reactions to the divergences between these traditions, which we can refer to as compartmentalisation and contradiction. Compartmentalisation arguments say that the different traditions are talking about different things and so it is acceptable for them to reach different conclusions. Contradiction arguments say that the subject matter of the different approaches overlaps, to a significant degree, and thus they contradict one another and we must seek to reject some or all of them.

Three particularly notable instances of the compartmentalisation argument have appeared in the recent literature from three of the leading theoreticians in the area. In one way or another, they argue that the content of the reasoning dealt with by exponents of the different traditions differs, and thus there is no contradiction involved in their differing conclusions about the development of moral reasoning. Kohlberg (1984) argued that his work was on moral judgement (a term he often preferred to moral reasoning), whereas that of Loevinger was on ego development. Haan (1977, 1991) argued that her work was about bargaining during negotiations for moral exchange, whereas Kohlberg dealt with logical deductions from moral rules or principles. Loevinger has produced the most elaborate of the compartmentalisation arguments. This is the topic of her book *Paradigms of personality* (1987), in which she argues that there have been five major paradigms in the study of human personality. Two of these have produced divergent approaches to the development of moral reasoning.

None of these three versions of the compartmentalisation argument is very convincing. Thus, Kohlberg's (1984) comment is just a flat statement that Loevinger's approach deals with ego development and his own with the development of moral judgement, with no supporting argument, or mention of the fact that Loevinger (1970, 1976, 1983) disagrees with his claim. As we shall see later, there are reasons for thinking that the content of Kohlberg's and Loevinger's work is substantially different. However, this cannot be established just by appeal to the terms "ego development" and "development of moral judgement", as the general understanding that ego psychologists have about the scope of moral reasoning tends to subsume Kohlberg's understanding of this term. The reasons for this were discussed in the introduction, in dealing with the rival definitions of the topic given by these two schools of thought. It happens that the particular techniques used by Kohlberg and Loevinger to study moral reasoning do tend to focus on different aspects of the topic, but this cannot be established just by appeal to general labels in the way Kohlberg attempts. Haan's version of the compartmentalisation argument, as mentioned in Chapter 3, is also weak, as she misreads the nature of Kohlberg's work, which is not primarily, especially in its later versions, about deduction from moral premises.

Loevinger's version of the argument is the most extensive and carefully considered, but the details of her treatment also reveal how much she cannot explain by it. Thus, the three traditions outlined in Part 1 fall into only two of the five paradigms of personality she identifies, psychoanalysis and cognitive developmentalism, as she places contributions from ego psychology in the cognitive developmentalism paradigm, rather than making this a distinct strand. Considering the notably different ways that cognitive structuralism and ego psychology have viewed the stages, nature, and driving forces of development, this is a very questionable decision.

However, even more serious is her failure to explain why the various approaches described as belonging within the cognitive developmentalism paradigm have reached such different conclusions. A paradigm in the sense that this term is used by Kuhn (1970) refers to an approach within natural science to a given topic, that advances a particular theory about the topic and uses certain methods of investigation. The struggle between paradigms is conducted on the basis of their ability to account for available empirical evidence. A small amount of disconfirmation may be absorbed by the dominant paradigm, but substantial disconfirmation will initiate paradigm shift. Competing paradigms only exist in the interregnum between dominant paradigms.

Loevinger (1987) herself, in her preface, admits that this natural science model may have only limited validity in the social sciences, but she seems unwilling to recognise quite how limited the parallels are. It is more plausible to view the social sciences as frequently offering competing views of the same topic, without the capacity to decide definitively between them. This seems to be partly because they lack common intellectual methods, particularly appeal to agreed empirical data, to show when a theory or approach is inadequate. In addition, the passions aroused by the subject matter are often too great for practitioners to abide by the findings of such methods, even where they exist. Whatever relative weight we give to these factors, together they help to explain why we find competing views of the same topic persisting without adequate resolution. Thus, the views of ego psychology and of Kohlberg both persist, without adequate resolution of their disagreements. Why this situation arose and persists is not explained by the paradigm model, but it is explained by the alternative view of the social sciences just sketched.

At this point, it is worth noting that the argument of the preceding paragraph might appear to negate all hope of agreement in the social sciences, and thus negate the argument deployed in the next three chapters that one route to greater consensus is through a return to agreed methods of description. The earlier comments, however, refer to what the social sciences have been; my argument is directed to what they might be.

Loevinger's case is also weakened by the way she uses the notion of paradigm. The object of study to which psychoanalysis applies is said to be the dynamic unconscious, and that to which cognitive developmentalism applies is said to be character development. This is a very doubtful division, as psychoanalysis also studies the development of the conscious ego and thus of conscious efforts on the part of the ego to realistically attain goals in the environment. As cognitive developmentalism, in the versions of it propounded by Piaget and Kohlberg, studies just the same thing, this contradicts the claim that the two paradigms study different things. Psychoanalysis studies more than cognitive developmentalism, as it studies unconscious as well as subconscious and conscious mental processes, but this is not the division Loevinger is seeking to draw. In addition, her claims that cognitive developmentalism studies character development and that the views of

Piaget and Kohlberg are a major part of this tradition are weakened by the absence of a clear definition of "character development". In its usual senses it would seem to exclude the views of Piaget and Kohlberg.

Notwithstanding the weak and sometimes erroneous way the compartmentalisation argument has been deployed in the literature, it can be stated in a more convincing way. It is at its strongest in contrasting the methods of Loevinger and Kohlberg. The stems that the former offers for completion offer little scope for the consideration of first order moral norms, being mainly designed to elicit responses to controversial rather than consensual moral issues. This differs from Kohlberg's interviews, which centre on norms. On the other hand, there is probably considerable overlap between the issues discussed in Haan's involved discussion groups and those raised in Kohlberg's interviews. Thus, in considering how they will regulate the new society arising after global catastrophe in Haan's Humanus interview, discussants are likely to consider what norms should be adopted and why. They will, however, also consider controversial moral issues to which no first order norms apply.

Thus, although we should try to avoid overplaying the compartmentalisation argument, it would also be a mistake to ignore the following circumstances: moral reasoning can be defined in different ways and elicited by different techniques; students of moral development are often studying different kinds of things. Consideration of the extent to which the different definitions adopted, and the different techniques used to elicit responses, have been responsible for divergent findings follows in this and later chapters.

Until recently, it was very difficult to obtain any clear view of what the influence of the subject matter variable might be on findings in the area, as studies carried out within the different traditions have differed in: subject matter; methods of analysing interview data and other material; and in the theoretical interpretations given to findings, with theoretical interpretations often inextricably entangled with the scoring method used in analysis. The greatest volume of studies has been in the Kohlbergian tradition and has used Kohlberg's interviews and Kohlbergian scoring methods. An interesting study by Adams (1988) showed that an adapted version of Kohlberg's scoring methods could be applied to discussion within undergraduate cliques similar to those studied by Haan (1977, 1986, 1991). This provides empirical support for the contention that there is substantial overlap between the content of the reasoning studied by Haan and Kohlberg, but in general far too little attention has been devoted to this problem.

Interviews are widely considered a central method for the formal study of moral reasoning. The next two chapters will discuss studies that have used weakly interpretive scoring methods to analyse

Kohlbergian and other kinds of interview data. The purpose of these chapters is to show how studies using methods of this kind can enable us to get a clearer view of which aspects of findings are due to the subject matter of a study, which to the scoring method, and which to theoretical interpretation. Some other favoured methods, especially question-naires, semi-naturalistic moral discussion (of the kind advocated by Haan), and completely naturalistic moral discussion observed in real-life situations, will be covered in the following chapter. Before proceeding to describe studies of these kinds it will be useful to draw together and extend some conclusions drawn in previous chapters about the problem of theoretical interpretation.

THEORETICAL INTERPRETATION

There are a number of descriptive features of the development of moral reasoning that are agreed on by most variants of the research traditions outlined in the first part of the book. The aim of this section is to illustrate the problem of interpreting descriptive findings, using two such trends in descriptive features that are reasonably clear from the traditions previously outlined.

1. The expansion of consideration of interests.

This refers to the general finding that the young child thinks mainly about the interests of the immediate family and itself, and this later expands to consideration of the interests of members of the peer group, of the child's own school, and of other groups to which it belongs. Finally, it expands to members of the nation and possibly to even wider groups, such as the human race. The only traditions that have produced much formal empirical evidence for this descriptive trend are the Piagetian and Kohlbergian (see Chapters 4 and 5), but the others have generally assumed it.

Some theoretical notions advanced to explain this expansion are as follows. According to Freud it occurs for four main reasons: expanded defensive identifications; expanded libidinal investments; sublimated sexual attraction; the development of the ego ideal. The infant and young child identify with and have libidinal investments in the parents and other members of the immediate family circle and, as development proceeds, this circle is broadened. The later, expanded, identifications and investments are strongly contaminated by feelings and tendencies derived from their original models. The notion of libidinal investment encompasses that of reciprocity, and even quite young children are held to expect that by helping other people they will receive help in return.

Sublimated sexual attraction increases in importance and extends to a wider circle with the rising level of libido that occurs both in infancy and in adolescence. The development of the ego ideal also encourages the emergence of general moral ideals that advocate taking account of the interests of all groups within the nation state, sometimes extending even beyond this. The effect of this mechanism is again an expansion in the breadth of consideration accorded to the interests of others.

According to the Murphys, the expansion in the consideration of the interests of others occurs for all the reasons given by Freud, but the erotic components are considerably reduced and the onset of reciprocity is set later. In the place of the erotic components, a much greater role is given to the expansion of sympathy and non-defensive identification. Relationships begin with sympathy and end with a developed form of non-defensive identification; sympathy (primitive identification) ripens into developed identification through the rewarding experience of imitating the actions of others, which is rewarding as it results in heightened arousal. The scope of sympathy and identification broaden as the child comes into contact with a wider circle of individuals at school and in the wider society.

The Murphys use Piaget and Lerner to argue for a later onset of reciprocity. The young child suffers from both egocentrism and sociocentrism; these produce an inability to coordinate its own perspective with that of the groups to which it belongs, as well as an inability to coordinate the perspectives of groups with one another. This is later replaced by reciprocity, which is the ability to see that mutual assistance is beneficial to all parties within a social group. As the child becomes aware that reciprocity can operate in a wider circle of individuals than just its immediate group, so its tendency to take account of a wider range of interests also increases.

Sullivan and Loevinger view the expansion of concern in rather similar terms to Freud, but they add to his mechanisms the broadening of sympathy.

Piaget explains the expansion of concern largely in terms of the shift from egocentrism (concern for the child's own interests) to heteronomy (concern for adult wishes) and then to reciprocity (concern for the interests of wider groups in the expectation of return consideration). Piaget uses formal interview evidence to buttress his claims about these mechanisms. He is able to point to convincing examples of appeal to authority in young children during his third stage, though he is not so clear about just how frequent these are. Evidence from his interviews that the principle of reciprocity is first explicitly stated in early adolescence is also far from convincing, due to his highly selective use of the interviews.

Kohlberg's theory is difficult to translate directly into predictions about the scope of interests considered, even though his scoring system undoubtedly scores replies that take account of wider interests at higher stages. This is because there are at least three reasons given by the theory that could result in a broadening of interests, but it is not entirely clear how they will work together. The first of these reasons is the shift from the combination of heteronomy and egocentrism found at Stage 1 to the notion of reciprocity found at Stage 2. At Stage 2 the individual still helps others for selfish reasons, but now realises that by entering into moral agreements and helping others they themselves will be better off. This shift will result in a broadening of the interests considered from those of the self and of authority figures, chiefly the parents, to the peer group and other wider, though still relatively immediate, groups.

However, this is then followed by a second shift that also bears on the scope of interests considered. This occurs as the sociomoral point of view shifts from Level 1 (Stages 1 and 2) concern for the interests of the self as the ultimate reason for any helping of others, to the acceptance of the interests of groups, initially mainly small groups and dyads, as the ultimate reason for considering others' interests. That is to say that, from being a means to the end of self-interest, the interests of the other members of the group now become ends in themselves.

The initial focus of this new level of thinking will be somewhat narrower than that of the previous stage, as at first it tends to focus on permanent relationships within the family and on close friendship bonds. However, as elements of Stage 2 thinking will persist alongside it, it is unlikely that any actual diminution in the scope of interests considered will occur. When we reach Stage 4, the scope of this second kind of consideration now widens further and includes consideration of the interests of "society" as a whole, usually meaning the nation, as the ultimate reason for considering the interests of others.

At Stage 5 the reciprocity argument returns in a new form, as the individuals comprising society are now seen to derive benefits from their participation in the social contract, and this provides another reason for considering the interests of the wider society. Stage 5 moral principles are also highly general in their application and this provides a third mechanism for broadening consideration, to add to reciprocity and change in sociomoral point of view. For reasons that will be made clearer in the following chapters, Kohlberg's attempts to ground his account of the developmental course of these mechanisms in the replies of interviewees is, like that of Piaget, flawed.

The available interpretations for the expansion of the child's consideration of interests do not end with those discussed by the theorists included in the first part of this book. Other theoretical traditions, that have not been prominent in formal research or theoretical discussions defined by textbook treatments of the topic, can often offer explanatory ideas that can be used to provide interpretations of descriptive phenomena of this kind. General theories of personality development are a particularly fertile source of such ideas. Two notions culled from this source are particularly relevant.

The first is the ethological view of bonding and attachment (see especially Archer, 1992; Bowlby, 1984; Eibl-Eibesfeldt, 1989; Rushton, 1988; Sluckin, Herbert, & Sluckin, 1983). It can be argued that, like some other animals, human beings possess one or more innate biological bonding mechanisms that produce social attachments. One version of this argument says that there is a bonding mechanism that first bonds the infant to parents or other significant figures in the environment, either due to exposure, or to the way in which interaction between them triggers the bonding mechanism. This may operate in something like the way that exposure to moving objects triggers the imprinting response, causing the young of some species of bird to follow moving objects to which they are exposed during a critical period (Hess, 1973; McFarland, 1993; Sluckin, 1972). This initial set of attachments is then widened by extension of the same mechanism, which later attaches the child to significant members of the peer group and others. Alternatively, it could be that, as some animal ethologists think is the case with many birds, there are separate attachment mechanisms for initial bonding to the parents and later bonding with the peer group. It could be that part of the widening of consideration of interests is due to the broader scope of operation of the second, later, attachment mechanism.

Another explanation is based on Pavlovian conditioning. This was implied by the Murphys, though not spelt out in detail. Thus many forms of human gratification take place socially, from eating meals and playing board games to sex games among children. Perhaps the conjunction, of the pleasurable experience of participating in such activities with the sight of others enjoying themselves, causes the two to be associated by Pavlovian conditioning; this leads to the enjoyment of others becoming pleasurable in itself. As the social activities of the child broaden, so the circle of people associated with gratification broadens.

We can distinguish in these approaches a number of different reasons for the broadening of the consideration of interests during development and it is useful to isolate some of these:

1. Expanding sympathy (called empathy by Sullivan). Here it is assumed that, especially by witnessing the pleasure or pain of another, the child will catch this pleasure or pain themselves. Thus they act to promote the interests of others in order to be able to

catch their pleasure and to avoid catching their pain. The ability to sympathise with others by hearing about or reading about their emotions, as well as attendance at meetings of larger groups outside the home, result in expansion of sympathy during development.

2. Widening of viewpoint. Here the child no longer seeks to act solely on its own behalf, but to act on behalf of a wider group as the primary aim of action.

3. Identification. In the purely Freudian sense this is largely a defence against the anxiety generated by thoughts of opposing the wishes of a powerful person. The child comes to adopt the viewpoint of the other, not for cognitive reasons but for emotional ones.

4. Prudence in the face of authority. The child does what authorities want to avoid punishment or displeasure and to gain favour. This may include helping other group members to please group authorities. As the child becomes a member of wider groups, such consideration of others' interests will expand.

5. Reciprocity. The child takes account of the interests of others so as to gain consideration from them.

6. Libidinal investment. The child considers another person because they have invested libido in them. This is a special case of reciprocity, where the calculation of mutual interest has solidified into an established relationship or "object choice".

7. Sublimated sexual attraction. Although some may argue that Freud overplayed this factor, it is likely to play some role, for instance in the adolescent peer group. It will expand with development as sexual feelings intensify.

8. Biological bonding mechanisms. This argues that the scope of such mechanisms expands during development.

9. Pavlovian conditioning. Again, the scope of this can be predicted to expand during development.

The inability of theorists to produce a convincing account of the mix of these mechanisms responsible for the course of development has resulted from two main factors. The first is that many theorists, especially those in the Freudian and ego psychology traditions, have simply taken the descriptive principle of the expansion of consideration for others, and then read explanations for this trend from their general theoretical preconceptions. Thus, Freud discounted sympathy and emphasised sexuality because this fitted his general theoretical views, rather than because he could give any particular reason for this emphasis grounded in facts about the development of moral reasoning and emotion.

The second reason is that those theorists, like Piaget and Kohlberg, who have tried to use interview evidence to support their explanatory account of this trend, have used strong interpretation of such evidence in a way that makes it impossible to discover whether it really does support their accounts. The object of the following chapters is to assess how far weakly interpretive methods of analysing interview evidence and other kinds of data can remedy this situation. It should be emphasised at the outset that no claim is made that a definitive answer can currently be given. The aim is rather clear delineation of areas of knowledge and ignorance.

2. The self-other-self cycle.

This is a second descriptive developmental phenomenon that has been interpreted in various ways by theorists. It is the tendency, assumed by all the main theorists covered except Haan, for the focus of moral reasoning to shift during development from an initial focus on the self, to an intermediate focus on outside social groups and then ultimately, though not necessarily in everyone, at least partially back to the self again. This is not in general in conflict with the continual broadening of the interests considered described earlier, as the self that is promoted in the third phase is typically a moral self that acts to promote general human interests. However, in cases where the moral ideal of the self in the third phase is not conventionally moral but, as occurs in a significant minority of cases for a period, that of a moral individualist who defines morality as what benefits himself or herself (Kohlberg's college relativists), the breadth of human interests considered will shrink. This ideal does not appear to persist in a sufficiently large fraction of the population, in most Western societies, to outweigh the general tendency for the breadth of interests considered to expand with age (see especially Langford, 1991b).

The self-other-self cycle occurs for the following reasons, according to Freudian theory. The infant is relatively narcissistic; it later adapts to reality by investing libido in those around it and by identifying with those around it. Ultimately the ego ideal, at least in many adults, is capable of reattracting libidinal energy and converting this once again to a new form of narcissism, this time experienced on a higher plane. This theme in Freudian theory was taken up by all the main ego psychologists discussed, except Haan, though they generally reinterpreted it to remove Freud's hydraulic model of libidinal energy flow and replace it with their own preferred theory of motivational dynamics.

The same descriptive trend is assumed by Piaget when he argues that development goes from the initial egocentrism of the child, through heteronomy and on to reciprocity and autonomy, in which the adolescent once again becomes independent and relatively self-centred in moral outlook. The force that powers development in the initial part of this sequence is improved ability to entertain differing viewpoints. Just why the adolescent returns to a new kind of self-centredness in later development is less clear, but one reason could be the pride in his or her newfound intellectual accomplishments emphasised in Piaget's (1972) treatment of the period of formal operations.

The theme of the self-other-self cycle is even more obvious in Kohlberg's account of his three levels of moral reasoning. Here we find that the sociomoral perspective of the first level is that of egocentrism, of the second level that of the group, but in the third level the viewpoint of the individual returns, at first, at Stage 5, in a subordinate role, but then, at Stage 6, in the dominant role. At Stage 6 the most prominent feature of reasoning is commitment to self-chosen moral principles. As for Piaget, these developments are chiefly driven by improved cognitive capacity.

We can also look to general theories of personality development for explanations of aspects of the self-other-self cycle. One relevant theory here is that of Jung. According to Jung, in the first half of life there is an initiation into outward reality. This sees the consolidation of the ego, differentiation of the individual's main style of psychic functioning, and dominant attitude type, and formation of a social persona or outward image. This is followed by the mid-life crisis and a turning inward to explore the person's inner fantasies and reality. This will occupy the second half of life if the person is to achieve satisfactory resolution of their inner tensions, though this may not occur. This turning inward is often referred to as an alteration of moral outlook (e.g. Jung, 1952; Jacobi, 1968, pp.105–7).

In the first half of life, the direction of flow of libido is outward; in the second, it is inward. Libido for Jung is a general psychic energy that seeks an outlet not only in sensual or sexual gratification but also in activity in a wider sense (Jung, 1952). The direction of this flow turns to the inner fantasy world, and away from the outer world, in the second half of life. This is because: the tasks of establishing the person in the outside world through family and career are now completed, and these activities can be put on automatic pilot with reduced expenditure of energy; and the imbalance in the personality that has built up as a result of efforts to adapt to the outside world leads to inner pressures for structural readjustment.

Although this Jungian view cannot be used in its original form to explain why the direction of moral interest seems to turn inward in some respects from late adolescence, rather than from mid-life, an adapted version of the theory would explain this. Thus, it could be argued, late adolescence often involves a break in the search for adaptation to the outer world, that results in an initial turning inward in search of relief from structural tensions in the personality that have already built up, later followed by a resumption in the outward direction of movement and final inversion in mid-life.

Another possibility is suggested by Rank's view that, as adolescence proceeds, fear of death becomes more prominent and defences against this fear come into play (Becker, 1973; Lieberman, 1985; Menaker, 1982; Rank, 1931, 1968; Schumaker, 1990). It could be that intellectual developments in late adolescence lead to a further crisis in this area, resulting in increased resources being diverted to the building of a moral ideal as part of the individual's "immortality project". The immortality project is one that offers the person the hope of immortality, whether real or illusory. Striving towards a moral ideal, either conceived as part of a timeless and unchanging realm, or as a lasting contribution to human progress, may well offer such a hope in late adolescence.

Once again, the material on weakly interpretive methods covered in the following chapters cannot presently establish the relative contributions of these mechanisms to the self-other-self cycle. However, such methods are able to establish the way in which the trend is manifested in interview evidence, in a manner that constitutes an advance on previous accounts, and can hopefully pave the way for a fuller understanding of such mechanisms in the future.

CONCLUSIONS

The existence of general descriptive trends, of the kind outlined in this chapter, can be established both by using formal methods of inquiry like interviews and by common observation and clinical practice. In one sense, the two descriptive trends discussed here hardly require formal methods to establish their general outline, though formal methods can help in making clear their details. However, other trends are less obvious from general experience and casual observation.

The next two chapters will focus on attempts that have been made to establish detailed descriptive trends in the development of replies in interviews, using weakly interpretive scoring methods. This will provide a much clearer view of the extent to which such evidence really does support the dominant Kohlbergian account of the mechanisms underlying development. Kohlberg's use of strongly interpretive methods to analyse interview evidence makes it hard to know whether the evidence supports the theory or not. Weakly interpretive methods are able to clarify this issue by providing information about the developmental course of particular kinds of reply, rather than about that of bundles of disparate kinds of reply, which are the only trends reported in Kohlberg's developmental research on his stages. Kohlberg's theory, as well as other theories reviewed here, make definite predictions about the developmental course of some particular kinds of reply, such as those providing explicit explanations of reciprocity, which can be used to test these theories when evidence is analysed using weakly interpretive methods.

CHAPTER SEVEN

The Kohlbergian interview and weakly interpretive scoring methods

INTRODUCTION

It has been common to think that Kohlberg concentrated upon one particularly central way of eliciting moral reasoning and that he succeeded in successfully describing, and explaining, the development of this kind of reasoning, in his stages and the theory used to explain progress through them. It should already be clear that this is far from true in an uncomplicated sense. It would be more accurate to say that he isolated and concentrated upon one central kind of moral reasoning; his way of describing its development inextricably confounds description and explanation, in a way that makes it hard to see whether the explanation really fits the description, or just recycles the theory through it, in a self-validating circle that allows little scope for testing the theory.

Loevinger (1970) pointed to the existence of three ways of scoring projective instruments like the Kohlbergian interview: that which concentrates on surface forms of language; that which concentrates on explicitly expressed meanings; and that which interprets underlying and unexpressed meanings. She rightly points out that this was a long-established classification of scoring methods among those concerned with the development of projective tests.

We have already seen that Kohlberg's method of scoring the interviews to which he gave his name was emphatically of the third of these kinds. This has the drawback that it is impossible to engage in the normal scientific enterprise of reviewing possible alternative explanations for phenomena and assessing their relative ability to provide an explanation. This is because Kohlberg's stages do not just describe what is said in his interviews at different points in development. Replies are often assigned to stages by interpreting what is said so that it fits the stage description, even though there are other interpretations of such a reply available. The methods of interpretation deployed in the 1987 manual are also so flexible that they permit the assignment of many replies to a wide range of stages.

We can divide replies in Kohlbergian interviews as scored by the later methods into the following categories: those that are unambiguously assigned to a stage by the theory and provide an explicit statement of the underlying meaning of the reply ascribed to it in the theory; those that are unambiguously assigned to a stage by the theory but need to have additional meaning given them, which is not explicitly stated, in order to reveal the underlying meaning assumed by the theory; those whose stage level is not unambiguous but which are assigned by the arbitrary use of methods of interpretation that give the statement some meaning it does not have on the surface, when some completely different meaning could have been given to it using the interpretive methods offered by the theory. It is not at all clear from Kohlberg's own way of reporting his findings how numerous each of these three categories of reply is. Clearly, if the third category is large, the theory derives reduced support from the evidence on sequentiality of stages that has been used to support it, as the claim that the stages in some sense explain such replies is flimsy. If the second category is large, this will also reduce support for the theory obtained by the scoring methods in question, as there may be ways of explaining replies falling into this category, other than those offered by the theory.

There are two ways in which we could respond to this situation. One would be by developing other strongly interpretive methods of analysing findings from Kohlbergian interviews. If such methods could be developed, then this would show that Kohlberg's theory is only one among several candidates in this area. This strategy seems not to have been pursued in a systematic way.

However, there are good reasons for preferring an alternative strategy, which is to devise methods that are weakly interpretive, in the sense that they concentrate on explicitly expressed meanings rather than interpretation of underlying but unexpressed meanings. The main reason for this is that the number of potential theories that can be used to explain the development of moral reasoning is large. It includes not only the three traditions and their various variants dealt with in the first part of the book, but also new combinations of concepts derived from general personality theory that have not been used much in the literature for this purpose, but are quite suitable for it. To devise a separate strongly interpretive scoring technique corresponding to each of the resulting theories would be a very arduous undertaking.

A much simpler and less labour-intensive strategy, that has in fact been pursued more widely, is to concentrate on devising a weakly interpretive method of scoring, and thus to separate the business of description from that of interpretation. This means that, at least as an ideal, we can do the work of description once and then review possible explanations for our description at a later stage. This is a much easier route to take, as the process of scoring transcripts from interview studies, using two or more scorers to establish the inter-rater reliability of each method, is extremely labour-intensive. Although the labour of working out interpretations for descriptive findings from studies is almost equally arduous, by pursuing this route we can at least avoid having to do the work of devising scoring methods and undertaking transcript scoring many times.

Two difficulties disturb this ideal picture of such a research strategy. The first is that it is probably not possible to have a weakly interpretive method that is entirely devoid of all theoretical presuppositions. However, one of the surprising features of the history of attempts to devise such methods is how little this difficulty has appeared to disturb progress so far. This is at first sight surprising, as it is quite natural to form a picture of replies in many interviews, including Kohlbergian ones, as like a complex and chaotic abstract painting. The painting acts like a Rorschach ink blot, in which we can make out all sorts of different shapes and outlines. Rorschach supposed that a person's personality and unconscious preoccupations would bias their perceptual system to grip onto certain outlines in the ink blot that were relevant to their preoccupations, and make these look like "a robber" or "a naked man". It is natural to think that dividing up kinds of reply to an interview is like making an outline salient in an inkblot, and that the dividing lines that might appear descriptively important to one investigator would appear descriptively unimportant to another, depending on their theoretical preoccupations and personality. This relativistic picture of the process of interview analysis tends to draw further support from the current fashion among some literary critics for the deconstructive methods of Derrida, one of whose best known slogans is "the reader is the text", which is to say that the reader projects onto the text their own preoccupations, rather than seeing what is in it.

However, there is another picture of what happens here that is also plausible. This is that interview transcripts are not so much like chaotic abstract paintings as like the realistic paintings of, say, Holbein or Rembrandt. That is to say, the replies of the interviewee are intended to call up in the mind of the hearer the limited number of socially agreed meanings that are conventionally thought to be relevant in replying to such questions. The interviewee is like the painter who intends to convey tables, chairs, the human body, apples, and so forth in a clear and unambiguous manner. If artists intend to draw clear and unmistakable objects they leave the viewer with little choice but to see these objects, at least on the level of perception. The viewer can then go on to say "The skull lying on the table is a typical sixteenth-century reference to the omnipresence of death." Someone else might say "The skull lying on the table is a reflection of the desire of the sixteenth-century church to retain control over the population, by harping on the subject of death." This could lead to a discussion about why skulls were used in paintings in this period. What is not in doubt is that there is a skull on a table; its underlying meaning is debatable, but its presence as an object is not.

The history of attempts to devise weakly interpretive methods of analysis that can be applied to Kohlbergian and other kinds of moral reasoning interview, as well as examination of aspects of Kohlberg's own strongly interpretive methods, tend to suggest the second of these pictures rather than the first. The most prominent weakly interpretive methods have been those suggested by Williams (1969), Wilson (1973), Davidson, Turiel, and Black (1983), Trainer (1982, 1983), and Langford and D'Cruz (1989). The first of these methods was also used in studies by Steward (1979) and Turner (1987); the third in studies by Tisak and Turiel (1984, 1988), Arsenio and Ford (1985), Tisak and Ford (1986), and other studies discussed in Turiel and Davidson (1986), Helwig, Tisak, and Turiel (1990), and Turiel et al. (1991); the fifth in a range of studies dealt with later in this chapter and the next. Although only the third and fifth of these methods have been applied in studies of Kohlbergian interviews, they all could be with slight modifications.

It is striking that these methods all bear a strong family resemblance to one another (for detailed discussion of this see Langford & D'Cruz, 1989; Langford & Claydon, 1989). This is despite the widely differing theoretical presuppositions of their originators. Thus: Williams had his own distinctive theory of the development of moral reasoning; Davidson, Turiel, and Black were sympathetic to Kohlberg at the time they devised their method; while Wilson, Trainer, and Langford aimed chiefly at description without interpretation.

Before proceeding, one or two comments on Williams's interview methods will be in order, as his rather different view of descriptive developmental trends, from that offered in this and the next chapter, might otherwise seem to contradict my claim that all weakly interpretive methods lead to similar descriptive conclusions. However, they will of course only do this if applied to similar material. The differences between Williams's findings and those from other techniques seem to owe more to his concentration on unusual methods of eliciting replies than to his method of analysing them. He concentrated almost exclusively on interviews relying on the prompt "Who told you that?" and requests for definitions of moral terms. The use of the former technique encourages belief-based replies and discourages others, thus accounting for many of the peculiarities in his descriptive findings. The idiosyncrasies of the latter technique are discussed in Chapter 9.

Consideration of the scoring manual of Colby and Kohlberg (1987b) suggests that Kohlberg himself also viewed the purely descriptive features of his later scoring system in much the same way as the authors of descriptive methods of assessment listed earlier. Thus, Colby and Kohlberg argue that justifications always make implicit or explicit reference to a first order moral norm and explicit reference to a moral element in the justification. (Moral elements are justifications other than norms and were outlined in the previous chapter.) This can be translated into the statement that we will find in a justification either explicit mention of one of the moral elements alone or of a moral norm together with one of the moral elements. This gives us a descriptive system that to this point is strikingly similar to the methods of classification outlined earlier, especially that of Langford and D'Cruz (1989). There are three main points of difference.

First, Colby and Kohlberg's list of moral elements is rather more discriminating and fine-grained than the corresponding list of categories used by the other authors. Second, because Colby and Kohlberg cross-classify replies using both the type of norm and the moral element, they do not have to decide between them in assigning replies. Langford and D'Cruz (1989) discussed this option, but decided for reasons of simplicity to assign replies that contain only explicit reference to a norm by the norm, and replies that contain both a norm and another element of justification by the latter. Third, as explained shortly, provision is also made by Langford and D'Cruz for situations where we find two of these further elements of justification in the same reply; thus "Everyone can see we should consider Joe's interests" contains both belief ("Everyone can see") and interest elements ("consider Joe's interests"). Where there are two such elements in a reply, one is scored as the more reflective using explicit rules for deciding reflectiveness. In Colby and Kohlberg's method we usually take the combination of elements to the scoring manual and find it listed there, thus obviating the need to decide between the elements.

None of these differences is one of principle. Very similar sets of basic elements of meaning are identified in both cases. The key difference, between Colby and Kohlberg's scoring method and weakly interpretive methods, is that the former uses the initial identification of a type of reply purely as a means for the scorer to find out the deeper meaning of the reply from the scoring manual. They then report findings only in terms of this deeper meaning, which assigns it to a stage. Furthermore, only proportions of replies falling into stages are reported, not proportions falling into detailed categories of reply, whether interpreted or not. Weakly interpretive methods report on the number of replies containing chosen elements of uninterpreted, explicit meaning. Thus information is available on proportions of detailed types of reply, rather than just about proportions of replies aggregated into stages. This means that a detailed descriptive picture of uninterpreted meanings emerges from findings, which does not emerge from those reported according to Kohlberg's stages.

THE LANGFORD AND D'CRUZ SCORING METHOD

The bulk of this chapter will deal with findings from two studies of Kohlbergian interviews reported by Langford and D'Cruz (1989) and Langford and Claydon (1989), which used the scoring method of Langford and D'Cruz (1989). The reason for concentrating on these studies is that the scoring method used is the most detailed of the weakly interpretive methods mentioned in the previous section, and overcomes some of the difficulties associated with other methods. It has also been found to show satisfactory inter-rater reliability (see studies just mentioned and those to be discussed shortly). Three of the most important additional features it contains are as follows.

The first relates to the division of the broad categories of justification, which correspond roughly to Colby's and Kohlberg's norms and elements of justification, into subcategories corresponding to the level of generality of the reply. Thus a reply that mentions justification by human interests can mention those of an individual (the least general category), those of a small group (the next most general category) or those of a very large group or of people in general (the most general category). This division into levels of generality is implied in the Colby and Kohlberg method by the way that particular types of reply (called criterion judgements) are described in the scoring manual, but it is not formally stated as an aspect of most elements of justification (the exception here is interest-based elements), although it undoubtedly is.

The second additional feature is the provision of a rule that deals with situations, which are extremely common, where we find more than one element in a reply. Here we need to take account of the fact that, in the terminology of Langford and D'Cruz (1989), an element of justification includes both norms and rules and other elements of justification, rather than just the non-rule elements of justification, which is what Colby and Kohlberg mean by this term. This rule will be explained shortly and enables the scorer, in most instances, to discover which element of the reply is to determine the score, without recourse to personal judgement.

The third additional feature is that the method takes account of the logical organisation of replies, whereas the other methods do not. The view taken of this was originally proposed by Trainer (1982, 1983). The ability of the interviewee to integrate the various "thought units" contained in their replies is held to pass through three phases.

In the first phase, which predominates until mid-adolescence, there is very little attempt to relate one justification to another. Thus, in the transcript given in Chapter 5 as typical of Kohlberg's Type 1, we find that most justifications are not coordinated with one another. For instance, in response to the second, third, and fourth questions the interviewee says:

(Q: Should he give it or refuse?) Give it to him. Well you should be nice to your parents and do what they say. (Q: Would it be wrong for him to refuse?) Yes. Well, he wanted to go to camp and his father said he couldn't and he wanted to go on a fishing trip and if he refused to give his father the money, he could have taken away most of his privileges, and stuff too. (Q: Does Joe have a right to refuse?) Yeah, he has the right. Well, his father said that he could go to camp if he saved up enough money and his father changed his mind and wants to go on a fishing trip; while Joe will be sad because he wanted to go and his father wouldn't let him.

Here, the first justification given is that you should be nice to your parents; the second, contained in the same sentence, is that you should do what your parents say. The third involves an initial review of the problem and then comes to the conclusion that the need to avoid punishment is the decisive factor. The fourth is that his father had made a promise; the fifth that it is against Joe's interests to give in to his father. None of these justifications is related to another; instead, they are just listed one after another, despite their disparate nature.

As adolescence proceeds, there is greater coordination of replies into chains of reasons. This often occurs in the coordination of replies of the same kind. An example of this can be found in the transcript of replies given as typical of Kohlberg's Type 3 in Chapter 5:

> I think that Joe worked very hard to get to that camp, and since his father's short of money for maybe other purposes—I don't think it said why he was short of money did it? If he was short of money and he needed to put a payment on his house, that Joe should sacrifice a little for his father and give him the money. And his father will most likely repay him in some other respect.

The main theme of this reply is the need to balance Joe's interests against those of his father. It lists the interests that both have in the situation and weighs them against one another. The reply begins by mentioning that Joe worked very hard for the money. It then goes on to say that his father might be short of money to put a payment on the house; then adding into the scales that Joe's father will probably repay him for his kindness. Thus three kinds of human interest that are involved in the situation are weighed against one another; and the implied result is that the second two outweigh the first. Other examples of ways in which chains of reasons within a particular type of reason may appear are: by moving from the consideration of the interests of individuals to the general interest; or from the need to avoid family conflict to the need to avoid conflict in society at large.

Chains of reasons that coordinate fundamentally different kinds of reply together also appear in this phase, when interviewees assess the weight they attach to two or more different factors in the situation. Thus, they may weigh human interests against the value of upholding a first order norm, when the two conflict; or they may weigh human beliefs against the value of upholding such a norm. Although weighing replies of this kind coordinate two different kinds of reason, they do so according to an intuitive sense of the relative importance of the reasons in the particular situation considered, rather than by providing an explicit statement of a common underlying criterion, or set of criteria, that can be applied to all situations. For this reason, they belong to the second rather than the third phase in the integration of reasoning.

A minority of individuals in late adolescence and early adulthood reach an advanced level of this second phase of coordination, in which a single principle, or group of principles, is used to integrate all the various kinds of justification that were considered earlier. In this kind of reply, the interviewee will continually seek to relate all replies back to one, or a small number, of basic principles that are integrated into a system. This kind of integration was studied by Kohlberg, but in an inconsistent way. Kohlberg (1958) apparently failed to find convincing examples of this kind of reasoning among his interviewees, and thus, in identifying examples of Stage 6 reasoning from his interviews, he discussed only individuals who clearly had not integrated their thinking by using general principles. Apparently already partly aware of the problems involved in doing this, Kohlberg also cited passages from the writings of novelists and philosophers, illustrating moral reasoning integrated by unifying principles, thus showing that it does indeed exist in some adults.

Colby and Kohlberg (1987a) were ultimately to admit that reasoning not integrated by general underlying principles should not have been scored as it was then, and claimed that examples of Stage 6 reasoning have a very low rate of incidence in Kohlbergian interviews. They appear to have been driven to this conclusion because they failed to clearly separate the content from the structure of reasoning, requiring that reasoning have both a high level of logical structure and a certain content in its principles to qualify for Stage 6.

If we clearly separate the logical structure of replies from their content, there does appear to be an appreciable incidence of advanced second phase reasoning showing a high degree of purely logical integration in Kohlbergian as well as in some other kinds of interview. We know this because Kohlberg and Kramer (1969) found appreciable numbers of examples of "college relativists" who showed consistent reasoning in Kohlbergian interviews integrated by the principle that "What is right is what benefits me." Kohlberg and Kramer were reluctant to accord this Stage 6 status, as the content of this principle does not belong to Stage 6, but if we look only at structure such interviews do show an integrated structure.

The two studies of Kohlbergian interviews using weakly interpretive methods discussed in this chapter did not yield convincing examples of advanced phase two reasoning, probably because they involved only relatively small numbers of younger undergraduates. But the examples discussed by Kohlberg and Kramer (1969) show that studies with larger numbers of older undergraduate or postgraduate students would almost certainly yield appreciable numbers of examples of this kind of reasoning. Further details of formal methods used to score such reasoning, as well as examples from transcripts manifesting it in non-Kohlbergian interviews, are given in the next chapter. Although Kohlbergian interviews, due to their concreteness, are not ideally suited to the exploration of this kind of reasoning, its general form is probably similar in Kohlbergian and some nonKohlbergian interviews.

Phase three in the structure of reasoning adds to the general principles of advanced phase two reasoning the adoption of a compatible metaethical view (i.e. a view about the meaning and logical functions of ethical concepts in general). Trainer (1982, p.177) comments that "Most people seem to have virtually no explicit ideas on these sorts of issues ... ", and the attainment of phase three reasoning appears to be largely confined to those with philosophical training.

Other dimensions of moral reasoning

The description of findings from moral judgement interviews under consideration is multidimensional. That is to say, we can most usefully describe the reasoning of an individual by looking at where they stand on a number of different dimensions. A peculiarity of the particular kind of multidimensional approach to development being advocated here is that it claims that, as the development of moral reasoning proceeds, change takes place along a number of dimensions, not just one, and that such change may be of three kinds.

Some dimensions show unidirectional change, with development proceeding in one direction from less developed to more developed, as with the dimension of organisation just described. Some show directional shift, with change beginning in one direction but later going into reverse; this is sometimes called U-shaped development. Some show individuation, with some individuals progressing in one direction along the dimension and others in another, resulting in a range of individual differences in the adult population. Examples of these three kinds of change will be given here.

Several of the dimensions used by the scoring method are based on "broad" categories of reply. We can get an idea of the main broad categories by turning to the four kinds of reply most often given to justify moral judgements in dilemma interviews: those based on punishment, human interests, human beliefs, and first order moral norms. These are already familiar from our discussion of Kohlberg's work. To these can be added three other less frequent broad categories of reply: inevitable behaviour; social harmony; religious.

In inevitable behaviour replies, the interviewee argues that a course of action is right because it is the one the actor will inevitably adopt. For example, in justifying the judgement that Joe should have given his father the money in Kohlberg's first moral dilemma story, the interviewee may say "He's going to have to give it to him anyway" or "It's no use fighting against the inevitable."

In social harmony replies, the interviewee justifies a judgement by arguing that the course of action is right because it promotes social harmony, prevents quarrelling and fighting, or preserves harmonious relationships. Many of the replies that Kohlberg thinks most typical of his Stage 3 belong here. Thus, in justifying giving the money to Joe's father the interviewee may say things like "It will avoid a quarrel" or

"He should put their relationship first." In religious replies there is reference to divine inspiration or sanction for the rule or action being justified. Thus, giving the money to Joe's father may be justified by saying "Jesus wants us to avoid quarrels", "It says in the Bible 'honour thy father and mother'" or "My Buddhist faith makes me think so."

There are three kinds of dimension connected with the broad categories just described. The first kind involves ordering the categories in order of depth or importance. At present, it includes only one dimension: that of reflectiveness. At the lowest level of reflectiveness we have the statement of first order norms, like "You should not lie or cheat." To justify a judgement about a situation purely by appeal to such a rule can be considered a relatively superficial justification, as it tells us nothing about why we have the rule, just that we do have it. At the next level of reflectiveness, we have three kinds of justification that seem to offer somewhat more in the way of rationale for a judgement. These are justifications in terms of human belief, of possible punishment, and of inevitable behaviour. Finally, we come to three kinds of justification that seem to provide deeper reasons: those based on human interest, on social harmony, and on religion.

It must be admitted straight away that this division into levels of reflectiveness is open to some objections, which will be discussed directly. In its defence it can be said that, at least for some people, it has intuitive plausibility; it also helps in understanding some features of empirical findings.

Although the use of a dimension like reflectiveness involves a theoretically loaded way of looking at things, thus apparently building into the scoring method precisely that kind of theoretical bias for which I have criticised Kohlberg's methods, this disadvantage is less serious in the present coding method than in that of Kohlberg. This is because anyone who wants to use results from the method to investigate other kinds of theoretical presupposition, can easily stop looking at reflectiveness as an ordinal scale with three points on it, low, medium, and high, and instead fall back on the idea that broad categories belong only to a nominal, unordered, scale. This comprises the seven categories formed by the seven main kinds of justification: rules, belief, behaviour, punishment, interest, social harmony, and religious. Most studies that have been reported using this method have in fact done this, as well as looking at reflectiveness as an ordinal dimension.

However, to thoroughly disentangle the scoring method from assumptions about reflectiveness, one further step would be necessary. This is because one problem, which should be overcome by any method of scoring of this kind, is that of dealing with justifications that contain more than one of the broad categories just reviewed. Thus, a justification like "I think stealing is wrong" contains two elements, a belief element, indicated by the words "I think", and a rule element, indicated by the words "stealing is wrong". A justification like "Everyone knows we would all be worse off if that was allowed to happen" contains a belief element, indicated by the words "Everyone knows", as well as an interest element, indicated by the words "we would all be worse off".

This means that to apply this kind of coding method, we should either allow some justifications to be scored in more than one category, or use a precedence rule that says which of the elements is to determine the category in which the reply is scored. To date, all published studies using this method have used the second of these options, following the suggestion of Langford and D'Cruz (1989) that the element at the highest level of reflectiveness is to determine the category into which the reply is placed, when two or more elements differ in reflectiveness. When the reply contains two or more elements at the same level, which is relatively unusual, the scorer must decide which is being given the most emphasis by the respondent. This precedence rule makes the scorer's task easier; it also simplifies the presentation of results and statistical analyses. Having some replies scored once and others twice poses presentational and statistical problems.

This precedence rule produces an inbuilt bias in the scoring. The main effect is to provide a larger estimate for the proportions of interest, social harmony and religious replies than would be the case if every element within a reply were scored. This needs to be borne in mind in considering findings from it. However, it is not likely to interfere substantially with the main use to which it will be put here, which is to throw light on the developmental trends applying to the detailed categories of reply underlying Kohlberg's stages, though care must be taken over one point here, which will be described directly.

There are two respects in which the precedence rule has few disadvantages for the purpose just mentioned. First of all, the scoring method of Colby and Kohlberg (1987b) also makes use of a similar precedence rule, by claiming not to score the norm element of a reply at all, instead scoring only the other elements within it. This principle is applied in a slightly inconsistent way, but in general only some norm-based replies are hidden by the Langford and D'Cruz precedence rule, whereas nearly all are hidden by the Colby and Kohlberg method. Thus, the absence of information about some norm elements of reply in the former system is not a handicap in trying to understand the behaviour of the latter's detailed categories of reply. Second, punishment replies are seldom overridden by interest or religious elements, whereas inevitable behaviour replies are relatively unusual and do not play a key role in Kohlberg's theorising.

The point about which care must be taken here arises because numbers of replies mentioning the beliefs of individuals or groups are hidden by the Langford and D'Cruz precedence rule, when they are found in conjunction with elements mentioning human interests. Some of these hidden elements are used by Colby and Kohlberg to assign these replies to stages. The two most common examples of this in the 1987 scoring manual are replies mentioning that authority will recommend attention to certain interests and those mentioning that general social belief will recommend such attention. Examples are: "My father would know I wanted to go to camp" and "Most people would think we should consider Joe's needs." When we come to detailed consideration of Colby's and Kohlberg's scoring categories later in this chapter this issue will require attention.

A second kind of dimension related to broad categories is the level of abstraction found within the categories of reply just outlined. In general, only the rule, belief, and interest categories are sufficiently common to make such assessment worthwhile for individuals. Rule replies are scored as being at the lowest level of abstraction if they mention first order rules without saying that these are rights. They are scored at a higher level of abstraction if they mention first order rules that are said to be "rights". This has been done mainly because Kohlberg claimed that rules said to be rights are particularly important in assessing the moral reasoning of an individual.

Langford and Claydon (1989) suggested that one reason that older children and adolescents give a greater proportion of replies in this second category is that they have learned that one can give linguistic emphasis to a moral rule by using the term "right", especially when there is a social tradition of calling it a right. This use of the term can be purely instrumental, designed to get one's wishes. On the other hand, fuller understanding of the term would include the notion of legal entitlement and of the reasons that such entitlements have been granted. Thus when we say that people have civil rights, rights of possession, or rights under a contract we are, if we understand the full legal meaning of the term, referring to legally established rights, the pattern for many of which is the Bill of Rights enacted by the British parliament in 1689 (an association endorsed by the *Oxford Dictionary* account of the term "right"). This can be used to confirm Kohlberg's view that some statements of rights are associated with Stage 4 and with the idea of upholding the legal system. However, it is far from clear that all those who use the term rights are aware of this fuller meaning.

Even less clear is when individuals are using Kohlberg's Stage 5 meaning of rights, in the sense of universal human moral rights that are independent of particular legal systems. Interviewees rarely explain this meaning of the term explicitly and although it seems likely that most adults would understand the term "human rights" in this sense, this term does not often appear in replies to Kohlbergian interviews.

Both the instrumental and the more fully understood legal and universalistic uses of the term rights can be predicted to increase in late adolescence, as the instrumental use is picked up from adults and other adolescents and the other two are likely to increase with greater understanding of, and participation in, the legal system and wider experience of political debate. However, we have little means of knowing what level of understanding interviewees have of the term. Thus it is useful to separate statements about rights from other appeals to norms, without attempting to ascertain what kind of right is in question, as interviewees may have different meanings in mind and it is hard to know which is intended.

Within the category of belief replies we can distinguish three levels of abstraction. The first is replies based on the beliefs of an individual, such as "Because I think so", "Because my mother thinks so", or "Because my teacher thinks so." The second applies to replies based on the beliefs of a local group, such as "Because my friends think so", "Because my parents think so." The third applies to the beliefs of a wider group, such as "Because everyone thinks so."

There are also three levels of abstraction within the interest category. The most concrete mentions the interests of an individual, such as "Because X will benefit." X is often a person mentioned in the initial interview scenario, such as Heinz's wife or Joe. An intermediate level of abstraction involves mentioning the interests of a local group. An example of this is where an interviewee says, in attempting to justify why Joe should not go to camp "It will be better for the family." The most abstract kind of reply based on interest refers to the interests of a large group of people or of people in general, as when it is argued that we should avoid stealing because "Everyone will be better off."

A third kind of dimension based on broad justification categories is religiosity. This is calculated as the proportion of an individual's replies that fall into the religious category. The rationale for singling out religious replies in this way is that there are only two main kinds of reply at the level of maximum reflectiveness, namely interest/social harmony and religious. Social harmony replies are conceptually similar to interest replies because individuals in a group have an interest in the contentment that comes from living in harmony. Thus, by calculating a person's leaning to the use of religious replies, we can in effect obtain a measure of the relative importance of these two main kinds of highly reflective reply in their thinking.

A synoptic view of the various dimensions outlined so far is given in Table 1. This also lists some dimensions described in the next section.

TABLE 1
Some dimensions along which replies can be assessed using the Langford and D'Cruz scoring method

A dimension of logical organisation:
1. Phases of logical organisation (3 levels on an ordinal scale: little integration; moderate to full integration in content; full integration in content and metaethical reasoning)

Five easily assessed dimensions connected with common categories:
2. Reflectiveness (assessed on a ratio scale by any measure that assesses replies in categories at higher levels of reflectiveness as a proportion of total replies, e.g. those that are in the interest, social harmony, and religious categories)
3-5. Abstraction within the rule, belief, and interest categories (assessed on a ratio scale by any measure that assesses replies at higher levels of abstraction within each of these categories as a proportion of the total number of replies in the category, e.g. those that are at the highest level of abstraction)
6. Religiosity (assessed on a ratio scale by religious replies as a proportion of total replies)

Two less easily assessed dimensions connected with less common categories:
7-8. Abstraction within the social harmony category and within reciprocity replies (assessed on a ratio scale by any measure that assesses replies at higher levels of abstraction within each of these categories as a proportion of total number of replies in the category, e.g. those that are at the highest level of abstraction)

Empirical findings about broad categories

Although the two studies discussed here were performed on Australian rather than American samples, and the latter were the main Western sample used by Colby and Kohlberg (1987a), it is unlikely that this had any great influence on findings, as the Australian samples produced very similar findings to the American ones when scored by Kohlberg's method. The main difference is likely to lie in the area of religiosity, which is not adequately revealed by Kohlberg's scoring method. Most studies agree that on measures like church attendance Americans are significantly more religious than either Australians or the British (Langford, 1992b). This, however, makes little difference to the main thrust of the findings reported.

Both studies used Kohlberg's Form A interview, a standard short form of his Dilemmas I and III. Replies were tape recorded and transcribed for scoring by two independent raters. Raters were trained by an initial explanation and reading of the scoring manual of Langford (1987c), followed by trial scoring of a section of transcript, followed by discussion of errors and further trial scoring until a reasonable level of accuracy was reached. The extent of each scorable item of justification (idea unit) was marked on transcripts by the chief investigator prior to scoring. Inter-rater reliability averaged 82% over the two studies.

Both reported studies agree that age influences: degree of integration within reasoning; levels of abstraction within the rule, belief, and interest categories; and religiosity (Langford & Claydon, 1989; Langford & D'Cruz, 1989). Integration of reasoning and abstraction in the rules and interest categories increase with age. Religiosity and level of abstraction within the belief category both peak in mid-adolescence and decline thereafter. Younger children rely more on the beliefs of authority than older subjects, though the beliefs of authority are never used as often as the beliefs of self, even by 7-year-olds. Those in mid-adolescence rely more on general social belief and those in late adolescence and adulthood more on their own beliefs.

A striking finding has been that there seems to be little or no shift with age in preference for use of the more popular broad categories of justification, especially those emphasising rules, beliefs, and interests. The only age-related changes in use of broad categories occur for two of the less popular kinds of justification. Religious replies, as already mentioned, peak in mid-adolescence, whereas punishment-based replies decline with age.

This means that we find very little shift in the overall level of reflectiveness of justifications between the ages of about 7 years and adulthood. This can probably be extended back to 5 years, if we accept parallels from studies using non-Kohlbergian interviews (see Chapter 8).

These findings, on the surface, might be thought to give some support to Kohlberg's view of the development of moral reasoning, as some of the trends in broad categories support it. Thus, younger children rely more on the interests of individuals, the views of authority, and the possibility of punishment in justifying moral judgements. Those in mid-adolescence rely more on general social opinion than those at other ages. Those in late adolescence and adulthood rely more on wider interests, personal belief, and rules stated to be rights than those at other ages. Note that this confirmation of Kohlberg's findings on age trends in wider belief replies shows that the tendency for the Langford and D'Cruz system to mask some replies of this kind, noted earlier, does not fundamentally alter the picture of such replies derived from the Colby and Kohlberg method.

However, other aspects of the picture are not in accord with Kohlberg's theory. Thus, reliance on the beliefs of authority is never predominant even at 7–8 years, with 34% of belief replies being based on the beliefs of authority, 13% on those of persons of equal status, and 51% on those of the child itself (Langford & Claydon, 1989). In the 15–16-

year age range this changes to 14% based on authority, 30% on the beliefs of equals, and 55% on those of the self. In the 19–21-year age range 10% are based on authority, 21% on the beliefs of equals, and 68% on the beliefs of the self. Although these are cross-sectional results and so do not provide an ideal method of assessing Kohlberg's view of stages, they support the notion of gradual rather than stage-like changes in the nature of belief replies. It is true that, as noted earlier, we have to be somewhat cautious in comparing authority belief replies scored by the Langford and D'Cruz scoring system with those scored by Kohlberg's methods, but it seems unlikely that the difference in method of assessment could have produced this degree of deviation from the theory.

A second problem for Kohlberg's theory is also raised by findings from these studies. This is that, averaging across both studies, even at 7–8 years 34% of replies, advocating attention to the interests of an individual, advocated attention to those of a character other than the main protagonist in the dilemma. Furthermore, this percentage changes little with age up to the 19–21-year age range. This contradicts Kohlberg's theory, which contends that those at Stage 1 will show a markedly lower proportion of such replies, and thus predicts that this proportion will rise appreciably in the age range 7–15 years, as Stage 1 declines.

A third problem is the peaking of religious justifications in the 15–16-year age range. This, as we have seen, is predicted by the 1987b scoring manual, which assigns them to Stage 3, but there is no basis within the theory for making this assignment and we must therefore count this as pointing to a weakness in the theory.

Some refinements to the scoring method

Examination of developmental trends in common types of reply has already revealed significant problems for Kohlberg's theory. Just as crucial for the explanatory part of the theory are developmental trends in some uncommon types of reply, which provide direct indices of developmental changes in reciprocity and sociomoral point of view.

Published studies using weakly interpretive methods have concentrated on the more common types of reply for two reasons: that it was initially desirable to obtain a general picture of what can be found from weakly interpretive methods before going on to details; and that it is difficult to stabilise scores from a more fine-grained scoring method in order to apply statistical methods to findings. However, the question naturally arises as to how findings would appear if more finely-grained analyses were undertaken.

Two particularly significant kinds of reply, for the purpose of giving an interpretation of underlying meaning in terms of Kohlberg's stages, are those labelled as "social harmony" in the Langford and D'Cruz scoring method, and replies that refer to reciprocity, in explaining why interests other than those of the speaker should be taken into account. Both occur in two significant forms. In "local" social harmony replies, the interviewee refers to harmony within the family or other local group as the reason we ought to do something. In "wider" social harmony replies the interviewee refers to the harmony of wider social groups, such as "society" (presumably the nation), or people in general. These replies are significant in Kohlberg's interpretive thinking, as local social harmony is one of the underlying concepts behind the Stage 3 point of view, whereas wider social harmony is one of the underlying ideas behind Stage 4 thinking.

The two studies already referred to give a consistent figure of 4% for total social harmony replies among interviewees between 7 and 21 years of age. These were not subdivided into local and wider harmony replies in the tables of results in the original reports, as it is difficult to obtain meaningful figures for individuals with these relatively uncommon categories, although replies were coded using them. Inspection of the original data shows that there is a substantial shift in the overall frequency of these two types of reply between the ages of 7 and 21 years, from a preponderance of local social harmony replies (88% in the two studies), to a preponderance of wider social harmony replies (68%).

The developmental course of social harmony replies is instructive in revealing how Kohlberg's scoring method conceals, and even to some extent distorts, the descriptive picture, in its quest for an interpretive solution. Kohlberg's theory would lead us to expect that local social harmony replies would be at a fairly low level among 7–8-year-olds, would rise in the age range 12–16 years, and then decline again. This is because they appear from the description of Stage 3 to be a central feature of thinking at that stage. But in fact the developmental course of such replies is that they are at their most common from 7–12 years, remaining fairly constant in that period, and then declining substantially thereafter.

The real developmental course of local social harmony replies is hidden from us by the Kohlbergian scoring system because it does not report proportions of replies of this kind alone, but only in conjunction with a number of other more common replies. Thus, although replies of this kind are mainly scored at Stage 3, and they do not in fact follow the predicted developmental course for Stage 3 replies as a whole, this is masked by the scoring system due to the presence of other, more frequent kinds of reply. These are also scored at Stage 3 and do in fact peak in the 12–16-year age range. This is a serious defect of the scoring method, as many of these more frequent kinds of reply do not give any explicit statement of the underlying principles of reasoning that are claimed to typify Stage 3, whereas local social harmony replies do. This is an example of a general problem with Kohlberg's later scoring methods. We sometimes find that theoretically crucial replies fail to follow the predicted developmental path, while theoretically neutral replies are used to bolster stage scores, so as to ensure that these do follow the predicted developmental path.

The developmental course of wider harmony replies also throws doubt on Kohlberg's analysis. The obligation to seek the stability of society as a whole is typical of Stage 4 reasoning in the theory and such reasoning is predicted to increase in later adolescence. This is what actually happens to wider social harmony replies. However, the presence of appreciable numbers of such replies in the period 7–12 years contradicts a strict version of the theory, as such replies should be very rare in this period, few individuals in this age range showing appreciable Stage 4 scores. A weakened version of the theory that acknowledges that individuals may be simultaneously at more than two stages, and that passage through them is less sequential than Kohlberg allows, could possibly encompass this finding.

The reason that explicit reciprocity replies are not scored, in the Langford and D'Cruz scoring system, is that they are even less frequent than social harmony replies and it is thus difficult to obtain reliable scores for proportions of such replies given by individuals. In local reciprocity replies, the interviewee will argue that a person should consider the interests of another person or persons, within an immediate local group, such as the family, because these people will in return consider their interests. In wider reciprocity replies, the same argument is applied to individuals in a wider social group. These kinds of reply are of significance, as the former provides evidence for one of the underlying interpretive notions separating Stage 1 from Stage 2. Thus at Stage 1 others are only helped out of deference to authority, whereas at Stage 2 they are helped in an effort to obtain reciprocal benefits. Wider reciprocity replies are of significance as they distinguish Stage 4, at which the welfare of society is sought solely as an end in itself, from Stage 5, at which the welfare of society is sought in part because of the reciprocal benefits that individuals receive from being members of society.

In the Langford and D'Cruz scoring system, reciprocity replies of both these kinds are scored in the interest category, as they both advocate paying attention to human interests. Local reciprocity replies fall into the local interests category, wider reciprocity replies into the wider interests category. Rescoring of the original transcripts, from the two studies mentioned, provided figures for the incidence of these two categories at each age. Due to the instability of scores in such infrequent categories, these show quite widely differing values at the top three age ranges in the two studies (the lowest age group, 7–8 years, was only included in one of the studies). Pooling the findings from the two studies, however, probably results in a fairly accurate picture over the 11–21-year age range, as pooling low incidence scores of this kind in the two studies tends to produce fairly smooth developmental trends for these and other kinds of reply.

Kohlberg's theory predicts an initial increase in local reciprocity replies in the period about 7–11 years, with a decline setting in shortly thereafter, as Stage 2 replies peak in early adolescence. This later decline was observed in the pooled scores. As the value for the youngest age group (7–8 years) was based on only one study it cannot be regarded as reliable. Thus findings here support Kohlberg at present, though further work with larger samples of younger children is desirable.

The developmental course of wider reciprocity replies is almost exactly the reverse of that for local reciprocity replies, over the period for which pooled results are available, beginning at 0.7% at 11–13 years and increasing to 1.1% at 19–21 years. This finding can be reconciled with Kohlberg's view that this kind of reply is typical of Stage 5 reasoning, on the ground that it peaks in the right age range. The developmental course of such replies, however, suggests that there are more in the age range 7–13 years than would be predicted by Kohlberg's theory. Once again, we must be cautious in drawing firm conclusions from rather unreliable scores, but in this case we have a total of three values in the age range 7–13 years from the two studies, and their mean is more than half the mean at 19–21 years. According to Kohlberg, Stage 5 thinking, to which wider reciprocity replies belong, should be much less frequent before 14 years than after 19 years. This effect is hidden in Colby's and Kohlberg's scoring system, as although such replies will often be scored at Stage 5, so long as they are less than 10% of total replies they will be dismissed as error, explaining how Colby and Kohlberg (1987a) can claim that the level of Stage 5 replies is effectively zero at 11 years.

Having looked at these four particularly important kinds of uncommon reply, we turn to other such replies. A good way to identify these is by reference to the Colby and Kohlberg 1987b scoring manual. This may alert us to other infrequent kinds of reply, which these authors regard as important from an interpretive viewpoint, even though they are uncommon.

It will help to begin here with an analysis of that part of the (1987b) scoring manual that deals with Dilemma III, which is Heinz's dilemma over stealing a drug to save his wife. If we examine the scoring manual for this dilemma, we find that the descriptions given of criterion judgements enable us to subdivide some of the categories of reply already mentioned into smaller categories. Table 2 shows the results of doing this and then counting the number of criterion judgements listed in the 1987b manual falling into the resulting categories. A criterion judgement is defined for this purpose as a single sentence defining a type of reply in the manual. (Where the manual gives several such sentences for one combination of element and norm these are separated by OR in caps.)

It can be seen that the great majority of Colby and Kohlberg's descriptive categories belong happily within the descriptive categories of Langford and D'Cruz (1989), except those concerned with society (31–33). Although these three categories are not common, with replies of this kind occurring at the relatively infrequent Stages 4/5 and 5, they are of considerable theoretical significance and it is a defect of the Langford and D'Cruz system to have omitted them. In the Langford and D'Cruz system categories 31 and 32 would be scored as the opinion of the interviewee; category 33 as an example of a rule said to be a right. Rescoring of the transcripts of the two studies discussed earlier shows that these three kinds of reply are very rare before late adolescence, when their frequency becomes detectable, though they are all found in less that half of 1% of replies in the age range 19–21 years. These findings are in accord with Kohlberg's theory.

If we could understand the developmental trends impacting on each of the categories in Table 2, we would discover what Colby and Kohlberg's descriptive system of assigning replies tells us about developmental trends. We have already looked at the developmental behaviour of some of the categories (20, 26, 28, 29, 31–33). The behaviour of many others can be deduced from that of the corresponding categories in the Langford and D'Cruz scoring method. Our earlier consideration of trends using that method focused on broad brush issues, but by combining it with the Colby and Kohlberg (1987b) manual we can learn more about details.

To do this we need to note that several kinds of reply are found distributed over two neighbouring stages, rather than being confined to a single one. In such cases, we nearly always find that those at the lower stage are simple examples of the reply, whereas those at the higher stage are what Langford (1992a) called "weighing" replies, in which two factors are weighed against one another and are either said to cancel one another out, making the issue undecideable, or, more commonly in Kohlbergian interviews, one is said to be more significant. An example was given earlier in the chapter. Weighing replies are cognitively more

TABLE 2
Number of criterion judgements assigned to descriptive categories by Colby and Kohlberg

Wider rules:
1. The claim that laws are not perfect: Stage 4 contains 2 judgements.
2. The claim that laws can be over-ruled by a higher value: Stage 4 contains 2 judgements; Stage 4/5 contains 3.
3. The rule that we ought to be able to dispose of our own property: Stage 1 contains 6 judgements; Stage 2 contains 1; Stage 3/4 contains 2.

Rules said to be rights:
4. The claim that the wife has a right to life: Stage 3/4 contains 2 judgements; Stage 4 contains 2; Stage 4/5 contains 1; Stage 5 contains 3.

Individual belief:
5. Permission or wishes of authority: Stage 1 contains 1 judgement; Stage 1/2 contains 1; Stage 3 contains 1.
6. Interviewee believes it wrong of the main protagonist to be selfish: Stage 2/3 contains 1 judgement; Stage 3 contains 2.
7. Interviewee believes it wrong of another protagonist to be selfish: Stage 2/3 contains 1 judgement; Stage 3 contains 4; Stage 3/4 contains 1; Stage 4 contains 1.
8. The protagonist would have guilty feelings or a bad conscience: Stage 3 contains 2 judgements.

Wider belief:
9. We should act to preserve social decency: Stage 3 contains 1 judgement.
10. The social importance of someone other than the main protagonist: Stage 1 contains 1 judgement.
11. A person's general social reputation would be damaged by an action: Stage 3 contains 3 judgements.
12. The social contract has been agreed on by all members of society, who thus assent to it: Stage 4 contains 3 judgements; Stage 4/5 contains 3; Stage 5 contains 3.

Inevitable behaviour of an individual:
13. The argument that the main protagonist will inevitably behave in a certain way: Stage 2 contains 2 judgements; Stage 3 contains 1.
14. The argument that if you or I were the protagonist in question we would behave in a certain way: Stage 2 contains 1 judgement.

Punishment:
15. To act in a certain way would invite punishment of the main protagonist: Stage 1 contains 2 judgements; Stage 1/2 contains 3; Stage 2 contains 3; Stage 2/3 contains 1;Stage 3/4 contains 2.
16. To act in a certain way would invite punishment of another protagonist: Stage 2 contains 3 judgements.

Promoting the interests of an individual:
17. We ought to promote the interests of the main protagonist: Stage 2 contains 3 judgements.
18. We ought to promote the interests of the wife: Stage 2 contains 2 judgements; Stage 3 contains 1.
19. Due to feelings of care for another's interests: Stage 3 contains 4 judgements.
20. We ought to promote the interests of someone other than the main protagonist as this will result in reciprocal promotion of the main protagonist's interests: Stage 2 contains 1 judgement; Stage 2/3 contains 1; Stage 3 contains 2.
21. To exact retribution on a person who harms the interests of the main protagonist: Stage 2 contains 1 judgement.

Promotion of wider interests:
22. We should act to help people in general: Stage 2/3 contains 1 judgement; Stage 3 contains 4; Stage 3/4 contains 4; Stage 4 contains 4; Stage 4/5 contains 1.
23. The right to life justified by its benefit to society: Stage 4 contains 2 judgements.
24. Society would be improved by the act concerned: Stage 4/5 contains 2 judgements; Stage 5 contains 1.
25. Society should function to promote the general interest: Stage 4/5 contains 2 judgements.

Local social harmony:
26. To foster the relationship of the main protagonist and another person: Stage 3 contains 6 judgements; Stage 3/4 contains 3; Stage 4/5 contains 1.
27. Because relationships involve an implied contract: Stage 4 contains 1 judgement.

Wider social harmony:
28. Social harmony in society at large would be damaged by an act: Stage 2/3 contains 1 judgement; Stage 3 contains 2; Stage 3/4 contains 1; Stage 4 contains 4.
29. The right to life is justified by the benefit to social stability: Stage 4 contains 1 judgement.

Religious:
30. Religious justifications: Stage 3 contains 1 judgement; Stage 3/4 contains 6.

Society:
31. Society would be unjustified if an act occurred: Stage 4/5 contains 2 judgements.
32. Protagonist has own standards distinct from those of society: Stage 4/5 contains 1 judgement.
33. Society protects fundamental human rights: Stage 5 contains 3 judgements.

---

complex than those involving only consideration of a single factor, and tend to become more common with maturity.

Categories 1 and 2 listed in Table 2 involve claims about laws, assigned to Stages 4 and 4/5. We have already noted that statements about laws tend to reach their maximum in late adolescence, the period in which these stages are predicted to peak. Thus findings here are in accord with Kohlberg's theory. Category 3 is a statement of a property rule, assigned mainly to Stages 1 and 2. Rules like that contained in Category 3 decline at the expense of rules as rights in later adolescence. Kohlberg's theory predicts that this will happen to Stage 1 and 2 replies and findings are thus again in accord with the theory. Category 4 involves a statement of the right to life, which as a rule stated to be a right can be expected to gain in importance in late adolescence. This is appropriately placed at Stages 4 and 5. As these stages reach their maximum in late adolescence, findings again accord with Kohlberg's theory.

Categories 5–8 correspond to the individual belief category. As we have already seen, younger children tend to give a greater proportion of individual belief replies based on the beliefs of authority, whereas those in late adolescence rely more on their own beliefs. Category 5 is authority beliefs, placed at Stages 1–3; Categories 6 and 7 involve the beliefs of the interviewee, placed mainly at Stages 3 and 4; Category 8 is the belief of the main protagonist, placed at Stage 3.

We can expect Category 5 replies to decrease in adolescence, producing developmental findings in accord with Kohlberg's theory. Replies relying on the beliefs of the interviewee (Categories 6 and 7) will show something like the developmental behaviour appropriate to Stages 3 and 4, in that they increase in frequency during adolescence. However, as already noted, there are far more of such replies in the 7–11-year age range than is appropriate for these stages. The beliefs of the main protagonist (Category 8) are those of someone the interviewee presumably regards as of equal status, and thus will begin from a relatively low level at 7–8 years, peak around 15–16 years, and then decline slightly at 19–21 years. This accords with what we would expect from a Stage 3 reply, which is where Category 8 is placed, but it is hard to see why such replies particularly belong to Stage 3.

Categories 9 and 11 are both simple examples of wider belief replies and both are placed at Stage 3. This is in accord with the theory, and as such replies peak in mid-adolescence, findings support it. Categories 13 and 14 are inevitable behaviour replies, which are placed at Stages 2 and 3. Inevitable behaviour replies do not change in frequency much with age. The fact that they are relatively unusual allows for their placement at these stages in the middle of the sequence without significant disturbance to findings on stage trends, although their developmental behaviour is not in accord with the theory. Categories 15 and 16, assigned primarily to Stages 1 and 2, correspond to the "punishment" category, which is quite common in the 7–12-year age range, but declines significantly thereafter. This accords with Kohlberg's theory.

Categories 17, 18, and 19, assigned to Stages 2 and 3, correspond to the individual interest category, involving concern either for the interests of the main protagonist or others in the story. Individual interest replies as a whole remain static at around 5% of replies throughout the period 7–21 years, with the proportions of such replies suggesting attention to the interests of the main protagonist and to those of other characters remaining constant throughout this period (Langford & Claydon, 1989). These findings are not in accord with Kohlberg's theory, which suggests that attention to the interests of the main protagonist will be greatest in the period 7–12 years, when Stage 1 is most common.

Categories 22–25 correspond to Langford's and D'Cruz's category of wider interests and are assigned to Stages 3–5. The developmental course of these common categories of reply is that they increase regularly from about 8% to 22% of replies over the period 7–21 years.

This has the effect, combined with that of the increased complexity of the weighing and other replies included in the higher stages, of appropriately swelling the ranks of Stage 3 replies in mid-adolescence, and of Stage 4 and 5 replies in later adolescence. Thus findings here support the theory.

As already mentioned, the assignment of Category 30, religious replies, to Stages 3 and 3/4, seems to owe more to pragmatism than theory. Religious replies peak in the 15–16-year age group and this is the empirical behaviour required of these stages. However, the theory nowhere makes reference to religious replies and their placement at this stage is an arbitrary decision.

This leaves only Categories 10, 12, 21, and 27. These all fall into the Langford and D'Cruz coding system, but refer in addition to subtle aspects of replies that are not captured by that system. In all cases we can see that replies assigned to higher stages involve greater cognitive sophistication than those assigned to lower stages. It is desirable that future versions of weakly interpretive methods be extended to cover replies of these kinds. However, they all represent rare replies and their presence does little to disturb the overall outline of developmental trends established through existing weakly interpretive scoring methods that has just been given.

Langford and Claydon (1989) showed that the style of explanation just applied to Colby and Kohlberg's (1987b) Dilemma III can also be extended, with minor modifications, to Form A as a whole (comprising Dilemmas I and III). Examination of the scoring manual suggests that it can also be extended to other dilemmas.

We can divide the failures of Kohlberg's predictions that we have encountered into three kinds. The first involves a number of kinds of reply that show trends that, although not in accord with the strong 1987 version of the theory, can be accounted for by a weakened version that admits that subjects can score at more than two neighbouring stages and may not pass through the stages sequentially. Two notable examples of this are developmental trends in wider social harmony and wider reciprocity replies.

The second involves two kinds of reply whose behaviour cannot be predicted by the theory, but where the theory could perhaps be saved by declaring that it does not apply to replies of this sort. These are religious and inevitable behaviour replies. In both cases it is hard to see what such replies have to do with Kohlberg's fundamental notion of sociomoral point of view, and for this reason a revised version of the theory might simply exclude them.

A third kind of reply raises even more fundamental problems for the theory, in that they index something that is clearly important to it, but show developmental trends that are substantially at variance with its predictions. Local social harmony replies index a fundamental aspect of the sociomoral point of view of Stage 3, but they fail to follow the predicted developmental trend for this stage. Mention of the beliefs of the speaker also fails to follow predicted trends. This comprises at least half of replies mentioning the beliefs of individuals at all ages from 7–21 years, increasing only moderately with age. This contradicts the notion that individuals at Stage 1 are overwhelmingly influenced by the beliefs of authority, with the views of individual authorities never forming more than 34% of individual belief replies. Attention accorded to the interests of the main character also fails to follow predictions. There is little shift in this with age as a proportion of all individual interest replies, although Kohlberg's theory suggests that such interests should be given considerably greater attention by younger children, who are thinking predominantly at Stage 1.

Testing Kohlberg's predictions against findings from weakly interpretive methods reveals serious problems for the theory. Just as damaging is the fact that merely stating these developmental trends, in the way outlined, suggests that they could be susceptible to other explanations than that offered by Kohlberg. The task of exploring such explanations in detail will be left until the next chapter, which fills out the descriptive picture with findings from some kinds of non-Kohlbergian interview.

TWO DEFENCES OF KOHLBERG

Rest's (1979, 1986, 1989) work appears on the surface to offer evidence for Kohlberg's view of the development of moral reasoning from a source other than the Kohlbergian interview. Rest and his collaborators have devised multiple-choice methods of assessing moral reasoning and these are claimed to support the theory. However, detailed inspection of findings shows that they can also be explained in terms of the descriptive developmental trends already outlined, without recourse to the theory.

Rest, Turiel, and Kohlberg (1969) and Rest (1973) originally devised a test in which the subject was first given a Kohlberg dilemma story. They were then offered statements that made the underlying reasoning found at a stage explicit, rather than implicit, as is the case with many interview replies. They were asked to rank a number of such statements according to which gave the best arguments or which were more like the subject's own thinking confronted with the dilemma. It was found that almost all subjects, including children as young as 7 years, tended to give the highest ratings to high-stage statements. This apparently supports the view of Haan (1991), confirmed by weakly interpretive methods, that the reasoning of younger children is in some respects qualitatively similar to that of older children and more sophisticated than claimed by Kohlberg. Although a narrower range of interests tends to be considered, the reasons given for considering others are not very different from those given by adults.

However, instead of accepting this conclusion, Rest (1979) argued that the failure was due to a tendency to project simpler ways of reasoning onto the more complex moral positions expressed in the statements. He therefore devised the method used in the *Defining Issues Test*, a widely used research instrument. This asks subjects to say what are the most important issues in thinking about moral dilemmas. It also presents a selection of statements for rating, according to this criterion, that focus on certain aspects of reasoning found in interviews, but omit others. This instrument has been found, in a large number of studies, to have good test-retest reliability and shows sequential passage by individuals through the stages; this second finding is claimed as support for the theory.

However, examination of the statements included in the DIT shows that these results only offer support for some of the broad brush descriptive and non-interpretive aspects of the theory. The statements offered cover only some of the features that show sequential development according to the theory. These are precisely those that weakly interpretive methods find to show developmental change of the kind predicted. However, the instrument does not contain many of those kinds of theoretically crucial statement, also predicted by the theory to be typical of particular periods in development, that weakly interpretive methods have found not to show the predicted developmental progressions. Findings about those theoretically crucial statements that are included are often misinterpreted.

In addition, as in the Colby and Kohlberg (1987b) scoring manual, some assignments of statements to stages in the DIT have been made largely on the pragmatic ground that they tend to occur at a certain period in development, rather than because their presence at these points can be unequivocally predicted by the theory. Thus, in the statements offered for Dilemma III (Heinz and the drug), there is no statement diagnosing a Stage 1 issue; the only statement discussing a Stage 2 issue discusses punishment, which could more plausibly be termed a Stage 1 issue; the only statement discussing a reciprocity issue is assigned to Stage 3, though it belongs more naturally at Stage 2, according to the theory.

Another possible line of defence of Kohlberg's ideas may in the future emerge from the work of Turiel and his collaborators. At present, it is not entirely clear that this is his intention, but as the work of his group suggests some lines along which this might emerge it requires consideration here. Turiel and Davidson (1986), Helwig et al. (1990), and Turiel et al. (1991) summarise a large number of studies by Turiel and his collaborators on differences in the domain-specific characteristics of reasoning, concentrating on the moral, social conventional, and personal domains. Most of these used adaptations of the weakly interpretive scoring method of Davidson et al. (1983), referred to earlier in this chapter.

The meaning that Turiel, Killen, and Helwig (1987) and Turiel et al. (1991) give to the term "moral issue" is similar to that given by Kohlberg. Thus, for them morality centres on universalisable notions of welfare, justice, and rights. Although Turiel does not usually make mention of the notion of conflict between norms, or of norms under challenge, in his definition, this is usually assumed, as his studies usually involve such conflict when they deal with moral issues (though there are notable exceptions to this, for example some studies reported by Turiel et al., 1991). As with Kohlberg, although first order as distinct from second order norms are not specified, they are usually intended.

Turiel's object in emphasising the notion of welfare in this definition is to distinguish rules that bear on human welfare from those that do not, the former being moral and the latter conventional. Moral rules are also distinguished by being recognised in all societies and by being linked to what it is to be human, whereas conventional rules are specific to particular societies.

The personal domain involves decisions that impinge only on the welfare of the actor and are recognised as being a personal matter, such as, nowadays, what length a man wears his hair. Some individuals may not recognise this as a personal decision, but consider it conventional, and this is recognised by Turiel. Domains to some extent, especially in distinguishing the conventional from the personal, reside in the eye of the beholder.

It has already been pointed out that the Davidson et al. (1983) method lacks the detail of either the Langford and D'Cruz (1989) method or the descriptive system underlying Colby and Kohlberg (1987b). It is clear, from the descriptions of Turiel's research programme given in Turiel and Davidson (1986) and Turiel et al. (1991), that this is because the system was not designed for and has not primarily been used to investigate developmental issues (see also Saltzstein, 1991). It is quite similar to Langford and D'Cruz's list of broad categories, which as we have seen do not shift much with age. The main aim of this method of scoring, rather, is to investigate general differences, of the kind that can be captured by such categories, between domains of reasoning. As we might expect, general human welfare and, among older individuals, rights are considerably more important in the moral than in the conventional or personal domains.

One key motivation behind this programme was described in Turiel and Davidson (1986) as being to show why, in reviewing the empirical literature on the sequentiality issue in relation to Kohlberg's stages, Rest (1983) found that there were considerable variations in the range of stages at which an individual was located, using the then current scoring methods. Many individuals scored at more than two stages and there was considerable variation in the average stage level displayed by an individual, from one dilemma to another, and from one kind of task to another (e.g. substantial differences between recognition, that is choice between passages, and production, mainly interview, measures of moral reasoning).

However, whether these issues are as crucial for the programme of cognitive structuralism in this area as Turiel thinks is open to some doubt. Thus, orthodox cognitive structuralists have long known that recognition precedes production of abilities (e.g. Inhelder & Piaget's, 1964 comparison of recognition and production of classification abilities). Likewise, orthodox cognitive structuralists have long recognised that horizontal *decalage* will mean that an ability may appear earlier in relation to one topic than in relation to another (Piaget & Inhelder, 1969). In the period 1983–1987 the fact that individuals often scored at more than two adjacent stages was a problem for Kohlberg's theory, but this was apparently solved by the new scoring system of Colby and Kohlberg (1987a, b), a system that Turiel does not appear to be on record as having criticised.

One reason for Turiel's original concern about the Rest (1983) survey was that he apparently wanted to find evidence for a particularly orthodox version of cognitive structuralism, and was not willing to accept that some weakening of its basic assumptions might be called for. The notion that some studies had been mixing up different kinds of reasoning, and this had caused the deviations from strictly orthodox predictions, provided a potential explanation for such deviations. One result of Turiel's programme here is that he has now discouraged the unwary from embarking on studies that they think are of moral reasoning, but which are not. At the same time, the new list of moral dilemmas, new scoring system, and new findings on really moral reasoning (in the Kohlberg–Turiel sense), reported in Colby and Kohlberg (1987a, b), can be interpreted as having shown that a rather strong version of cognitive structuralist sequentialism is valid and we are now back on track.

A possible future additional payoff for which Turiel may hope is that, as already pointed out, even some of Colby and Kohlberg's (1987b) dilemmas involve rules, especially those connected with authority and sex, that are doubtful as true moral norms. Turiel may hope to further clean up Kohlberg's list of dilemmas by removing these and other "impurities" and obtain even better results. Thus, one further issue arising from Rest's (1983) review that worried Turiel and Davidson (1986) was that stage transition did not occur suddenly enough in results to that date. They may hope for further progress on this front.

However the reader of Turiel and Davidson (1986) and Turiel et al. (1991) must notice that although these things have evidently in part motivated their programme, the lack of specific commitment to the Kohlberg (1976) sequence of stages is almost deafening. Turiel and his collaborators continually talk in nonspecific terms about the possibility of devising a truly cognitive structuralist series of stages within moral development, but it is Piaget's stages of development, rather than those of Kohlberg, that are held up as examples. This suggests that Turiel may be thinking that, once truly moral dilemmas are identified and appropriately scored, a new stage sequence will be identified. The authors are at least agnostic between this possibility and definite commitment to Kohlberg's view of stages.

Turiel's work is also notable for his having devised, in Turiel (1977, 1983), a separate sequence of stages, through which he believes reasoning about conventional, as opposed to moral, reasoning passes. Some reference was made to his important findings in this area in dealing with the work of Piaget in Chapter 3, but, as the topic lies outside the scope of this book, details will not be pursued further here.

In summary, Turiel's work on domain characteristics might be preliminary to some possible future defence of the Kohlbergian approach to the development of moral reasoning. Alternatively, it might be preliminary to a future attempt to devise an alternative structuralist account of such development. However, at present it offers nothing that can directly offset the serious difficulties identified in Kohlberg's work, as these do not primarily relate to the relatively minor difficulties for the theory raised in Rest's (1983) review, but to the much more serious difficulties reviewed earlier in this chapter.

CONCLUSIONS

Although the studies that were the main focus of this chapter adopted a cross-sectional methodology, thus providing a less stringent test of Kohlberg's theory than would be provided by longitudinal studies, they make clear three things. The first is that the assignment of replies to stages by his scoring system is sometimes made on the pragmatic ground of the point in development at which the reply occurs, rather than because the theory is able to predict that it occurs at the suggested point. The second is that some crucial types of reply indexing the underlying theoretical concepts of the theory do not show the developmental course it predicts. The third is that there are descriptive developmental trends in the relative frequency of replies that stand in need of explanation. Some of the explanations that can be given for such trends have already been discussed in the previous chapter. Further explanations are considered in the next.

CHAPTER EIGHT

Other interview techniques in the light of weakly interpretive methods

This chapter first deals with nonKohlbergian interview techniques and then with the theoretical interpretation of interview evidence in general.

NONKOHLBERGIAN INTERVIEW TECHNIQUES

Kohlberg's interview techniques are one good way of realising his notion that moral reasoning should be defined as the study of reactions to first order norms under challenge. However, his methods are limited in two ways. First of all, they are only one way of realising this notion (see especially Kitwood, 1990). Second, many investigators would prefer a broader definition of the topic that includes first order norms not under challenge and decisions affecting human interests where no such norm is relevant. This section will first explore other ways of realising Kohlberg's definition and then turn to interviews based on broader definitions. Both will be viewed in the light of weakly interpretive methods.

Other ways of realising Kohlberg's definition

Dilemma questions
Kohlberg's interviews tend to present dilemmas that involve an individual deciding which first order norm to follow, under conditions where their decision most obviously affects the interests of another

individual or a small group. The exceptions to this in the original 1958 interviews are topics V and VI, which present a situation in the Korean war where the individual must make a decision that affects the interests of a company of marines, which is a medium-sized group lying between small groups like the family and wider groups like the nation. In Colby and Kohlberg (1987b) V was retained, but VI omitted.

Apart from these exceptions, the Kohlberg dilemmas all deal with situations where the interests explicitly mentioned are those of an individual or a small group. The result of this is that, in order to discuss the effect of a decision of the main protagonist on the wider interests of society in general, the interviewee has to infer that these might be indirectly involved, as they are not directly so. Although topics V and VI encouraged the discussion of the interests of a medium-sized group, the same kind of inference must be used in these cases to discuss the interests of society in general.

Now discussion of the interests of society in general is one of the defining characteristics of Stages 4 and 5, and Kohlberg's theory as a whole assumes that such interests will not be considered before these stages are reached, which in most Western societies occurs in late adolescence. An obvious objection to Kohlberg's claim here is that discussion of wider interests might be possible at a younger age if these were explicitly involved in the dilemma. A dilemma that involves an individual or a group deciding whether to follow one or more first order norms, under conditions where their decision obviously affects the wider society, or people in general, still falls under Kohlberg's definition of moral reasoning; but it might tell us something about such reasoning that is not learned from the more concrete dilemmas Kohlberg uses.

Evidence bearing on this issue comes from one of the studies of Langford and D'Cruz (1989). This used two interviews, E and A. Interview E began:

A group of teenagers did some work for a neighbour. They all did the same amount of work. As a result he wanted to reward them and gave them a thousand dollars. How ought they to divide it among themselves? Can you justify your answer?

This last question was then repeated in the style of a Kohlbergian interview until no further justifications were offered. Four further questions developed aspects of this division problem. Although the first question did not involve a dilemma for most interviewees, the four further questions did, as when it was asked:

> Two of the teenagers were known drug addicts and would be
> likely to use their share of the money to buy heroin and harm
> themselves. Should they be restrained from doing this?

Both interviews ended with the following three standard questions. In the first, the interviewer is asked to "Provide a summary of the various justifications they have given, ask if this is correct and whether the justifications can be taken any further." The second asked "Is there any religious justification for your thinking on this?". The third was "In societies other than our own, people have had different beliefs from your own. [An example is given.] How do you react to this?".

Interview L also began with a non-dilemma question:

> Three teenagers wanted some money to buy a new car. They
> bought a gun and robbed a service station. They decided that
> if anyone tried to stop them they would shoot them. During
> the robbery the station attendant tried to knock the gun out
> of one of the teenagers' hands and he fired at the attendant
> and killed him. Was this right? Can you justify your answer?

Three further questions that did involve dilemmas asked about small group situations involving killing, two of which related to the ethics of killing enemy soldiers in battle.

The scoring procedures were those of Langford and D'Cruz (1989), applied as for the studies of Kohlberg's Form A interview described in the previous chapter. Inter-rater reliability in the studies of Langford and D'Cruz (1989), and other studies using this method of scoring these interviews, has, as for Form A, averaged just over 80%. Findings were compared with results from Kohlberg's Form A (Dilemmas I and III). There was a statistically significant and substantial tendency for the generality of the interests considered to be greater in interviews E and L, than in Form A.

This shows that it is possible to devise interviews that provide less of a barrier to abstract thinking than Kohlberg's. Interviews E and L comprise three kinds of question: the non-dilemma initial questions; dilemma questions involving the interests of small and large groups; and the final synoptic questions. It was found from examination of replies to particular questions that all three kinds showed a marked tendency for the generality of interests considered to be greater than for Form A questions. That this applied to the second kind of question, confirms the suggestion made earlier that, for dilemmas meeting Kohlberg's definition of moral reasoning, the scope of interests explicitly involved in the dilemmas influences the abstraction of replies in the interest category.

The dilemmas concerned here increased the generality of the explicit interests involved in two ways: by having a small group rather than an individual protagonist; and by having the issue bear on the interests of the wider society in some interviews and on those of the small group in others. Examination of findings from particular questions within the interviews showed that, when the decision bore on the wider interests of society, the generality of interests considered was even greater than when the decision bore on the interests of a small group. This suggests that both the size of the group making the decision, and the size of the group explicitly said to be affected, influence the generality of the interests considered.

The dilemmas presented in this study realised Kohlberg's definition in a slightly different way to that in which he realised it, as the challenges to the first order norms, of equity, and the prohibition against murder, came from either a second order norm (we should promote the welfare of others) or from loyalty to one's country. It may be that these features contributed to observed differences between findings from these interviews and Form A, and further studies to determine this are desirable. It seems unlikely, however, that these features could be the sole origin of such differences, as the generality of the explicit interests involved was found to have an impact on the generality of reasoning within the two interviews concerned. If the presence of challenges other than those from first order norms also proves to have an influence on findings, this would provide evidence of an additional way in which the Kohlbergian interview is not representative of moral reasoning that falls within Kohlberg's definition.

One way to summarise findings from interviews, relevant to the issue at hand, is to cite average levels of abstraction found within interest-based replies at different ages. For the two nonKohlbergian interviews already discussed, about 30% of all interest-based replies in the 12–13-year age range involved wider interests. This is considerably more than are found at this age range with Kohlberg's interviews, for which the corresponding figure was only 13%.

Another revealing way of looking at such findings is to examine whether individuals give at least one reply taking account of wider interests. This provides an index of the ability to think in terms of such interests. An objection to Kohlberg's way of looking at interview findings that has come into clearer focus, as a result of stepping outside his particular interview technique, is that he assumes that individuals have an adequate opportunity to manifest their best level of reasoning in his interviews. Thus, a report of the overall distribution of their replies is justified, as this gives an unbiased picture of their thinking. However, once we abandon this perspective to think of the interview as offering opportunities to manifest high levels of reasoning, with some hindrance to this, even in Langford and D'Cruz's most abstract dilemmas, then the practice of reporting the distribution of replies, although very useful for some purposes, has limitations.

Langford and D'Cruz (1989) and Langford and Claydon (1989) found that a large majority of 12-year-olds were able to give at least one wider interest reply, in an interview that facilitated such replies. This again suggests that the moral reasoning ability of younger adolescents, and probably of younger children as well, is substantially underestimated by the Kohlbergian interview.

Another general finding from Langford and D'Cruz's nonKohlbergian interviews was that although abstraction within the interest category (and in some other categories, notably social harmony) was increased at all ages, compared to Kohlberg's Form A interview, the main developmental trends were as for Form A. The logical organisation of reasoning increased with age. There was little shift in the proportions of broad category replies with age, except that punishment replies decreased in older interviewees and religious replies peaked around 15–16 years. Abstraction increased with age within the interest and rules categories, and peaked around 15–16 years in the belief category. The same kinds of age-related shifts in authority-based, equals-based, and self-based replies within the belief category were found, as were reported in the last chapter for Kohlbergian interviews. These findings suggest that generalisations about developmental trends derived from Kohlbergian interviews can be extended to nonKohlbergian dilemmas involving norms under challenge, although the average level of abstraction found in some broad categories of reply may differ from one interview to another.

By varying the format and features of nonKohlbergian dilemma interviews, some other phenomena have also been identified. Thus, it has been shown that when a dilemma involves weighing the value of upholding a moral norm against human interests, or other factors suggesting it be set aside, the relative weight—of the factors suggesting upholding the norm and those suggesting it be set aside—will influence the incidence of broad categories of justification. If the norm predominates, then rule-based justifications citing the norm will be relatively more frequent, as well as some other kinds of reply supporting its validity, especially the human interests served by upholding it; if human interests or other countervailing factors suggesting setting aside the norm predominate, then replies citing the interests served by breaking the rule or other countervailing factors, such as human belief, will be more frequently cited (Langford, 1992a).

These findings are of interest as they suggest that the relative preponderance of broad category replies found in answers to a battery of dilemma interviews, whether Kohlbergian or not, is likely to be influenced by the overall balance between the factors pitted against one another in the dilemmas, and by the particular norms concerned in them. Although studies using Kohlbergian methods have shown that average Kohlbergian stage level differs from one dilemma to another (see especially Gibbs, Widaman, & Colby, 1982), this provides a more direct insight into one of the origins of such differences than studies scored by Kohlbergian methods.

Another aspect of the style of interview also seems to have an influence on the proportions of broad category replies in the kind of interview under consideration. Langford (1992b) varied a number of factors related to interview style, and found that the presence or not of closely related items in the interview had a demonstrable influence on such proportions. It seems that if interviewees are asked to make a number of judgements about dilemmas in closely related situations, they turn towards justifications based on human interest and away from those based on other factors, especially beliefs. This is probably because neither general rules, nor widely accepted social beliefs, nor those of the individual interviewee, have much to say about how to distinguish between closely related situations. On the other hand, the probable effects of different courses of action on overall human welfare do provide a basis for making such distinctions. This provides one reason for thinking that consideration of human interests plays a foundational role in the moral reasoning of contemporary Western children and adolescents. Some other reasons for thinking this will be discussed directly.

NonKohlbergian dilemma interviews similar to those of Langford and D'Cruz (1989) were also the subject of a study that attempted to refine Trainer's (1982) description of advanced second phase reasoning (Langford, 1991b). In dealing with this sub-phase, we face some initial definitional problems. As already mentioned, in such thinking one or more general principles is used to integrate everything else that is said. Unlike individuals in the earlier phases, who shift from one kind of reason to another in their justifications, such people generally stick to using only one reason, or to some deliberate way of distinguishing different kinds of moral judgement and using one reason for each.

Four such general principles are particularly common. The first is the religious view that relates all moral reasoning to the will of God, conceived as an external and objective reality. This is revealed in religious texts such as the Bible and in the traditions of churches.

Second, we have religious subjectivism, which says that all ethical decisions and principles can be decided by my own direct religious experience. This is a kind of belief system that has expanded in the West in recent years, being particularly associated with "born again" Christianity and, in a different form, with the New Age movement and so-called religious cults. Instead of referring ethical issues to the Bible, or the traditions of churches, it refers them to a direct personal relation with God, Jesus, or spirits.

The third kind of criterion is individual subjectivism. This says that moral values are determined by the individual's own choice, decision, or preference. In philosophy, this stance is often associated with Nietzsche and Sartre. Although some philosophers tend to blame the supposed prevalence of individual subjectivism in contemporary society on these two authors (e.g. Bloom, 1987), when we meet individual subjectivists in moral judgement interviews they only rarely mention the influence that philosophers have had on them. They seem, rather, to be developing a particular combination of ideas and feelings about life that suits them at a certain point in personal development. Some examples of this are given later.

Lastly, we come to "social subjectivism", which is the view that ethics is based on the beliefs, decisions, or welfare of large groups of people, like nations, or humanity in general. Here it is the subjective state of people in general, or people in large groups, that provides the criterion for deciding what is right. The commonest form of social subjectivism is utilitarianism, which is a doctrine particularly associated with the philosopher Jeremy Bentham, but in a rather vaguer form has been popular throughout the history of Western philosophy. In its broadest form, it states that we should act so that everyone's interests or happiness are considered. Bentham's criterion, that we should "Act to ensure the greatest happiness of the greatest number", is a more specific version of this principle. Although philosophers have puzzled over such questions as "What is happiness?" and "Is happiness the same as pleasure?", in moral judgement interviews we find only a small amount of attention to such issues. Most interviewees seem satisfied they know what other people's happiness or welfare is, though they puzzle very hard about how to achieve these things in particular situations.

Quite often, difficulties arise in knowing whether a given interview can truly be considered to show consistent use of a criterion. Interviews showing use of such criteria sometimes contain an initial section where the interviewee seems to be feeling their way. Quite often interviewees who hold strong views about general criteria are at first unwilling to discuss them, as they realise they may be controversial or socially unacceptable. They will respond to the first few questions as they think other people would and then confess they do not really mean these replies.

To deal with this difficulty, I have suggested the following way of assessing the consistent use of such a criterion: that the interviewee indicate on at least one occasion that one particular criterion or set of criteria is preferred and could be used to assess all moral claims (Langford 1991b). This avoids the difficulties that would arise if we said that the interviewee could not mention alternative criteria, which are sometimes mentioned and then repudiated. The reverse problem, of an individual saying briefly that they have an overall criterion that should be applied to all cases, and then abandoning this criterion in favour of a prolonged demonstration that they do not really know how to stick to a single criterion, but in practice use the haphazard methods of the intuitive thinker, is not common.

The following four summaries of moral reasoning interviews showing consistent use of criteria are adapted from Langford (1991b). This used one interview on the value of life (L) and another on the division of earnings (E). These were similar to those used by Langford and D'Cruz (1989), except that protagonists were either groups or individuals.

1. The Fundamentalist. The interviewee's first reply was "Look I don't know if I'm going to be much use to you for this." "Why not?" "Well I'm afraid I can't even start what you've asked me to do because I ... I live with Jesus you see, it's the most real thing in my life, and I couldn't, well imagine myself killing another human being ... It's to do with my relationship with Jesus." "Can you tell me anything more about that?" "Well it changes everything you know. You should try it. How can I explain it to you? He is here, all the time, with us. It's the most important thing we can know." "And how do you know that Jesus doesn't want us to kill?" "It says so in the Bible. But it's more than that. It's like direct knowledge. It's like being in love and then thinking about hurting the other person. God is love. It says that in the Bible too. Does it make sense at all?" Throughout the rest of the interview nearly all justifications were referred to direct experience of Jesus or of God, with occasional references to the Bible and "what makes sense". That God wants human beings to be happy was mentioned once, but the main emphasis was on direct experience that makes moral values obvious, backed up by the Bible.

2. First Individual Subjectivist. This interviewee answered the first question in the E interview in a conventional manner. The second question asked if it was right for two members of a group of six teenagers to bully the other four out of money they had worked for. The interviewee initially replied "No", but when asked to say why this wasn't right he said "If two of your friends bully you that's a fact of life, I can't say whether it's right or wrong. It's wrong for me, but whether it's right for them is another thing. It's a contingency, it's not a thing you can apply." "So it's not a proper subject for moral judgement?" "Whether their actions are right or wrong? No." "What is a proper subject for moral judgement?" "Whether your own actions are right or wrong." The interviewee then went on to explain that he would use moral terminology in a dispute, such as might arise over the distribution of the money in the question, but this was just to settle disputes and was a "practical" use of moral language, rather than representing a case where morality was involved "in principle".

The interviewee also went on to explain that the "source" of all moral judgements was in himself: "In the end you must be answerable for them." Later on he sums up his position as follows: "You start with the foundation that your parents put in place in your upbringing, that's often difficult to rationalise, even though you may wish to later on. Then on top of that a rational judgement is formed from the experience of an adult and then the highest priority in determining the way I act in any circumstance, is when I get up in the morning can I live with it? That may be some strange mix of unaccountable background and the more accountable rational overlay." This interviewee's system of belief differed from what we can call standard individual subjectivism because he was quite clear, and stated several times, that even when other people's actions affected him, they were not to be considered as moral or immoral, but only from a "practical" point of view. Only his own actions were to be considered as moral or immoral, and we could know which they were from the test: "Can I live with myself knowing I did this?".

3. Second Individual Subjectivist.   This interviewee showed the most dramatic defiance of conventional values of all those in the study. When asked, in the first question of interview L, if it was right for a group of teenagers, of which he was a member, to shoot someone during a service station robbery, he replied "To me sounds fine, the plan, there's some reason behind the plan, and if they get away with it successful." "Why does the plan justify this?" "I am not fully sure why we decided that we shoot whoever, but if someone did try to stop us and held somebody back or found out information, so that we might get caught and put in jail, pretty horrid time in there." During the second question, about a girl who kills her boyfriend out of jealousy, he explains that although he has given answers (if unconventional ones) to earlier questions, there is really no such thing as morality. Asked if people should do what they need to do in order to satisfy themselves (an idea he had appeared to endorse), he says "People do do, and also they don't have a great deal of control over their actions. I don't see any morals being an entity at all." "So strictly speaking these questions are all meaningless." "Yes. Totally meaningless."

The rest of the interview revealed that he had been sitting on a bus the previous week and it had suddenly come to him that there is no such thing as morality. In the future he would do what pleased him rather than what pleased others. He had spent some time since this realisation attempting to reorganise his beliefs and behaviour, to fit in with these principles. One could argue that this position is not so much ethical as antiethical, as he denies that the term morality has any meaning at all. However, it seems that this is largely a terminological difference, as he has not given up making those kinds of decisions about action that we normally call moral decisions. Rather, he has now decided to make them in a new way.

4. *The Social Subjectivist (a Marxist).*   This interviewee began by answering the first question in interview E, about the division of money earned by a group, by saying that equal pay for equal work was justified by Marx's labour theory of value, which states that the value of a product is proportional to the socially necessary labour time involved in its production. She then went on to expand this into a defiance of conventional opinion by saying that a brain surgeon should get the same as an unskilled labourer, but older people should be paid somewhat more than younger people. An important concept in her moral belief system emerged in reply to the third question, which asked if people should be restrained from spending their money to achieve (conventionally) immoral ends. Here she says "It doesn't matter what sort of organisation of society you are living, you can't get away from social control. That point has become the arbitrator of how you run society and how you should function otherwise." After several references to the importance of having benign rather than the current malignant forms of social control, she comes to the core of her beliefs. In reply to a question about where basic rights come from, she says: "From our own humanity. Once we started whatever state we were, some sort of animal. Communication power and the ability to organise and create better conditions for ourselves, inherit the ethical ideas and concepts, which have been thought through by more intelligent people."

This interviewee showed less inclination to dwell on the foundations of her beliefs than the other three or to continually relate them to particular aspects of beliefs. However, she rapidly ascended up her chain of reasons from the evils of social control, through to basic rights, and then to the foundations of basic rights in "our own humanity" and human social evolution, showing that she had a thought-out view on such issues. This was related to her opposition to religion, as an ethical system that claims to be supported by divine sanction, but is in fact an instrument of malignant social control, a view she expanded at some length.

These interviews provide fairly clear evidence of advanced phase two reasoning. There are in addition some signs of third phase or metaethical reasoning in the second and third interviews, where the definition of morality is explicitly discussed. There are even signs that in these cases such reasoning about the definition of morality is quite well integrated with the substantive ethical criterion adopted.

Langford (1991b) found that, among 60 Australian undergraduate students from 19 to 24 years of age, only 7% showed advanced phase two reasoning with consistent use of general normative criteria. This is probably a reasonable estimate of the incidence of such reasoning in Western undergraduate populations in this kind of interview. Its incidence in Western adult populations as a whole is almost certainly appreciably less. Only 3% of undergraduates showed signs of being at phase three by integrating metaethical reasoning with their substantive position, although this figure must be seen as very approximate.

Synoptic questioning in dilemma interviews

The synoptic questioning method involves giving a request, usually at the end of an interview on more detailed issues, for interviewees to provide an overall survey of their views on given topics involving moral issues. This has been used for both Kohlbergian and nonKohlbergian interviews realising Kohlberg's definition of moral reasoning (Kohlberg, 1958; Langford, 1991b; Langford & D'Cruz, 1989). In Colby and Kohlberg (1987b) the separate section of synoptic questions, found in Kohlberg (1958), was dropped from the interview schedules, though occasional examples of such questions persist in the probes given after dilemma stories. As these probes are few, and findings from them are amalgamated with the far more numerous specific questions, in the later work it is hard to know how replies to them differ from those to other questions.

Findings from this method bear on the issue of the representativeness of the non-synoptic parts of the standard Kohlbergian dilemma interview. Not only is there some doubt about the opportunity that these non-synoptic parts of Kohlberg's interviews give for the production of abstract replies, but there must also be doubt about their ability to encourage the most logically integrated replies an interviewee is capable of, as this too may be inhibited by the concrete nature of the questions. The synoptic method is ideally suited to elicit an individual's most abstract and integrated replies.

Examination of the specimen transcripts given by Kohlberg (1958), as well as of the original transcripts from the other two studies mentioned earlier, suggests that the logical integration of replies is not substantially different when synoptic and concrete questions are asked, but that the abstraction of replies is substantially increased.

The first of these findings is less surprising when we look at the typical course of a non-synoptic dilemma interview that reveals a high level of logical integration, as described by Langford (1991b). This is for the interviewee to tend to play along with the piecemeal and concrete form of the questions for a short initial period, followed by a decision to adopt a more synoptic view of the problem. This usually occurs within the first 15 minutes of the interview. As most dilemma interviews last at least this long, they provide an opportunity for the interviewee to reach this point. Thus, piecemeal and concrete interviews probably do not present much of a barrier to the expression of highly integrated views.

That the abstraction of replies is substantially increased in synoptic interviews accords with findings from studies reviewed in the previous section, as synoptic questions will usually direct attention to abstract and general issues in a way that Kohlberg's non-synoptic dilemma questions do not. Further research contrasting the synoptic with other methods is desirable.

Interviews based on wider definitions

There are three kinds of interview based on wider definitions that are of particular interest: the Piagetian style of interview that asks for justification of a first order moral norm that is not under challenge; interviews that ask for justification of second order norms, like the principle that we should seek to advance the general welfare; and interviews about issues where human interests are at stake but no first order norm is involved. Interviews of all three kinds may be synoptic or not.

Interviews about first order norms not under challenge

Although this kind of interview has been extensively used following its use by Piaget (1932), studies have generally been analysed using strong interpretation (for a review see Tomlinson, 1980). No formal study of the method using weakly interpretive methods has been reported. However, something of what might be found here can be gleaned from Piaget's original description of his findings. According to him, when asked to say why we should not lie, children up to about 10 years of age (the end of stage 3) tend to give reasons like "You get punished", whereas those in stage 4 say that the rule is there so we will all be better off. Given Piaget's tendency to omit reasons that are not significant in his theory, we could expect some other kinds of reasons to be prominent, especially those based on beliefs, whether of the interviewee, of authorities like parents, or of people in general. However, it is notable that the punishment and interest replies that Piaget cites are mainly of a general and abstract kind, even for the younger children. This confirms what we would expect to find, on the basis of findings reviewed in the previous sections, which is that the absence of a concrete dilemma situation provides a better opportunity for general replies to be given than Kohlberg's dilemmas, and thus justifications are more abstract.

Piaget's studies used non-synoptic interview techniques, but as the initial question is in this case a fairly general one, findings would probably be similar with synoptic techniques.

Interviews about second order norms

Langford (1992a) provided interviewees with a number of first and one second order norm, and then suggested situations in which the reasons they might be broken varied from weak to strong. The second order norm was "We should help other people." Findings indicated that when asked to justify this rule, the great majority of replies between the ages of 12 and 21 years involved restatement of the rule. This suggests that such principles are regarded, even prior to the period in which generalised ethical criteria are used, as ultimate explanations that are not capable of further elucidation.

Interviews about controversial social issues where no first order norm is relevant

Non-synoptic methods.   Langford (1991a) asked for justifications for moral judgements about situations that did not involve a first order norm. Questions asked whether authorities or subordinates or both should have control in situations in the home, school, workplace, and political decision-making. The most notable finding was that the percentage of interest-based replies was constant and in the region of 80% throughout adolescence, which is higher than for any situation that has been studied where a first order norm applies. This is not in one sense a surprising result, as replies based on such norms are a substantial component of the mix of replies when they are relevant to a situation, and other kinds of reply will naturally increase when these are not available. However, it is significant that it is interest-based and to a lesser extent religious replies, rather than other kinds of reply, that expand when the opportunity to appeal to a rule is removed.

Turiel et al. (1991) reported rather similar studies focusing on controversial topics, in which they asked questions of the form "Is homosexuality all right or not all right", with the terms "abortion", "incest" and "pornography" also substituted for "homosexuality". High school and college students were asked to justify judgements about these issues and the findings analysed using an adaptation of the Davidson et al. (1983) scoring system, which is similar to analysis in terms of Langford and D'Cruz's broad categories. A parallel procedure was also adopted to assess justification of moral norms, by substituting the terms "killing", "rape", and "theft" in the statements.

In their first study, for the moral norms 83% of replies were norm-based. For the controversial topics, the predominant justifications showed a more complex pattern. The two issues of abortion and pornography showed the same tendency as in Langford's studies to be predominantly justified in terms of human welfare, 65% of justifications being of this kind. The somewhat lower figure for interest-based justifications here, compared to Langford's studies, may have been due to the latter having asked groups of questions about related situations, which Langford (1992b) showed increases the incidence of such justifications. For those who approved of homosexuality, interest-based justifications were also the commonest, constituting 42% of justifications. Other findings from the homosexuality and incest issues will be more appropriately discussed later.

These results add further weight to the suggestion that consideration of human interests plays a foundational role in the moral reasoning of Western populations. This can also be supported by another finding, from adolescent subjects, which it is convenient to mention here, although the technique used involved first order norms under challenge. As already mentioned, Langford (1992a) provided interviewees with a number of first order norms and then suggested situations in which the reasons they might be broken varied from weak to strong. The analysis separated justifications given for upholding the norm, when the reason for breaking it was judged insufficient, from those given when the norm was rejected or the problem judged undecideable. It was found that the broad categories of reply, given for upholding the various norms offered, were similar for a range of central first order norms and, among these, interest-based replies were clearly predominant. Thus, for the rules that you should not kill another person, that people should be allowed freedom of speech, that we should avoid telling lies, and that everyone should have an equal opportunity to get a good education, a substantial majority of replies were based on human interest, nearly all mentioning wider interest.

This seems to confirm that interest-based replies are particularly fundamental. They provide a foundation for the common reply based on first order norms and they expand when such a norm-based reply is not available. This applies throughout adolescence; Langford and Claydon (1989) also found indications that it obtains during middle childhood. This is also in keeping with the explanatory role that second order norms relating to interests play in moral reasoning. Such norms are often used to justify first order norms, but the reverse is uncommon.

There is also evidence that these comments can be extended to the other most reflective type of justification, that involving religious considerations. Langford (1992b) found that, when the style of interview involved repeated judgements about closely related situations, not only did interest-based replies increase, but religious replies also increased considerably more than other kinds of reply. This effect did not appear in the other two groups of studies that have just been cited as evidence for the foundational role of interest-based considerations (Langford, 1991a; 1992a). However, this is probably because religious justifications are usually only found in contemporary Western populations when the question mentions a specifically religious issue (Langford, 1992b). Such questions were not included in the two groups of studies concerned.

However, when an issue is perceived to fall in the religious domain, further evidence for the foundational role of religious replies can be obtained. Turiel et al. (1991) showed that religious reasons were the commonest justification among those who disapproved of homosexuality, such disapproval often being associated with Christian religious commitment (the study included a group of committed Catholics). For incest, religious replies, together with custom and tradition, also predominated for those who disapproved. This shows that, when a controversial issue is perceived to fall within the religious sphere by people who give weight to religious considerations, if there is no first order norm that is relevant then religious norms can become the most important type of second order norm used in justifications. In addition, a separate study involving only committed Catholics found that for this group the use of welfare and interest justifications decreased markedly for all questions and their place was largely taken by religious justifications.

The foundational role of religious norms is further indicated by the explanatory role that such second order norms as "Act in accord with the will of God" play in moral reasoning, being used to justify first order norms, but not being justified by such norms.

Developmental trends in justifications obtained in interviews about controversial issues, where no first order norm is relevant, have tended to be most noticeable in the abstraction of interest replies, which, as for other interviews, increases with age. Trends for other replies tend to be severely reduced by their relative scarcity (Langford, 1991a).

Synoptic methods. A study using synoptic methods with an interview focusing on controversial issues, rather than first order norms, was that of Perry (1970), previously discussed in Chapter 3. He claimed that his Harvard undergraduates went through nine positions, organised into three levels, in their epistemological and moral views. These were outlined in that chapter. The aim of this discussion is to show how his findings can be interpreted within the framework so far outlined.

Perry's method of interview analysis was not strongly interpretive in the sense that Piaget and Kohlberg used strong interpretation. It did, however, interpret the information derived from his interviews in a stronger way than is advocated here. This was because he assumed that his interviewees were all capable of advancing an integrated position on the topics covered. Examination of his sample sections from transcripts, however, indicates that many were not capable of fully integrating their views, giving advanced chains of reasons, rather than fully integrated ethical or epistemological views.

Perry's study focused on a particular topic, in a particular American social environment, that is less relevant now than when the study was performed. The first of these points was emphasised by the author in an exemplary way, but we still need to bear it in mind in considering his findings. The topic of the interviews was not morality in general, but the students' view of moral issues arising from their university experiences, particularly their experiences of study. They came to the process of study in a way that many students nowadays in comparable countries would not. They had emerged from an authoritarian schooling system, mostly with a strong religious orientation, and then had to adapt to the liberal outlook and educational philosophy of Harvard in the 1950s, which led to considerable culture shock. This aspect of the study had two results.

The first was that it led to a concentration, both by the interviewees and in the scoring method, on the content of the individual's views; this tended to shift from authoritarian admiration for a system where knowledge and values were handed down from above to an outlook where the individual undertook a commitment to his or her own beliefs. The scoring method enabled scorers to follow this shift in the content of individuals' views, under the assumption that they passed through the sequence with highly integrated reasoning. The high reliability of the scoring system was probably due to the relative ease of judging how far the individual had gone along this continuum. The continuum is certainly real, but it is largely one of content, ranging from authoritarian to liberal, rather than one based on the structural organisation of the reasoning, which is assumed to be highly integrated, even when it is not.

The second feature produced by the particular nature of the study was that interviewees probably had rather more integrated views about issues raised by the experience of study than they might have had on other topics. They were undergoing a very intense experience of adjustment to change, with their future careers depending on how well they could adapt, in the broadest sense, to this experience. Thus they probably did a lot more thinking about issues of this kind than about moral issues in general. Perry's way of viewing his findings fully incorporated this feature of development, and it fitted his theoretical views about how such reasoning develops. However, in comparing his findings with those from other studies, this needs to be borne in mind.

Finally, one example of how Perry's scoring method may produce a limited view of the experience of undergraduate students in general. Langford (1991b) found there was a minority of "born again" Christians on Australian campuses in the 1980s, which was also evident on campuses in other Western countries as well. Many of these had begun from the majority outlook of those in late adolescence in this period, which we can label "intuitive utilitarianism". This involves poorly integrated reasoning justifying moral judgements in various ways, concentrating on a foundation in human interest justifications. One kind of born again Christian then advanced to reasoning integrated around the principle "Act according to the will of God/Jesus."

This kind of developmental progress combines a shift from a more "liberal" to a more "authoritarian" content in the views expressed, with one from a less advanced structural organisation to a more advanced one. Without separating content from structural organisation, this kind of development is hard to describe accurately. This is a weakness in the developmental scheme advocated by Perry.

This is also an opportune moment to comment on the difficulties of the method of analysing text and interview complexity advocated by Schroder et al. (1967) and Suedfeld and Tetlock (1977), previously mentioned in Chapter 3. This ranks material from a point of minimum complexity, at which answers and replies are generated by a single fixed rule, to a point of maximum complexity, at which the individual realises that there are two or more equally valid alternative views of the topic in question. This provides an index of complexity that is independent of content, but it suffers from two related difficulties. The first is that it may not adequately capture developmental progressions. Seeing two or more alternative views of a topic may be a developmental precursor to integrating them through a single superordinate rule or viewpoint. This is precisely what Perry's students did as they advanced to his final three positions. The Schroder et al. method fails to distinguish simpler and earlier rules and views from later and more encompassing ones (for a review of this problem see Hunsberger et al., 1992).

The second difficulty of the method is that it is content-independent, claiming to be applicable to all kinds of content. This problem is highlighted by the work of Jaques (1986), who devised a separate series of conceptual levels to deal with people's understanding of their work environments. Although he found the general framework offered by Harvey, Hunt, and Schroder (1961) appealing, the content-independent methods of analysing conceptual complexity, to which it gave rise, did not appear appropriate to this topic. This also seems to apply to the structure of reasoning found in moral reasoning interviews, which is again difficult to fit into the content-independent sequence offered by Schroder et al. (1967).

Other dimensions

NonKohlbergian styles of interview have also thrown light on a number of dimensions that have not been covered so far. Some of the studies investigating these dimensions have used dilemma interviews involving first order norms, but as the majority have not it is convenient to review them together here. Four further kinds of dimension are known to be of importance: those that index autonomy, generalised ethical criteria, intentionality, and reification. These are not all directly assessed by the scoring method of Langford and D'Cruz (1989), but have all been assessed by weakly interpretive methods of assessment.

The list of criteria for autonomy versus heteronomy drawn up by Tappan et al. (1987), discussed in Chapter 5, shows that a rather wide range of concepts have on occasion been thought relevant to the assessment of this dimension. In the following discussion, only assessments relating to some core aspects of the distinction will be considered.

Autonomy in moral reasoning in these selected core senses can either apply to justifications or to the content of moral judgements. Autonomy in justifications can be assessed by subdividing replies scored in the belief category into: those that cite the beliefs of authorities, like parents, police, or teachers; those that cite the views of people other than authorities or the interviewee, including most replies citing general opinion; and replies citing the opinion of the interviewee. The ratio of the first two kinds of reply to the third gives an index of autonomy in justifications (Langford & Claydon, 1989). Autonomy in the content of judgements refers to the tendency to make judgements in favour of giving decisions to a subordinate rather than to an authority, or in favour of rules that suit the subordinate (Langford, 1991a; Laupa & Turiel, 1986, 1993). Such subordinates may be children (as opposed to parents or teachers) or may be other kinds of people playing subordinate roles in an organisation, such as factory workers, who are subordinate to management. In any interview where issues of this kind are involved, individuals can be scored as showing greater or lesser moral approval of autonomy (Langford, 1991a).

Generalised ethical criteria as a dimension in moral reasoning means the tendency to favour one or other criterion for making moral judgements when individuals have reached at least advanced second phase reasoning and are able to make consistent use of a single criterion or group of criteria. It can be assessed from interviews by the methods already discussed. Existing interview studies have chiefly thrown light on the content of such criteria, though studies investigating beliefs about their origin and perceived permanence are desirable.

Intentionality is significant, as young children tend to say that when someone does something unintentionally they should still be held accountable for it. This was originally studied by Piaget (1932), who asked children questions about a child who broke some cups by accident and one who broke them on purpose. Young children tend to judge the objective effects of the action, rather than the subjective intention, saying that a child who breaks many cups by accident deserves a greater punishment than one who breaks one on purpose. Older children and adults take the intention of the action into account. Thus the intentionality of an individual can be assessed by looking at their judgements in cases where the intention of the actor is varied (see Ferguson & Rule, 1982; Karniol, 1978; Keasey, 1978; Lickona, 1976; Shultz et al., 1986; Tomlinson, 1980).

Reification refers to the tendency to see social relations, including moral arrangements, as natural or as a consequence of agreement. This is best indexed in interviews that ask whether social arrangements could or should be changed (see Connell, 1971; Hess & Torney, 1967; Jahoda, 1979, 1981; Piaget, 1932; Seif, 1993; Tomlinson, 1980; Turiel et al., 1991).

Turning to findings from these techniques, autonomy in judgements and justifications shows a steady increase with age in some areas, especially in reply to questions about some core issues connected with the family; but the view derived from Piaget (1932) that this applies uniformly in all areas has received substantial disconfirmation in recent years. For example, Damon (1977) found that children in the 4–10-year age range generally accepted parental directives to clean their rooms, but not parental instructions to steal others' possessions or harm others. Laupa and Turiel (1986) found that children rejected directives from teachers at school, when obeying them would cause harm to others. Laupa and Turiel (1993) found that children from 5–11 years said they would obey a school principal's instructions inside the school, but not outside.

In addition, children do not just consider whether a person is an adult or older child before deciding whether to obey them, but instead have a quite sophisticated notion of duly constituted authorities, who should be obeyed, clearly distinguishing them from those who are not legitimate. Damon (1977) found that a peer could be a legitimate authority, to be obeyed, if they had been designated as such by the teacher or had special knowledge or skills. Laupa and Turiel (1986) found that the authority of teachers depends on their organisational status (e.g. whether they were hired to perform the function in question).

In other areas, particularly in the control of school learning, autonomy in judgements, at least among Australian children and probably also in other Western countries, decreases in the early school years, increasing again during adolescence (Langford, 1991a; Seif, 1993). Possible reasons for this are discussed later.

Generalised ethical criteria have usually been considered as a dimension involving individual differences, and thus we can expect developmental trends to involve individuation. Convincing studies of this have yet to be reported.

The studies previously cited from the literature on the assessment of intentionality show that the tendency to take this into account, in assessing moral responsibility, increases with age, with most children being able to use the criterion effectively by 5 years in American samples, rather than the 7 or 9 years suggested by Piaget (Shultz et al., 1986).

The reification of social relations declines with age, with both its absolute level and rate of decline strongly dependent on the topic discussed (see earlier references). In general, the rate of decline in topics defined as moral in the Kohlberg-Turiel sense is much less than that for either issues that are controversial among adults or those defined by social conventions (Turiel et al., 1991). However, a minority of the population in late adolescence and adulthood ultimately come to see even rules such as that against murder as based on personal or social agreement, rather than as having an absolute status beyond human decision (Langford, 1991b; Trainer, 1982, 1983).

Gender differences in moral reasoning

It is worth briefly mentioning the influence of gender on replies in moral reasoning interviews. Studies using the methods of scoring such interviews of Langford and D'Cruz (1989) have shown no appreciable influences of gender on scores along dimensions relating to justifications, even when, as for instance in the study of moral judgements about sex roles within the family of Langford and Claydon (1989), the topic of the interview might seem most likely to produce such differences. This is in accord with the general finding from Kohlbergian interviews, when scored by Kohlbergian methods, that such effects are slight or non-existent (for a review see Kohlberg et al., 1983). There are, on the other hand, some sex-related differences in the content of the moral beliefs of males and females, as assessed by questionnaire studies, particularly in relation to feminist issues (Bliss, 1988; Eysenck, 1954, Eysenck & Wilson, 1978; Renzetti, 1987).

These two sets of findings are not in conflict with one another if we accept, as suggested earlier, that the outcomes of actions in terms of human interests are the chief foundation of moral opinion in contemporary Western societies, both among children and adults, especially in dealing with controversial social issues where no first order norm is relevant. There is also a tendency for individuals to be swayed, although they tend not to admit it, somewhat in the direction of self-interest where this conflicts with the general interest (see Chapter 9). Thus, in dealing with the morality of controversial social issues, the predominant method of reasoning is calculation of the general interest for both sexes. However, where the interests of the sexes conflict, the impact of self-interest will produce differences in the content of moral beliefs about feminist issues, such as how much housework men ought to do.

The widely publicised claims of Gilligan that substantial gender-related differences in styles of moral justification exist, are based on such impressionistic methods of summarising replies from Kohlbergian and other interviews that it is difficult to give them much credence (see Gilligan, 1977, 1982; Gilligan, Lyons, & Hamner, 1990). Her methods are even more selective than those of Piaget, with excerpts that suit her case reported and those that do not ignored. It may be, however, that her claims have more validity if we read them as applying to the management of discourse in real-life situations. Males and females sometimes prefer to discuss issues using different styles of discourse, as when a man prefers to talk about the division of household duties in factual terms, relating to what traditional roles prescribe, rather than in terms of moral language that deals with what ought to happen (see Goodnow & Bowes, 1994). This is an interesting topic for future research.

THE PROBLEM OF THEORETICAL INTERPRETATION

We can organise the descriptive phenomena of development in moral reasoning, as revealed through interviews using weakly interpretive methods of analysis, under five general principles. These principles provide covering explanations for detailed trends in findings without taking us far from non-interpretive description. They are not, however, fully satisfactory from a theoretical viewpoint, as they do not explain underlying mechanisms. Some possible explanations in terms of underlying mechanisms are also reviewed, but it would be premature to attempt to decide between them on the basis of current evidence.

The expansion of social interest

As noted in the introductory theoretical chapters, the existence of some version of this tendency is obvious from informal observations, and has been recognised by virtually every major theorist. However, too little effort has previously gone into disentangling different versions of the principle. Two of these are particularly useful. The first is that preferred by Freud and the ego psychologists, which is the tendency for social attachments and bonds to expand in scope with development. The second is that mentioned in this and the previous chapter, which is improvement in the ability to relate concrete moral issues to their wider social context with age. In interviews centring on concrete issues, this too will result in increased consideration of wider interests with increased maturity. At present, it is hard to disentangle the influence of these two factors on interview findings.

We also need to separate the ability to draw wider implications from concrete situations from the more usual version of the cognitive incapacity argument, used by cognitive structuralists in relation to moral reasoning. For reasons already outlined, in some key areas we can reject the idea that, particularly during adolescence, development is mainly produced by an initial inability to entertain certain ideas due to cognitive incapacity, followed by the development of such capacity. Cognitive incapacity may play a role in relation to expansion in the scope of interest-based justifications, but it is mainly in hindering the inferences needed to draw the inexplicit out of the explicit, rather than in preventing certain ideas being entertained at all.

When we come to provide explanations of the mechanisms underlying the two versions of the expansion of consideration of interests principle, we are faced with a wealth of mechanisms and insufficient means of deciding their relative importance. Various contending explanations for the first version have been reviewed in Chapter 6, including expanding libidinal investments, expanding reciprocity, broadening of defensive identifications, expanding sympathy and broadening biological bonding mechanisms (more detailed attempts to suggest a plausible mix of the mechanisms involved here have been made by Vine, 1983a, b, 1986, 1992; and Rushton, 1988). One of the things we have learned from our review of interview methods is that it is hard to reach definitive conclusions about this kind of underlying mechanism using existing interview methods, as interviewees say too little about their reasons for considering the interests of others. Something is said about reciprocity in this connection, but such explanations are attached to only a small percentage of all statements suggesting other people's interests should be considered. It is hard to know whether this reflects the relative unimportance of the mechanism of reciprocity, or the difficulty that interviewees have in telling us about it. If we are to seek to disentangle the relative contributions of this and other mechanisms, we need to turn to evidence outside interviews or to devise more penetrating styles of interview.

One way that this problem might be pursued is by asking explicit questions about an interviewee's view of a mechanism, such as reciprocity, and also giving them dilemma interviews, to assess the relation between replies to the two kinds of interview. The possibility of involving naturalistic and experimental methods is also appealing, as such methods have been widely applied in the general study of attachment. Although they have not so far enabled any consensus to be reached, theories of attachment have evolved considerably over the years in response to theoretical and empirical advances, and we can expect further improvements in future (see especially Bretherton & Waters, 1985; Gewirtz & Kurtines, 1991; Greenberg, Cichetti, & Cummings, 1990; Lamb et al., 1985).

In seeking to explain the improvements in cognitive capacity involved in drawing the inexplicit from the explicit we are faced with a somewhat different problem. It is obvious both from common observation and from formal studies that the ability to draw inferences about the implications of a written or verbal text, that are not explicitly stated in the text, increases during childhood and adolescence (Duffy, 1986; O'Brien, Shank, Myers, & Rayner, 1988; Prawat, Cancelli, & Cook, 1976; Rayner & Polatsek, 1989; Whaley, 1981). However, none of the studies reported has involved the same kinds of inference that are involved in moving from the concrete to the abstract in Kohlbergian dilemma interviews. Nor has theory in this area focused directly on this kind of ability. However, it is not difficult to produce a variety of explanations for improvement in the abilities concerned.

Consider, as an example, the ability to infer that even though in one case of lying it is only the interests of the person lied to that are damaged, there is a principle involved that extends to the interests of people in general. It could be that older children are more likely to think of this general principle because others tend to discuss such principles with them in connection with concrete situations, to a greater extent than they do with younger children. Thus, simple verbal association between particular examples and general principles might increase with age.

Alternatively, a certain kind of mental models approach to cognitive development suggests that the mental models of younger children involve concrete situations, whereas those of older children involve models of classes of situations (Demetriou, Efklides and Platsidou, 1993; Halford, 1992; Langford & Hunting, 1994). Representations involving classes of situations would be more likely to suggest the need to consider general human interests, rather than those specifically mentioned by the interviewer. Our difficulty here is that, once again, we currently have no means of knowing what relative weight to attach to such alternative explanations as associative strength and style of mental model. This is an appealing topic for further research.

Other cognitive improvements

Other age trends seem to owe something to improvements in cognitive capacity. Thus, it is plausible to think that the tendencies for reification of social relations to decrease with age, for the use of intentionality to increase with age, and for the integration of reasoning (construction of longer chains of reasoning) to increase with age are all due, at least in large part, to such improvements. The tendency for punishment-based justifications to decline with age may also arise partly from improved ability to understand that a question asking why we won't do something (to which the mention of punishment is quite acceptable to an adult) is different from one asking why we shouldn't do something (to which mention of punishment is not acceptable to an adult). In these areas, it is again relatively easy to devise alternative explanations for these phenomena, but it is currently difficult to decide on their relative importance.

The self-other-self cycle

This is seen in interviews in two main ways. The first is the developmental course of belief-based justifications. Such justifications follow a rather complex course, with appeals to the beliefs of the self and of equals being present in substantial numbers at all ages. Although appeals to adult authority are never predominant, they do decline in middle childhood, with appeals to general social belief increasing to a peak in mid-adolescence. Appeals to the views of self then increase at the expense of those to general social belief, achieving a slight preponderance by late adolescence (Langford & Claydon, 1989). It is reasonable to follow Piaget in supposing that at some point early in development the views of the self were originally prominent, being displaced first by those of parents and other authorities and then by peers, before a turn back to those of the self in late adolescence.

The second way in which the self-other-self cycle is seen is in the emergence of integrated reasoning based on an individual subjectivist criterion in a minority in late adolescence, which involves reliance on the views of self to a degree not seen in middle childhood. It is likely that both trends can be explained by similar mechanisms, though possibly operating in rather different combinations.

The tendency in middle childhood to rely to some extent on adult authority in belief justifications, fits in with the young child's attachment to the family and its socialisation into the acceptance of parental authority, whereas the shift to the views of equals accords with the increasing commitment to the peer group during adolescence. The shift in later adolescence back to relying on the views of self could be due to contraction in the scope of social attachments, the views of Erikson providing some support for this supposition; although it is not at all clear that this is so. The Jungian explanation for this was reviewed in Chapter 6.

One alternative explanation for these trends in late adolescence is that they are mainly due to greater personal social status, which makes appeal to the individual's own opinions a more acceptable conversational tactic. A second is provided by the contention of Freudians and ego psychologists that a partial return of infantile narcissism occurs in late adolescence. Third, it could be that, as suggested by Baldwin and Kohlberg, the cognitive ability to consider the views of the self at the same time as those of society and other people is partly responsible. When the importance of the views of others is first discovered, according to this line of thinking, it crowds out the views of the self. The latter return when the two can be entertained together. The comments made earlier about the need for the application of a variety of methods, to establish the relative importance of these mechanisms, apply again in this case.

The peaking of religiosity

The peaking of religiosity in mid-adolescence is a wide-ranging problem for general developmental theory that again does not seem near adequate resolution at present. Two particularly appealing explanations will be mentioned. According to both Freud (1926) and Bovet (1928) the concept of God is initially patterned on that of the parents. It could be that, as belief in the all-knowing wisdom and power of the parents declines in adolescence, there is a need to strengthen that in a substitute parent to retain a feeling of being protected. This later declines due to an awareness of needing less protection and being better able to cope with the demands of life (see also Goldman, 1964).

An alternative theory is based on Rank's (1931, 1968) notion that awareness of death increases in adolescence, leading to a need to be reassured of personal immortality. It is less clear why religiosity later declines, but one reason could be that in Western society the young adult becomes more closely integrated into a society that offers many non-religious defences against the awareness of death (see especially Becker, 1973). Again, further work is needed to establish the relative importance of these and other influences.

Increase in autonomy

Although autonomy, both in justifications and judgements, especially in matters connected with the family, tends to increase continuously with age in some situations, studies by Langford (1991a) and Seif (1993) indicate that, when asked to make judgements about whether a child or its teacher should control such aspects of the learning process as the selection of books and writing topics for a 6-year-old child, development follows a curvilinear course. From about 5 to 13 years Australian children actually decrease the autonomy they think ought to be given in this situation. From about 13 years to adulthood the suggested level of autonomy then increases again. The most likely reason for this is that the level of autonomy allowed Australian children in controlling the process of learning at school decreases with age during the primary years, reaching its lowest level in the early secondary grades, and then increases again in the later years of secondary school and at university. Children and adolescents partly project their own socialisation experiences onto the 6-year-old child about whom they are asked to make judgements.

Although it is tempting to see projection of the child's own socialisation experiences as the only factor in producing such judgements about autonomy, particularly in younger children, Seif's (1993) studies showed that there is a complex interaction between the age of the child judging and that of the child judged, when the latter is varied. More studies using greater numbers of interviewees, sampling a wider range of backgrounds, are needed to make sense of these interactions. It is possible that the cognitive capacity to make realistic judgements, about the effects of allocating authority to subordinates or authorities on the overall welfare of those involved, will be found to be significant here.

CONCLUSIONS

Findings from nonKohlbergian interviews scored with weakly interpretive methods show three things. First, they show qualitatively similar developmental trends to those found with Kohlbergian interviews. Second, they suggest that such substantial quantitative differences exist between the two kinds of interview that it is unsafe to generalise about moral reasoning in general, even in Kohlberg's relatively restricted sense of this term, from Kohlbergian interviews alone. An indication of this is that in nonKohlbergian interviews the level of abstraction of replies is often substantially greater, showing that Kohlbergian interviews discourage abstract replies. Third, by focusing on particular issues not easily approached through Kohlbergian interviews, nonKohlbergian interviews provide evidence about aspects of reasoning and developmental dimensions not illuminated by their Kohlbergian counterparts.

This poses the problem of explaining the developmental trends found in various kinds of interview. It was argued in this and previous chapters that the theories of Kohlberg and Piaget can be ruled out when considered as a whole by the trends observed. However, there is a wealth of particular mechanisms suggested by these and other theories that offer explanations for them. Further research is needed to establish the relative importance of these mechanisms.

PART THREE
Other methods

CHAPTER NINE

Findings from other methods

INTRODUCTION

The interview is only one of several methods that can be used to study moral reasoning. The aim of the present chapter is to look at a number of others and to assess what they can add to findings from interviews. The use of friendship discussion groups has already been dealt with in the coverage of the work of Haan in Chapter 3. As we have seen, findings tend to support the general thrust of the argument presented here based on interviews, in the sense that they show young children to be more cognitively mature and more capable of appreciating the benefits of reciprocity than Kohlberg thought, although there is need for further work on the connections between the two methods.

This chapter will next offer brief comments on the following three methods: stem completion; choice between passages of prose describing moral outlooks; and requests for definitions of moral terms. This is followed by more detailed consideration of the following three methods: factor analytic studies of sociomoral attitudes and values; studies of outcome comparison; and the naturalistic study of moral discourse. It is argued that findings from these last three methods are of considerable importance in refining the descriptive picture of moral reasoning obtained from interviews.

The stem completion studies of Loevinger were described in Chapter 3. Some comments about her method of reporting findings from the technique are appropriate here. Although only the expressed meaning of statements is used to assign replies to stages, the result of reporting findings in terms of stages is to repeat some, though not all, the problems of Kohlberg's stage assessment methods. In particular, the reader of Loevinger's research reports is not in possession of information about the developmental behaviour or overall incidence of the particular kinds of reply that go to make up a stage.

An example of this difficulty relates to replies based on general social opinion (wider belief replies). These are given quite often in her stem completion test and will mainly be assigned to Stage 4, which emphasises morality based on this factor (see especially Loevinger, 1970, 1983). If stem completion taps similar thought processes to interviews, we can expect this kind of reply to peak in mid-adolescence, approximately when Stage 4 should peak, so this aspect of findings supports the theory. However, the general description of this stage also states that its morality is dominated by respect for general opinion. But if we look at the nature of the stems given, it seems most unlikely that it will ever be true that general opinion replies will predominate; we are certainly not presented with any evidence for this. Thus this aspect of replies probably contradicts the theory, but this is hidden by the practice of reporting the sum total of replies at a stage, without giving a breakdown of these into their various types.

Hence, Loevinger's demonstration that up to mid-adolescence we find a steady increase in stage scores, with some samples showing net regression in the college years, does not show that particular kinds of reply behave as the theory predicts. This suggests that there would be substantial dividends in reporting findings in terms of categories similar to those used in interview studies with weakly interpretive methods.

We have already looked at the best-known group of studies using the choice between descriptive passages method in reviewing the work of Rest in Chapter 7. In general, the method is good for providing an assessment of the moral reasoning of individuals when it is already known what range of outlooks we are likely to find in a given population. It should usually be used as a follow-up to more open-ended methods, such as interviews or naturalistic study of moral discourse. It should also be borne in mind that if we give subjects a choice between a number of passages, all expressing coherent moral outlooks, they will have to choose one of the choices, though their own outlook may not be coherent. Trainer (1982, 1983) made use of this method within the general approach to moral reasoning advocated in Part 2, but, as these studies add only marginally to the information we have gained from interview methods, they will not be described in detail.

The request for definitions method was used by Williams (1969). It appears that it is not a very successful technique, because most children and adults are poor at giving explicit statements about the meanings of words, even when they can manifest considerable knowledge and discrimination in using the words.

FACTOR ANALYTIC STUDIES OF SOCIOMORAL ATTITUDES AND VALUES

Studies of this kind typically present subjects with questionnaires relating to moral attitudes and values. The attitudes and values studied are usually moral rules or ends that are controversial. Thus they fall within the widest definition of moral reasoning considered in the introduction, but usually not within the narrower definitions of Piaget and Kohlberg.

In a typical study, the subject is asked for their degree of support for or dissent from a rule or aim. Such studies are particularly valuable in providing information about the ways in which individuals differ from one another in their moral attitudes and values. Some studies in which individuals were questioned as to why they held their attitudes or values were dealt with in Chapter 8. This review covers those much more numerous studies asking only what values individuals hold and not why.

The study of social attitudes in general has no direct bearing on moral reasoning, as many studies in this field ask questions about the person's attitudes to, or feelings towards, various kinds of social object that have no moral dimension. However, there are strong traditions of research in the study of social attitudes that do ask for judgements about moral issues, and are thus relevant to the study of moral reasoning.

The first tradition of this kind that is relevant stretches from Likert (1932) and Ferguson (1939), through Eysenck (1944, 1954, 1975) and Adorno et al. (1950), to recent contributions such as Ray (1982) and Fleishman (1988). We can call this method the moral maxims method, as subjects are offered sentences stating moral maxims and asked to express support or rejection. From the 1930s to about 1975 this was the predominant method of studying general social attitudes. Thus Eysenck's (1954) Inventory of Social Attitudes contains such items as "Our treatment of criminals is too harsh; we should try to cure not punish them" and "It is wrong that men should be permitted greater sexual freedom than women." Respondents were asked to say if they agreed, were neutral to, or disagreed with such statements. After the mid-1970s, however, particularly under the influence of Wilson and Patterson (1968), Rokeach (1973), Wilson, (1973), Sidanius (1976), and

Kerlinger (1984), it became popular to argue that asking for judgements about such statements was inadequate to assess "gut reaction" values, which are values that are held on an unreflective level.

The methods pioneered by these authors involved asking for an immediate, unreflective, and essentially emotional reaction to key words, phrases, and short slogans like "Socialism", "Religion", "More power for the rich", or "God is a fake." The words and phrases method does not assess moral attitudes as directly as the maxims method, as subjects are typically asked to say whether they feel positive or negative towards the key words and phrases, not whether they think the things denoted by them are right or wrong. However, in general it has been found that the overall structure of attitudes assessed by the key words and phrases method is rather similar to that found with the maxims method (Nilsson & Ekehammar, 1990, 1991; Sidanius, Ekehammar, & Brewer, 1986). This is no doubt because the moral implications of many of the words and phrases used are so obvious that the emotional reactions reported are largely those aroused by these implications. One could say that, for this reason, such questions use "moral language". In effect this seems to be the case, but in order to stay on firmer and more conventional ground, most emphasis in this discussion will be on the more obviously moral language of the maxims method.

Factor analysis is a means of summarising correlational data by the use of latent variables. If we ask people a number of questions requiring an attitudinal judgement, then some pairs of questions will tend to be answered in the same way by many people. Such items are said to be positively correlated. Replies to other pairs of items will bear no relation to one another, and these pairs are said to have zero correlation. Other pairs will tend to be answered in the opposite way, with people agreeing to one item generally disagreeing with the other. These are said to show negative correlation. Factor analysis is designed to provide an economical description of such data by eliminating the redundancy involved when we have correlations between groups of questions of the kinds just described. It does this by constructing latent variables (factors) that are fewer in number than the original items.

A simple example of this would occur if we had four questions and everyone who agreed with question 1 also agreed with question 2, but disagreed with questions 3 and 4. Also, everyone who disagreed with question 1 also disagreed with question 2, but agreed with questions 3 and 4. Questions 1 and 2 might express racial prejudice and questions 3 and 4 opposition to such prejudice. To summarise each respondent's replies we can replace their replies to the four questions with one score: whether or not they are racially prejudiced. If they are prejudiced, they will agree with the first two questions and disagree with the second two;

if they are not prejudiced, they will disagree with the first two and agree with the second two. We can summarise the replies of our respondents to all four questions using only one latent or constructed variable: degree of prejudice. Factor analysis operates just like the racism score just mentioned, with three differences: prediction of particular replies from the latent variables, usually called factors, is less than 100% reliable; the factors are usually graded to tell us how racist (or whatever) the person was; and several factors are used to summarise the data.

In factor analytic studies, of any kind of human attitude or ability, there is a strong tendency for the method to feed back to the investigator aspects of the design of the investigation (Harman, 1976). This is because the method tries to produce factors that account for replies to as many of the questions asked in a study as possible. Thus issues that are not included in the questionnaire cannot produce factors, and those canvassed in only one or two questions can produce only weak factors. In the history of studies using the maxims method this obvious difficulty has exerted considerable influence on the development of the field. Thus Eysenck (1975) argued that his earlier studies of social attitudes had tended to find only two major factors (social conservatism and tough-mindedness), because they had neglected to include enough items concerning economic issues. When Eysenck (1975) included more items on economic issues he found that a third factor appeared, namely attitude to capitalism (economic conservatism). Thus Eysenck (1975, 1978) recommended a three-factor model. This is the model that will be advocated here, although one of the factors (tough-mindedness) will be renamed "religiosity", so as to reflect in a more direct manner the actual content of the items.

Economic conservatism can be directly assessed by questions asking whether we ought to have a socialist or a capitalist society, and about the role that the state and private enterprise ought to play in the economy. Religiosity is assessed by questions that tap the moral attitude people hold to religion. Social conservatism is indexed chiefly by reactions to three issues: how nationalistic one should be; how severe punishments for crime should be; and how racist and ethnocentric one is. The key thing that binds these three issues together is authoritarian identification with the nation state. If one identifies strongly with such a state and hopes to receive benefits and avoid hardships by manifesting strong commitment to it, then one will advocate pursuing its interests over those of foreigners, and harsh punishments for those who endanger its good order by committing crimes against its laws.

The main support for the three-factor view comes from those studies that used sets of items consisting primarily of moral maxims, whose content was as broad and balanced as possible, and involved reasonably large and balanced samples. Such studies have found between three and six general factors in samples from the United Kingdom and the United States (Bales & Couch, 1970; Eysenck, 1975; Withey, 1965). This result has also been produced in Indian studies by Deb (1981, 1984). The three factors that are common to all these studies are the three mentioned earlier. This is what one would expect if these are the three that are most important in social life generally. Other, less general, factors assumed importance in particular studies when the investigator included a greater number of items dealing with them in the study.

Other significant studies of moral maxims that found only two factors can be included in this picture by looking at the spread of items. Thus Ferguson (1939), Eysenck (1954), O'Neil and Levinson (1954), Smithers and Lobley (1978), and Boivin, Donkin, and Darling (1990) did not find the economic conservatism factor, as they had few items on this topic; Rokeach and Fruchter (1956), Ray (1982), and Fleishman (1988) did not find the religiosity factor, as they had no items dealing with religion. A similar conclusion about the three main factors underlying sociomoral attitudes can be reached from studies attempting a broad survey of such attitudes using the key words and phrases method (Kerlinger, 1984; Nilsson & Ekehammar, 1990, 1991; Nilsson, Ekehammar, & Sidanius, 1985; Sidanius, 1976; Sidanius & Ekehammar, 1983; Sidanius et al., 1986).

Although the general nature of social conservatism is fairly clear from the studies already discussed, it will help to broaden the basis of our understanding to consider also the very extensive literature on the related concept of authoritarianism, originally popularised by Adorno et al. (1950). There were two significant complaints from critics about the work of Adorno et al. First, the subscales of the F-scale, used to measure authoritarianism, often correlated with one another weakly if at all, indicating that the scale was not measuring a single dimension. Second, the F-scale only measured right-wing authoritarianism, but Stalinists and Trotskyists, in particular, manifested a form of left-wing worship of authority that would have to be included in any general scheme of social attitudes involving authoritarianism.

Ray (1976, 1981, 1988, 1989) and Ray and Lovejoy (1990), expanding on the first point, questioned whether there was such a thing as a general tendency to admire authority at all, as distinct from a tendency to think that particular groups or institutions are best run on authoritarian lines. They showed that indicators of authoritarianism in different contexts often failed to correlate, substantiating this view. Adorno et al. (1950) postulated a tendency for some people to be authoritarian in all situations. Ray's findings, as well as those of others summarised in his papers, show that this is false.

However, in concluding that there is no general factor of authoritarianism that applies to all situations, we should not take this to mean that there are not one, or more, general factors indexing the tendency to have authoritarian beliefs about a particular range of situations and institutions. Such a general factor, which has received substantial attention in the past two decades, is authoritarian nationalism, which has turned out to be very similar to the social conservatism factor discussed earlier. It involves belief in authoritarian control of the state, as exemplified by support for a strong state and political leaders who are prepared to exercise their power to make independent and sometimes unpopular decisions.

Instruments to assess this attitude have been devised and used in a range of particularly interesting studies by Altmeyer and his associates (Altmeyer, 1981, 1988; Duckitt, 1989; Tarr & Lorr, 1991). One of the most fascinating of these was carried out in the Soviet Union shortly before its dissolution. It successfully identified the substantial overlap between the authoritarian nationalist attitudes of the anti-reform wing of the Soviet Communist Party and the "right wing" or "fascist" nationalists, with whom they later allied themselves (Tarr & Lorr, 1991). This finding also illustrates how the three-factor model of sociomoral attitudes deals with the problem of left-wing authoritarianism, mentioned earlier. Left-wing authoritarians will tend to score high on social conservatism/authoritarian nationalism and on economic radicalism; right-wing authoritarians will tend to score high on social conservatism/ authoritarian nationalism and on economic conservatism.

Before leaving the topic of authoritarianism, another aspect deserves mention. Studies by Langford (1991a) showed that for several of the most central of our social institutions, namely the family, schools, and the workplace, there is a general factor of authoritarian belief, at least in Australia, that is connected to economic conservatism. It is hard to see why Australia should be very different from other Western countries in this respect. This raises an apparent difficulty, however, as a large number of studies have shown, particularly those summarised in Eysenck (1954, 1975), that in British samples belief in strict child rearing (representing a kind of authoritarianism towards the family and schools) has been quite strongly associated with social conservatism, which is claimed to be independent of economic conservatism. It may be that the solution to this apparent paradox is that Eysenck's studies concentrated more on the severity of punitive sanctions, whereas my own concentrated on the issue of who should have control of decisions. Authoritarian attitudes of these kinds within social institutions outside the state deserve more attention in the future.

An alternative approach to individual differences in moral values to that adopted here, which has been very influential in the literature in the past two decades, is that proposed by Rokeach (1973, 1979; see also Feather, 1975; 1988). Rokeach used the key words and phrases method of analysing moral attitudes and divided such attitudes into: those that relate to the ends that are preferred; and those that relate to the means advocated to achieve the preferred ends. He claimed, on the basis of conceptual analysis of end-related attitudes, that these could be arranged along two main dimensions, one indexing attitudes to freedom and the other attitudes to equality. Means-related attitudes were claimed to be organised into distinct and independent dimensions.

However, there are four serious difficulties with Rokeach's work. The first stems from his having adopted something akin to a strongly interpretive method of analysis, which analyses dimensions in values from a purely theoretical and conceptual point of view, without regard to whether such dimensions actually reflect the kind of coherence found in the replies made by respondents. This contrasts with the largely descriptive method of factor analysis.

Second, he asked respondents to rank the words and phrases used in the assessment task from most preferred to least preferred. This is generally agreed to involve substantial methodological and statistical problems. Later studies that have asked subjects to rate each of Rokeach's items independently have not supported his original claims, as factor analysis of responses to the end-related items has not yielded the two predicted dimensions (Sidanius, 1990). Inspection of the content of Rokeach's items, and the study of Sidanius (1990), suggest that Rokeach's scale for end-related values is mainly an index of the single dimension of economic conservatism–radicalism. The other two dimensions of general social attitudes identified earlier did not emerge, as the pool of items failed to adequately sample attitudes related to religion or social conservatism. When Braithwaite and Law (1985) set out to remedy this defect of Rokeach's method, they came full circle back to the view of Eysenck (1975): the three major factors in their revised scale of moral "ends" were social and economic conservatism and religiosity.

A third difficulty is that Rokeach assumes that dimensions of end-related values are independent of those that summarise means-related values. This seems contrary to common experience, which suggests that the two are inextricably interlinked, and is again unsupported by empirical analysis. This objection is strengthened by the finding of Braithwaite and Law (1985) that the end-related values in their revised scale could be best summarised by the dimensions of social and economic conservatism and religiosity. These dimensions, like the items by which they were indexed, do not signify just the ends desired, but rather an inseparable mixture of means and ends. Advocates of social conservatism, for instance, advocate both the ends of national power and pride, and the means of authoritarian state institutions. In addition, two of the four most significant means-related factors were economic conservatism/efficiency and religiosity, again testifying to the fact that the kinds of key words and phrases we use to talk about sociomoral attitudes tend to involve reference to both means and ends.

The fourth difficulty with the Rokeach approach is that it is artificial to ask people how much they value means without telling them the particular ends that are being sought, as something that may be very effective in achieving one end might be very ineffective in achieving another.

Developmental studies by Becona and Gomez-Duran (1986), Katz (1986, 1989), Nilssen and Ekehammar (1991), and Langford (1991a) found that the economic and social conservatism factors emerge at least as early as the start of adolescence, with factor structures becoming more pronounced as adolescence proceeds. This is consistent with the finding that for adults social attitudes are more consistent, and factor structures stronger, among experts than among non-experts, presumably because the greater expertise of the former encourages them to hold logically consistent attitudes across a range of issues (Sniderman, Brody, & Tetlock, 1991; Sniderman & Tetlock, 1986; Tetlock, 1990). Knowledge of and expertise in economic, social, and political issues increases considerably in the course of adolescence.

Social conservatism can also be detected in younger children; in children of less than 11 years of age it tends to be greater than in those above this age (Katz, 1986, 1989; Nias, 1972; Srivastava & Ramani, 1988; Wilderom & Cryns, 1986). This is probably due to the tendency for young children to pay attention to parental authority and to see this as a major source of what is right. They appear to project this admiration for authority onto the nation, advocating strong punishments for adult criminals and strong national defence. In general, the ability of children of less than 11 years of age to understand economic issues is too limited for them to hold meaningful opinions on them (Berti & Bombi, 1988; Connell, 1971; Langford, 1987b, Chap. 3).

Turning to development during the adult years, there is some tendency for adults to shift towards greater economic conservatism in middle age. This seems to be more a function of the shifts in self-interest and changes in group membership that occur with age than of age as such (Sigel, 1989). One indication of this is that the elderly show an average shift back to the economic left, probably because they depend on the social welfare programmes that are more generously funded by the political left in Western countries (Light, 1985; Sigel, 1989).

A classic set of findings shows that, in the period from the 1950s to the 1970s in the United States, the experience of going to college tended to make college students less economically conservative, but this change was later partially reversed after they went into the workforce (Feldman & Newcomb, 1971; Jennings & Marcus, 1986; Lane, 1968; Steckenrider & Cutler, 1989). However, this effect is almost certainly specific to this historical period. With the emergence of a consensus in favour of economic conservatism on American campuses in the 1980s, the college experience seems rather to have resulted in increased economic conservatism among American college students as they progressed through college (Steckenrider & Cutler, 1989).

Social conservatism, on the other hand, seems to show little tendency to shift with age once adulthood is achieved (Danigelis & Cutler, 1991). The main reasons for the widespread belief that such conservatism is greater in the middle aged than in young adults seem to be: it is confused with economic conservatism, and thus with the tendency for the middle aged to vote for economically conservative political parties; and it is confused with old-fashioned tastes and manners.

STUDIES OF OUTCOME COMPARISON

There are many situations in social life in which individuals or groups are allocated pleasant things (rewards) in return for unpleasant things (social costs). A typical question used to study outcome comparison concerns wages. The subject is asked if they think that it is fair for X to be paid A and Y to be paid B, where A and B differ. The social costs X and Y have borne to produce these outcomes, in terms of the training and effort required for their work, may also differ.

One substantial problem with the outcome comparison literature is that it tends to assume that all kinds of comparison are judged using the same principles (Levine & Moreland, 1987; 1989). However, different kinds of comparison may be judged in different ways. For instance, the interests of foreigners may be considered in a different way from those of fellow nationals, and international conflicts may be judged using different criteria from local conflicts of interest. Thus, we should specify what kinds of outcomes are involved in posing questions to subjects and in considering findings. The majority of studies in this area have asked about relative rates of pay among fellow nationals, and thus findings should be interpreted as applying to this topic, rather than to the allocation of rewards in general (see also Prentice & Crosby, 1987).

Martin and Murray (1983) list three conclusions that are broadly established by studies of relative rates of pay, which have also been sustained by more recent studies (Levine & Moreland, 1986, 1989; Vogelaar & Vermunt, 1991). These conclusions are as follows. When given a choice, most people will choose to compare their rate of pay with someone who is similar to themselves, usually someone in the same occupation or social class, rather than with someone who is dissimilar. When asked if they are satisfied with the relation between two rates of pay, as distinct from whether or not they think it fair or just, most adult interviewees will say that they are satisfied for someone to receive increased pay for increased work or effort. More particularly, they seem to operate using the quantitative principle that individual X's pay, divided by their social costs to earn that pay, should equal individual Y's pay, divided by their social costs. The third conclusion reached was that the second conclusion is also roughly true, when the question asked concerns the fairness or justice of the pay rates.

An additional finding from studies by Messick and Sentis (1979, 1983) has been that if adult subjects are asked to set fair relative rates of pay for two people, they set their own pay somewhat higher than that for someone else in exactly the same situation. This is a particularly neat demonstration of the tendency for high moral principle to succumb to base self-interest. The extent of this tendency should not, however, be exaggerated: it is appreciable, but not overwhelming.

Hook and Cook (1979), Keil and McClintock (1983), and Laak and Aleva (1991) have reviewed a large number of developmental studies of wage allocation and concluded that, although the notion of fairness in the distribution of wages is present from as early as 4 years of age, the expression of this early idea of fairness is limited by the child's restricted arithmetical abilities. By 6 or 7 years, children have usually mastered the concept of numerical equality and thus attempt to allocate wages equally between participants, although often doling out an extra portion to those who do more work. It is not until about 13 years of age, in most British and American samples, that the idea of making two ratios equal can be dealt with. Accordingly, it is not until around this age that the adult notion of wage equity, as an equal ratio of costs and rewards, takes root.

A second set of studies has been carried out under the inspiration of the "relative deprivation" thesis of Stouffer et al. (1949). These initially focused on the satisfaction of individuals with their work or with their lives in general. Stouffer et al. (1949) found that American military policemen were more satisfied with their lot than men in the Air Corps, despite the fact that pay was no better and promotion slower. To explain this, they argued that the policemen compared themselves to groups they came into contact with that were worse off, whereas Air Corps members compared themselves to groups who were better off.

Although the original study asked about satisfaction, subsequent studies of groups like American blacks, the working class, and women showed that not only did such groups often appear unaccountably satisfied with their lot, but they also seemed to regard their position as just (Crosby, 1982; Folger, 1987; Martin & Murray, 1983; Szirmai, 1991). This was despite the fact that, in many cases, their pay was inequitable. Again, it seems that the tendency to compare oneself with similar people, whom one knows, rather than with those who are much better off, whom one doesn't know, plays some role in this.

The widespread commitment to pay equity in Western countries justifies treating it as a norm. The complexity of the rule involved here means that understanding develops much later than for norms like those relating to lying and stealing, confirming the argument, given in Chapter 4, that Piaget was wrong not to take the complexity of rules into account, in dealing with the development of understanding moral rules. It seems likely that commitment to this norm is so widespread because it provides a particularly useful way of ensuring that everyone's interests are considered, in a society where most people work for pay.

THE NATURALISTIC STUDY OF MORAL DISCOURSE

The naturalistic study of moral discourse is the study of moral conversations, debates, and arguments as they occur naturally in everyday life, as opposed to that of contrived interviews or laboratory situations. One reason for being interested in this area is that most interviews and laboratory situations are such that the subject remains calm and rational. This will enable them to present themselves to the investigator in a favourable and thus conventionally moral light. Although Haan (1977, 1986, 1991) has shown that laboratory discussions can be made more emotionally engaging, by the use of unsupervised discussions among groups of existing friends, such discussions are still quite remote from some of the heated and vitriolic debate on moral issues that goes on in society at large.

As with the Kohlbergian interview, so in this area the method of analysis used to interpret such exchanges is all-important. An investigator's findings have often been conditioned by strongly interpretive methods of scoring transcripts of naturalistic moral discourse. Thus Piaget (1932) viewed them through the lens of Piagetian methods; Adams (1988) through that of Kohlbergian methods. A wide range of studies eschew systematic analysis altogether and opt for the impressionistic methods of the participant observer and the hermeneutic school of naturalistic inquiry (for reviews see Musgrave, 1989; Selman & Schultz, 1989). This discussion will concentrate on three research programmes that have adopted a more systematic approach to the presentation of their findings, which are those of Sutton-Smith (1982, 1986, 1990), Hoffman (1963a, b, c, 1970, 1977, 1980, 1983, 1984, 1987, 1989, 1990, 1991a, b) and Dunn (Dunn, 1988; Dunn & Munn, 1985, 1986, 1987).

Sutton-Smith's main conclusion is aimed at regaining the obvious about children's peer groups and play from the sometimes misleading constructions of the experts. This is that the aim of peer groups and play, from the child's point of view, is not socialisation or moral debate, but fun. This is significant as is shows that the moral debate that goes on in the peer group is likely to be directed to obtaining group consensus as to how best to have fun. It will be debate about how everyone's interests can be taken into account, and will thus form ideal practice for dealing with situations involving conflicts of interest later in life. It is well known that children do not just learn purely intellectual strategies of moral debate in the peer group. They also learn not to fly into a temper if the group decision about what ought to be done on a particular morning goes against them. Like the family, the peer group is a proving ground for the emotional restraint and control, as well as the mental outlook, required by the attempt to take account of everyone's interests.

Hoffman has reported a number of naturalistic studies of his own, as well as summarising a large literature by other authors, on how child-rearing techniques induct children into the moral practices of Western, particularly American, society. He divides disciplinary episodes into those involving power assertion (telling the child what to do and backing this up with the threat of sanctions), love-withdrawal (telling the child that they will not be loved, turning one's back on them, isolating or ignoring them) and induction (explaining the reasons for disciplinary actions). One type of induction is singled out for particular attention, called other-oriented induction; this involves pointing out the effects that a child's behaviour has on others.

This is divided into three types as follows. The first directly points out the consequences of actions, as in "If you throw snow on their walk they will have to clean it all over again", "Pulling the leash like that can hurt the dog's neck", and "That hurt my feelings." The second points out the relevant needs or desires of others, as in "He's afraid of the dark, so please turn the lights back on", or "She doesn't like marzipan, so don't give it to her." The third involves explaining the motives for the behaviour of another person towards the child, as in "Don't yell at him, he's only trying to help" or "She wanted to get her handkerchief." In the young child, other-oriented induction, observed in naturalistic studies conducted in the home, tends to focus on the effects of the child's behaviour on other children, particularly brothers and sisters and playmates. In older children it tends to focus on the effects of the child's behaviour on the parent, as much of the child's interaction with peers now takes place outside the home.

As we might expect from common experience, the extent to which parents use these techniques varies considerably, with some relying mainly on only one of the three. However, most children receive at least some explanations for disciplinary actions and some of these will usually be of the other-oriented variety. Very young children tend to receive fewer explanations than older children, while the level of abstraction and complexity in explanations tends to track the capacities of the child quite well.

This confirms that children are informally inducted into moral discussion that focuses on the interests of the participants in a situation. It does not entirely prepare us for the extent to which, by the age of 5 years, most children are already using interest-based justifications to the same extent that they will in their late teens, though of a more local and concrete variety (Learner, 1988; Seif, 1993). Parental discourse to the child does not seem to be nearly as loaded towards this kind of reasoning at this age as is that of the child.

The missing factor here is probably the influence of the peer group, and of other experiences with adults and older children outside the home. By the age of 5, activities outside the home have come to predominate, if only because most children are at school. (Although this is not true in some states in the USA, the studies of 5-year-olds, showing that taking account of the interests of others is already well established at 5, involved children who were already at school.) The peer group will be particularly liable to eschew the appeals to adult power and authority that play such a considerable role in the parents' conversations with the young child. Instead, it is likely to focus on making sure that everyone's interests are catered for.

Unfortunately, Hoffman's work has not focused in detail on the kinds of induction that lie outside his category of other-orientation. We can probably interpolate what these will be like using the following reasoning. The parent who is using an induction technique will usually either be responding to a demand from the child for a reason (especially in the form of the ubiquitous "Why?" of children thinking about resisting a request), or be acting on their own initiative. In both these cases, the parent is in very much the situation of the interviewee in a moral reasoning interview, providing they remain calm, except that they are faced with the problem of translating their explanations into a form appropriate to the child's cognitive level. Thus they are likely to give mainly interest-based, rule-based, and belief-based replies at a level judged appropriate to the child's capacities.

Interest-based replies correspond to the other-orientation category, so most induction replies outside this category are likely to involve rule-based and belief-based replies, with smaller amounts of other categories of reply such as inevitable behaviour and religious. The level of abstraction in explanations is likely to be severely reduced for the young child. Thus the interests considered will be chiefly those of individuals in their immediate vicinity (this is borne out by Hoffman's studies of the content of other-oriented justifications); the rules will tend to be simple ones like those against lying and stealing; and the beliefs will often emphasise those of a parent or other authority figure, although they are also likely to mention those of equals.

As the child gets older, the interests considered in explanations will broaden, rules will become more complex, and beliefs will widen to include those of other adults, children outside the family, and of people in general. Adults will also give quite a few justifications for instructions or rules that are based on punishments ("If you do that, you will get a smack"). In Hoffman's scheme, these will be considered as power assertions, rather than as explanations, but from a logical point of view they are explanations of a sort; they undoubtedly influence the replies children give when themselves asked to justify moral decisions, as they are a fairly common kind of reply among young children in interviews (Langford & Claydon, 1989; Learner, 1988).

This kind of extrapolation from interview findings is obviously limited, as real-life moral debate with children is often more heated than this implies. For this reason, naturalistic studies using weakly interpretive techniques of analysis that capture this facet of moral discourse in children and adolescents are desirable.

Finally, the findings of Dunn and Munn (1987) are of interest, as they throw particular light on the justifications that very young children offer in disputes involving conflicts of interest with others. Very young children often do not offer any justification in their disputes with others. Thus justifications offered to mothers and siblings rose from being given in only about 3% of disputes at 18 months, to about 30% at 36 months; they occurred in about the same proportions for disputes with both mothers and siblings. In this age range, there is substantial egocentrism in the interests to which the child appeals in offering a justification, although appeal to ethical norms and other social rules instilled by the parents is already significant at 36 months. At this age about 50% of justifications offered referred to the child's own feelings or interests, with the remainder roughly equally split between appeals to social and ethical rules and those to the material effects of an action (e.g. asking another child not to do something as they might break a toy).

This last category (material effects of an action) is somewhat ambiguous, as in many cases it is neither clear whose interests might be involved, nor even whether the child is aware that human interests are involved at all. They may have heard a certain material consequence forbidden and take the avoidance of this consequence as an end in itself, rather than as a means of avoiding damaging another person's interests. Thus breaking crockery could be avoided for either of these reasons. However, the early appeals to rules by children, as well as the ability to sometimes take account of the interests of others, show that the child is already developing some of the key justification categories it will rely on in later years. Dunn and Munn (1985, 1986) showed that caregivers often appeal to moral rules even when dealing with infants, thus providing early experience of this kind of justification.

CONCLUSIONS

This chapter has concentrated on the presentation of descriptive findings from three techniques that are of value in the study of the development of moral reasoning. Theoretical interpretation of these findings has been kept to a minimum. Such interpretation is particularly called for in relation to the development of sociomoral attitudes, as these form a relatively distinct topic of study and have been the object of a very vigorous and extensive literature. As was the case with interview findings, there is no shortage of explanatory concepts that can be used to explain the existence of such attitudes and developmental trends in their strength, and there is a large literature devoted to such interpretation (for references providing surveys, see below). To give adequate consideration to this would require far more space than is available here.

Thus, I must be content with pointing, first of all, to the value of separating the business of description from that of interpretation in dealing with sociomoral attitudes. The argument that this is fundamentally impossible, as description is too intimately bound up with interpretation, although it may apply in some areas of scholarly endeavour, does not seem to apply to the topics discussed in this chapter, any more than it did to those of the previous two. Investigators from quite different theoretical traditions, such as Eysenck (a neoHullian behaviourist at the time of his contributions to this field) and Sidanius (an advocate of ego psychology) have been able to agree substantively on descriptive issues, provided they have both been attempting non-interpretive description. On the other hand, Rokeach and Sidanius, both from the same theoretical tradition of ego psychology, reached substantially different conclusions, because one was attempting non-interpretive and the other interpretive description.

Second, one particular feature of debate about why children develop sociomoral attitudes is so illuminating, in relation to general problems of interpretation, that it is worth brief mention. This relates to the role of aggression in such attitudes. There is widespread agreement that the attitude of social conservatism, in particular, is often a channel for aggressive impulses on the part of the individual child and adult. The belligerence that is often displayed by those holding this attitude towards foreigners, and anyone else conceived as an opponent of their national state, is ideally suited to this, and the literature shows there is in general a positive correlation between such attitudes and aggressiveness (for reviews see Eaves, Eysenck, & Martin, 1989; Eysenck, 1954, 1975; Eysenck & Wilson, 1978; Sidanius & Lau, 1989; Teevan, Heinzen, & Hartsough, 1988).

There are, however, substantial differences in the interpretations that theorists offer for the origins of this aggression. Thus, Eysenck has progressively moved towards the position that there is a strong hereditary component involved: some children are born to be more aggressive, just as some species of dog have been bred to be more aggressive (Eaves et al., 1989; Eysenck & Eysenck, 1985). Those influenced by ego psychology, like Rokeach and Sidanius, on the other hand, are more inclined to stress the role of displaced aggression deriving from punitive child rearing, social frustration, and external threat.

There are two interesting things about this debate. The first is that it has occurred at all. In recent theorising about findings from interviews, theoretical debates of this kind have been curtailed by the predominance of strongly interpretive methods of scoring that prevent a clear awareness of what it is that competing theories are trying to explain. The second is the relative sophistication of the debate and the way it has been carried on; both sides have looked for evidence beyond the initial descriptive data to settle the matter.

Eysenck has particularly looked to studies directly investigating the heritability of social conservatism and aggressiveness. Eaves et al. (1989) have summarised findings from investigations of this kind, which include those comparing correlations between the aggressiveness and attitudes of non-identical (dizygotic) twins and identical (monozygotic) twins reared in the same family. Dizygotic twins have no greater genetic similarity than brother and sister, whereas monozygotic twins have identical heredity.

For both social conservatism and aggressiveness, correlations between the scores of such monozygotic twins have been found to be consistently greater than those for dizygotic twins. It could be that this is partly due to a tendency for monozygotic twins to identify more closely with one another as a result of their physical resemblance. However, the fact that other kinds of genetic relationship can be shown to be associated with these characteristics suggests that such correlations are partly due to a substantial component of heritability. At the same time, it should be understood that the environment must play a considerable role in their production, as identical twins reared in the same family rarely achieve more than a moderate correlation in either respect.

The inference that it is aggressiveness that is inherited and that the heritability of social conservatism is derived from this is, however, far from certain. For one thing, this inference is based on deducing causation from correlation, which is always hazardous. There might be something else that is also inherited and causes social conservatism; although the link with aggression is plausible and we do not presently have many other plausible candidates for this linking role.

Those favouring the displaced aggression view, on the other hand, have pointed to the correlations that exist between both aggressiveness and social conservatism and the following three variables: low socioeconomic status (and thus presumably a greater experience of frustration); punitiveness in the parents; and external social threat (for reviews see Doty, Peterson, & Winter, 1991; Eaves et al., 1989; Sidanius & Lau, 1989; Teevan et al., 1988). Once again, this argument depends on deducing causation from correlation, but once again it is plausible.

This debate has taken us away from the position where 20 years ago most investigators would have given some credence to the displaced aggression produced by environmental causes argument, but little to the inherited aggression one. Empirical evidence has now obliged us to consider the inherited aggression argument much more seriously. Eaves et al. (1989) also review similar evidence suggesting that religiosity too has a substantial inherited component. The underlying psychological trait responsible here is less clear, though the susceptibility to trance-like states is an obvious candidate.

This kind of controversy and advance provides a model for the theoretical debate that is needed in the study of the development of moral reasoning more generally. Advances have been slow and the complexity of multifactorial explanations is tedious, but we gain a sense that cumulative advance using methods of this kind is possible. This contrasts with the blind alley into which strongly interpretive methods of description lead us.

More extended discussions of issues of theoretical interpretation in this area appear in the following sources: Eaves et al. (1989); Eysenck and Wilson (1978); Nilsson, et al. (1985); Rokeach, (1973, 1979); Sidanius (1985, 1988); Sidanius and Lau (1989); Woodrum (1988).

PART FOUR

Conclusions

CHAPTER TEN

Conclusions and future research

The dominant interview methods that have been used to study the development of moral reasoning, those of Piaget and Kohlberg, involve such strong interpretation that findings from the methods contain two significant defects. The first is that the connection between the findings and the theory used to explain them is obscured, to the point where it is hard to tell whether the two are in accord. The second is that it is impossible to tell what alternative explanations there might be for findings.

This led us to consider the use of weakly interpretive methods of analysing findings from interviews. Such methods enabled us to gain considerable further insight into the two issues left open by the use of strong methods of interpretation. Most attention was given to comparison of findings with Kohlberg's theory, as that of Piaget is widely acknowledged to be less satisfactory. It transpired that in significant respects the findings from weakly interpretive methods falsify Kohlberg's theory. One serious problem here is that replies emphasising local social harmony justifications fail to follow the predicted developmental course. Trends in other replies also disconfirm predictions from the theory.

In addition, weakly interpretive methods enabled us to draw up a descriptive picture of developmental trends found in both Kohlbergian and nonKohlbergian interviews. Such trends can be explained in a variety of ways, including notions drawn from Freudian theory, ego psychology, and other general theories of personality development. Assessment of the relative validity of the available explanations will require the combined use of a variety of tactics, including naturalistic and experimental methods.

Kohlberg's work suffers from another serious limitation. This is that it is based on a style of interview that provides a somewhat misleading view of the development of reasoning about norms under challenge in general, although Kohlberg uses it to develop such a view. His interviews only offer an explicit invitation to various concrete varieties of moral reasoning, as they focus on the actions of individual characters in dilemma stories. To break out of the set this creates, to discuss more abstract and implicit aspects of the questions, certainly requires intellectual maturity, and the ability to do so is an indicator of a certain kind of maturity in moral reasoning. It is also likely to be of considerable use in everyday life. It is wrong, however, to conclude from findings with this kind of interview that those who do not produce abstract or general reasoning are incapable of doing so, as they can often do so in an interview that presents less of an obstacle.

Future work should use a greater variety of interview techniques to minimise the dangers that arise from concentration on one particular kind. Of interest here would be an extension of interviews of the kind used by Lerner (1937a; b) to assess the progress of sociocentrism in the child. It is very plausible to view the child as developing from sociocentrism to autonomy in its moral outlook, but the extent and manner in which this occurs has remained largely unknown, due to the neglect of this issue in interview studies.

The content of this book has been limited in two significant ways. First of all, it has concentrated on children growing up in contemporary industrialised societies, especially the United Kingdom, the United States, Australia, and Sweden, as most available work has been done in these countries. There has, however, been a lively tradition of work on the moral outlooks of non-Western societies, involving both the choice of passages methods of Kluckhohn and Strodtbeck (1964) and Ibrahim and Kahn (1987) (for reviews see Carter, 1990, 1991; Carter & Helms, 1990) and the more usual participant observation and ethnographic methods of anthropologists and cross-cultural psychologists (see especially Shweder, 1986, 1989, 1990; Shweder & Miller, 1985). Findings from the former method can be interpreted to show that some of the same dimensions that produce variation within societies, such as religiosity and economic conservatism, also produce differences between them. Findings from the latter method have caused Shweder (1990) to suggest that the very definition of moral reasoning adopted by authors like Kohlberg and Turiel may be a serious bar to the progress of cross-cultural research in this area. This is because their emphasis on welfare, rights, and justice applies to a particular modern, Western, liberal notion of morality.

According to Shweder (1990), there are three fundamental forms of moral reasoning found in different societies: Code 1 is founded on welfare, rights, and justice; Code 2 on duty, hierarchy, and interdependency; Code 3 on protecting the spiritual self from acts that are degrading or disproportionate to our spiritual nature. These codes are very similar to what have here been termed second order moral norms: they are sets of reflective values by means of which more particular rules and decisions are justified. Thus, Code 1 corresponds to interest-based norms, Code 3 to religious norms.

Code 2 principles can also be used to justify first order norms, as when it is said that authorities have decreed them or that antiquity or the simple fact that "that's the way things must inevitably be done" is used to justify them. The principles corresponding to this code have been discussed here as belonging to a lower level of reflectiveness than the other two codes (being involved in the belief and inevitable behaviour categories). This can be justified, as these codes have less status in the West and the coding methods advocated here were designed for Western populations. However, in many non-Western societies, appeals to Code 2 principles are regarded as more important. In addition, we find that the notion of duty assumes greater prominence.

Both findings from the Kluckhohn and Strodtbeck kind of method and those from ethnographic methods tend to encourage stereotyping of moral outlooks, whereas it may well be that many cross-cultural differences are ones involving balance rather than rigid dichotomies. In illustration of this, Liu (1992) undertook a study on tertiary students in Australia brought up in the People's Republic of China, using an adaptation of the scoring method of Langford and D'Cruz. She found that the broad categories of reasons given for why people ought to do things were similar to those found in the West, although the Chinese studied gave more emphasis to duty as a reason than Westerners. But, like us, they gave most emphasis to human interests and rules.

An interesting example of the influence of Code 2 type thinking in Liu's study was that the Chinese sometimes use justifications based on analysis of the meanings and etymology of word roots in their language, that are virtually never given by Westerners. Such justifications are an implicit appeal to a tradition of word use.

It is reasonable to agree with Shweder (1990) that the three codes are three kinds of inbuilt natural moral outlook. Explanations as to why this is so will inevitably vary. Shweder's (1989) account leans heavily on the human need for explanation; human beings will always look behind phenomena for entities by which to explain them. It is implied that in moral phenomena only certain kinds of entities are conceivable: those belonging to the codes.

Alternative Freudian, Jungian, and Rankian explanations for religiosity have already been mentioned in this book, as have reasons for paying attention to others' interests. Freudian and other alternative explanations also exist for the tendency to admire authority and tradition.

Given Shweder's (1978, 1979, 1980) interest in the ideas of E.B. Tylor, it is reasonable to suppose that, for him, part of the reason that particular societies tend more towards one of the codes than another is that they have been found to be successful in the social and physical environment of the society. Another style of explanation is that offered by theorists of culture cycles, such as Nietzsche (1899), Spengler (1926), Russell (1946), Toynbee (1951-61), and Quigley (1963). Such theories, especially that of the latter, take account of the kinds of external shock that Tylor would find important in altering moral outlook, but they are also able to explain why internal social forces can shape what we term broadly "progress" and "decadence" in moral outlooks.

Crudely, aristocratic and static societies with a fairly constant level of material welfare are often governed for long periods predominantly by Code 2. These are sometimes followed by progressive periods with a rising level of welfare, power, and the political forms of democracy, generally allied to an emphasis on human welfare, usually restricted to that of citizens (Code 1). Social decadence and the decline in the self-restraint needed to maintain either democracy or welfare, or severe external shocks, can then ultimately lead to a rise in the influence of the otherworldliness of religion (Code 3).

Discussion in this book has also been limited to moral reasoning as opposed to moral behaviour. Most theories of moral behaviour assume that in deciding what to do in a situation that involves a moral issue, when not acting from habit, the individual makes a compromise between the morally desirable course of action suggested by processes of moral reasoning and self-interest (see especially Aronfreed, 1976; Cortese, 1984; Eisenberg & Mussen, 1989; Eysenck, 1960; Farrington, 1982; Power, Higgins & Kohlberg, 1989; Rushton, 1980, 1981, 1982, 1984; Wispé, 1991). The claim made here, that young children are more mature in their moral reasoning than suggested by Piaget and Kohlberg, has the implication that they are more responsible in their behaviour than suggested by those authors, provided we also make the assumption that they have no greater tendency to prefer self-interest than older children and adults.

However, that this is the case is by no means obvious (see especially Eisenberg & Mussen, 1989; Farrington, 1982; Rushton, 1980, 1981).

Thus, we can conclude from the findings reviewed here that young children are more capable of engaging in moral discussion, for such purposes as family or classroom debate on moral issues, than was thought by Piaget and Kohlberg (on this see especially Langford, Lovegrove, & Lovegrove, 1994; Turner, 1957). The drawing of firm conclusions about moral behaviour would, however, require greater space than is available here. Nonetheless, as contemporary discussions of such behaviour place substantial reliance on theories of moral reasoning, it is clear, even in the absence of extensive discussion, that the arguments put forward here have much to say about the key determinants of moral behaviour. (On the connection between theories of moral reasoning and moral behaviour see especially Bandura, 1991; Eysenck, 1960; Eisenberg & Mussen, 1989; Power et al., 1989; Wispé, 1991.)

One aspect of the connection between moral reasoning and behaviour is particularly worth noting, due to its neglect in the literature. This is that moral discourse is more likely to influence behaviour in situations to which an individual has been encouraged or obliged to apply it. Some situations, such as formal debates on moral issues, make such discourse almost obligatory, but it is far more common for participants to have the opportunity to manage the style of discourse to their own ends. Someone who wants to avoid a moral discussion of an issue may have ample opportunity to make sure that some other kind of discussion takes place. Naturalistic studies would offer more insight into this process than is available from standard interviews, where the interviewer sets the discourse style; though Goodnow and Bowes (1994) offer valuable initial orientation here using interviews that ask about discourse management.

References

Adams, P.S. (1988). Peer influence and moral decision making in undergraduate cliques. *Moral Education Forum, 13,* 9–15.

Adler, A. (1917). *Study of organ inferiority and its psychical compensation.* New York: Nervous & Mental Diseases Publishing.

Adler, A. (1927). *The practice and theory of individual psychology.* New York: Harcourt Brace & World.

Adler, A. (1954). *Understanding human nature.* New York: Fawcett.

Adorno, T., Frenkel-Brunswik, E., Levinson, D.J., & Sanford, S. (1950). *The authoritarian personality.* New York: Harper & Row.

Altmeyer, B. (1981). *Right wing authoritarianism.* Winnipeg: University of Manitoba Press.

Altmeyer, B. (1988). *Enemies of freedom: Understanding right wing authoritarianism.* San Francisco: Jossey-Bass.

Archer, J. (1992). *Ethology and human development.* Hemel Hempstead, UK: Harvester Wheatsheaf.

Aronfreed, J. (1976). Moral development from the standpoint of a general psychological theory. In T. Lickona (Ed.), *Moral development: Theory research and social issues.* New York: Holt Rinehart & Winston.

Arsenio, W.F., & Ford, M.E. (1985). The role of affective information in social-cognitive development. *Merrill-Palmer Quarterly, 31,* 1–17.

Atkinson, J.W., & Raynor, J.O. (1978). *Personality, motivation and achievement.* Washington: Hemisphere.

Ausubel, D.P. (1952). *Ego development and the personality disorders.* New York: Grune & Stratton.

Ausubel, D.P., Sullivan, E.V., & Ives, S.W. (1980). *Theory and problems of child development (3rd edition).* New York: Grune & Stratton.

Baldwin, J.M. (1897). *Social and ethical interpretations in mental development*. New York: Macmillan.

Baldwin, J.M. (1906–11). *Thought and things. Vols 1–3*. London: Macmillan.

Bales, R.F., & Couch, A.S. (1970). The value profile: A factor analytic study of value statements. In R.F. Bales (Ed.), *Personality and interpersonal behavior*. New York: Holt Rinehart & Winston.

Bandura, A. (1991). Social cognitive theory of moral thought and action. In W.M. Kurtines & J.L. Gewirtz (Eds.), *Handbook of moral behavior and development. Vol. 1*. Hillsdale, NJ: Lawrence Erlbaum Associates Inc.

Becker, E. (1973). *The denial of death*. Glencoe, MN: Free Press.

Becona, E., & Gomez-Duran, B.J. (1986). The effect of sex, age and type of school on the conservatism of Spanish children. *Journal of Social Psychology, 126*, 805–807.

Berlyne, D.E. (1960). *Conflict, arousal and curiosity*. New York: McGraw Hill.

Berti, A.E., & Bombi, A.S. (1988). *The child's construction of economics*. Cambridge, UK: Cambridge University Press.

Bliss, S.B. (1988). The effects of feminist attitudes in parents on their kindergarten children. *Smith College Studies in Social Work, 58*, 182–192.

Bloom, A. (1987). *The closing of the American mind*. New York: Simon & Schuster.

Boivin, M.J., Donkin, M.J., & Darling, H.W. (1990). Religiosity and prejudice: A case study in evaluating the construct validity of Christian measures. *Journal of the Psychology of Christianity, 9*, 41–55.

Bovet, P. (1928). *The child's religion*. London: Dent.

Bowlby, J. (1984) *Attachment and loss. Vol. 1. Attachment (2nd edition)*. Harmondsworth, UK: Penguin.

Brainerd, C. (1978). *Piaget's theory of intelligence*. Englewood Cliffs, NJ: Prentice Hall.

Braithwaite, V.A., & Law, N. (1985). Structure of human values: Testing the adequacy of the Rokeach value survey. *Journal of Personality and Social Psychology, 49*, 250–273.

Bretherton, I., & Waters, E. (Eds.) (1985). *Growing points of attachment theory and research*. Chicago: University of Chicago Press.

Broadbent, C. (1989) Personality and learning. In P. Langford (Ed.), *Educational psychology: An Australian perspective*. Melbourne: Longman.

Bullock, M. (1985a). Causal reasoning and developmental change over the preschool years. *Human development, 28*, 169–191.

Bullock, M. (1985b). Animism in childhood thinking: A new look at an old question. *Developmental psychology, 21*, 217–225.

Carter, R.T. (1990). Cultural value differences between African Americans and White Americans. *Journal of College Student Development, 31*, 71–79.

Carter, R.T. (1991). Cultural values: A review of empirical research and implications for counselling. *Journal of Counselling and Development, 70*, 164–173.

Carter, R.T., & Helms, J.E. (1990). White racial identity, attitudes and cultural values. In J.E. Helms (Ed.), *Black and white racial identity: Theory, research and practice*. Westport, CT: Greenwood Press.

Chodorov, N. (1978). *The reproduction of mothering: Psychoanalysis and the sociology of gender*. Berkeley, CA: University of California Press.

Chodorov, N. (1989). *Feminism and psychoanalytic theory*. Cambridge, UK: Polity Press.

Colby, A., & Kohlberg, L. (1987a,b). *The measurement of moral judgment. Vols 1 and 2*. Cambridge, UK: Cambridge University Press.

Coles, R. (1981). Psychoanalysis and moral development. *American Journal of Psychoanalysis, 41*, 101–113.

Connell, R.W. (1971). *The child's construction of politics*. Melbourne: Melbourne University Press.

Cortese, A.J. (1984). Standard issue scoring of moral reasoning: A critique. *Merrill-Palmer Quarterly, 30*, 227–246.

Crittenden, B.S. (1978). *Bearings in moral education*. Melbourne: Australian Council for Educational Research.

Crosby, F.J. (1982). *Relative deprivation and working women*. New York: Oxford University Press.

Damon, W. (1977). *The social world of the child*. San Francisco: Jossey Bass.

Danigelis, N.L., & Cutler, S.J. (1991). Cohort trends in attitudes about law and order: Who's leading the conservative wave? *Public Opinion Quarterly, 55*, 24–59.

Davidson, P., Turiel, E., & Black, A. (1983). The effect of stimulus familiarity on the use of criteria and justifications in children's social reasoning. *British Journal of Developmental Psychology, 1*, 49–65.

Deb, M. (1981). *Multidimensional value orientation scale*. Calcutta: Deb.

Deb, M. (1984). Factor analytical study of a multidimensional value scale. *Psychological Research Journal, 8*, 40–47.

Deigh, J. (1984). Remarks on some difficulties of Freud's theory of moral development. *International Review of Psychoanalysis, 11*, 207–225.

Demetriou, A., Efklides, A., & Platsidou, M. (1993). The architecture and dynamics of developing mind: Experiential structuralism as a frame for unifying cognitive developmental theories. *Monographs of the Society for Research in Child Development, 58*, 1–159.

Deutsche, J.M. (1937). *The development of children's concepts of causal relations*. Minneapolis: University of Minnesota Press.

Dixon, N. (1981). *Preconscious processing*. Chichester, UK: Wiley.

Doty, R.M., Peterson, B.E., & Winter, D.G. (1991). Threat and authoritarianism in the United States 1978–1987. *Journal of Personality and Social Psychology, 61*, 629–640.

Driver, R., Guesne, E., & Tiberghien, A. (Eds.) (1985). *Children's ideas in science*. Milton Keynes, UK: Open University Press.

Duckitt, J. (1989). Authoritarianism and group identification: A new view of an old construct. *Political Psychology, 10*, 63–84.

Duffy, S.A. (1986). Role of expectations in sentence integration. *Journal of Experimental Psychology: Learning, Memory and Cognition, 12*, 208–219.

Dunn, J. (1988). *The beginnings of social understanding*. Cambridge, MA: Harvard University Press.

Dunn, J., & Munn, P. (1985). Becoming a family member: Family conflict and the development of social understanding. *Child Development, 56*, 480–492.

Dunn, J., & Munn, P. (1986). Siblings and the development of prosocial behavior. *International Journal of Behavioral Development, 9*, 265–284.

Dunn, J., & Munn, P. (1987). Development of justifications in disputes with mother and siblings. *Developmental Psychology, 23*, 791–798.

Eaves, L.J., Eysenck, H.J., & Martin, N.G. (1989). *Genes, culture and personality*. London: Academic Press.

Eibl-Eibesfeldt, I. (1989). *Human ethology*. New York: Aldine.

Eisenberg, N., & Mussen, P.H. (1989). *The roots of prosocial behaviour in children*. Cambridge, UK: Cambridge University Press.

Entwistle, N.J. (Ed.) (1985). *New directions in educational psychology 1. Learning and Teaching*. London: Falmer Press.

Erikson, E. (1950). *Childhood and society (1st edition)*. New York: Norton.

Erikson, E. (1968). *Identity, youth and crisis*. London: Faber & Faber.

Erikson, E. (1977). *Childhood and society (5th edition)*. London: Paladin.

Eysenck, H.J. (1944). General social attitudes. *Journal of Social Psychology*, *19*, 207–227.

Eysenck, H.J. (1954). *The psychology of politics*. London: Routledge & Kegan Paul.

Eysenck, H.J. (1960). *The structure of human personality (2nd edition)*. London: Methuen.

Eysenck, H.J. (1975). The structure of social attitudes. *British Journal of Social and Clinical Psychology*, *14*, 323–331.

Eysenck, H.J. (1978). *Psychology is about people*. Harmondsworth, UK: Penguin.

Eysenck, H.J., & Eysenck, M.W. (1985). *Personality and individual differences: A natural science approach*. New York: Plenum Press.

Eysenck, H.J., & Wilson, G.D. (Eds)(1978). *The psychological basis of ideology*. Lancaster, UK: MTP Press.

Farrington, D.P. (1982). Naturalistic experiments in helping behaviour. In A.M. Colman (Ed.), *Cooperation and competition*. Wokingham, UK: Van Nostrand.

Feather, N.T. (1975). *Values in education and society*. New York: Free Press.

Feather, N.T. (1988). From values to actions: Recent applications of the expectancy-value model. *Australian Journal of Psychology*, *40*, 104–124.

Feldman, K., & Newcomb, T.M. (1971). *The impact of college on students: An analysis of four decades of research*. San Francisco: Jossey-Bass.

Feldstein, R., & Roof, J. (Eds.) (1989). *Feminism and psychoanalysis*. Ithica, NY: Cornell University Press.

Ferguson, L.W. (1939). Primary social attitudes. *Journal of Psychology*, *8*, 217–223.

Ferguson, T.J., & Rule, B.G. (1982). Influence of inferential set, outcome intent, and outcome severity on children's moral judgements. *Developmental Psychology*, *18*, 843–851.

Finkelstein, L. (1991). Neglected aspects of the superego. *Journal of the American Academy of Psychoanalysis*, *19*, 530–554.

Fisher, S., & Greenberg, R.P. (1976). *The scientific credibility of Freud's theories and therapy*. Hassocks, UK: Harvester.

Fisher, S., & Greenberg, R.P. (Eds.)(1978). *The scientific evaluation of Freud's theories and therapy*. Hassocks, UK: Harvester.

Fleishman, J.A. (1988). Attitude organisation in the general public: Evidence of a bidimensional structure. *Social Forces*, *67*, 159–184.

Folger, R. (1987). Reformulating the preconditions of resentment: A referent cognitions model. In J.C. Masters & W.P. Smith (Eds.), *Social comparison, social justice and relative deprivation*. Hillsdale, NJ: Lawrence Erlbaum Associates Inc.

Freeman, N. (1984). *Margaret Mead and Samoa: The making and unmaking of an anthropological myth*. Harmondsworth, UK: Penguin.

Freud, A. (1968). *The ego and the mechanisms of defence (Revised edition)*. London: Hogarth.

Freud, S. (1901). *The interpretation of dreams. Collected works, Vols 4–5*. London: Hogarth.

Freud, S. (1911). Formulations regarding two principles of mental functioning. *Collected works, Vol. 12*. London: Hogarth.

Freud, S. (1914). On narcissism. *Collected works, Vol. 15*. London: Hogarth.

Freud, S. (1915). Instincts and their vicissitudes. *Collected works, Vol. 15*. London: Hogarth.

Freud, S. (1922). *Group psychology and the analysis of the ego. Collected works, Vol. 18*. London: Hogarth.

Freud, S. (1925). Some psychical consequences of the anatomical distinction between the sexes. *Collected works, Vol. 18*. London: Hogarth.

Freud, S. (1926). *The future of an illusion. Collected works, Vol. 21*. London: Hogarth.

Freud, S. (1929). *Civilisation and its discontents. Collected works, Vol. 21*. London: Hogarth.

Freud, S. (1931). Female sexuality. *Collected works, Vol. 21*. London: Hogarth.

Freud, S. (1933) *New introductory lectures on psychoanalysis. Collected works, Vol. 22*. London: Hogarth.

Freud, S. (1939) *Moses and monotheism. Collected works, Vol. 23*. London: Hogarth.

Garner, R.T., & Rosen, B. (1967). *Moral philosophy*. New York: Macmillan.

Gay, P. (1988). *Freud: A life for our time*. London: Dent.

Gewirtz, J.L., & Kurtines, W.M. (Eds.) (1991). *Intersections with attachment*. Hillsdale, NJ: Lawrence Erlbaum Associates Inc.

Gibbs, J.C. (1979). Kohlberg's moral stage theory: A Piagetian revision. *Human Development, 22*, 89–112.

Gibbs, J.C., Widaman, K.F., & Colby, A. (1982). Construction and validation of a simplified, group administerable equivalent of the moral judgement interview. *Child Development, 53*, 895–910.

Gilligan, C. (1977). In a different voice: Women's conceptions of the self and of morality. *Harvard Educational Review, 47*, 481–517.

Gilligan, C. (1982). *In a different voice*. Cambridge, MA: Harvard University Press.

Gilligan, C., Lyons, P.N., & Hamner, J.T. (1990). *Making connections*. Cambridge, MA: Harvard University Press.

Goldman, R. (1964). *Religious thinking from childhood to adolescence*. London: Routledge & Kegan Paul.

Goodnow, J., & Bowes, J.M. (1994). *Men, women and household work*. Oxford, UK: Oxford University Press.

Graham, D. (1972). *Moral learning and development*. London: Batsford.

Greenberg, M.T., Cichetti, D., & Cummings, E.M. (Eds.) (1990). *Attachment in the preschool years*. Chicago: University of Chicago Press.

Grosz, E. (1989). *Sexual subversions: Three French feminists*. Boston: Unwin Hyman.

Grosz, E. (1990). *Jacques Lacan: A feminist introduction*. London: Routledge.

Haan, N. (1977). *Coping and defending: Processes of self-environment organisation*. New York: Academic Press.

Haan, N. (1986). Systematic variability in the quality of moral action. *Journal of Personality and Social Psychology, 50*, 1271–1284.

Haan, N. (1991). Moral development and action from a social constructivist perspective. In W.M. Kurtines & J.L. Gewirtz (Eds.), *Handbook of moral behavior and development. Vol. 1*. Hillsdale, NJ: Lawrence Erlbaum Associates Inc.

Hale, N. (1971). *Freud's reception in America*. New York: Van Nostrand.

Halford, G. (1992). *Children's understanding: The development of mental models*. Hillsdale, NJ: Lawrence Erlbaum Associates Inc.

Hare, R.M. (1963). *Freedom and reason*. Oxford, UK: Oxford University Press.

Hare, R.M. (1981). *Moral thinking: Its levels, method, and point*. Oxford, UK: Clarendon.

Harlow, H. (1953). Mice, monkeys, men and motives. *Psychological Review, 60*, 23–32.

Harman, H. (1976). *Modern factor analysis*. Chicago: University of Chicago Press.

Harvey, O.J., Hunt, D.E., & Schroder, H.M. (1961). *Conceptual systems and personality organization*. New York: Wiley.

Hebb, D.O. (1949). *The organisation of behavior*. New York: Wiley.

Helwig, C.C., Tisak, M., & Turiel, E. (1990). Children's social reasoning in context. *Child Development, 61*, 2068–2078.

Hess, E.H. (1973). *Imprinting: Early experience and the developmental psychobiology of attachment*. New York: Van Nostrand.

Hess, R.D., & Torney, J.V. (1967). *The development of political attitudes in children*. Chicago: Aldine.

Hoffman, M.L. (1963a). Childrearing practices and moral development: Generalisations from empirical research. *Child Development, 34*, 295–318.

Hoffman, M.L. (1963b). Parent discipline and the child's consideration for others. *Child Development, 34*, 573–588.

Hoffman, M.L. (1963c). Personality, family structure, and social class as antecedents of parental power assertion. *Child Development, 34*, 869–884.

Hoffman, M.L. (1970). Moral development. In P.H. Mussen (Ed.), *Carmichael's manual of child psychology (3rd edition)*. New York: Wiley.

Hoffman, M.L. (1977). Moral internalisation: Current theory and research. In L. Berkowitz (Ed.), *Advances in experimental social psychology*. New York: Academic Press.

Hoffman, M.L. (1980). Moral development in adolescence. In J. Adelson (Ed.), *Handbook of adolescent psychology*. New York: Wiley.

Hoffman, M.L. (1983). Affective and cognitive processes in moral internalisation. In E.T. Higgins, D.N. Ruble, & W.W. Hartup (Eds.), *Social cognition and social development*. Cambridge, UK: Cambridge University Press.

Hoffman, M.L. (1984). Parent discipline, moral internalisation, and development of prosocial motivation. In E. Stuab, D. Bar-Tal, J. Karylowski, & J. Reykowski (Eds.), *Development and maintenance of prosocial behavior*. New York: Plenum Press.

Hoffman, M.L. (1987). The contribution of empathy to justice and moral judgement. In N. Eisenberg & J. Strayer (Eds.), *Empathy: A developmental perspective*. New York: Cambridge University Press.

Hoffman, M.L. (1989). Empathy and prosocial activism. In N. Eisenberg, J. Reykowski, & E. Staub (Eds.), *Social and moral values: Individual and societal perspectives*. Hillsdale, NJ: Lawrence Erlbaum Associates Inc.

Hoffman, M.L. (1990). Empathy and justice motivation. *Motivation and Emotion*, *14*, 151–172.

Hoffman, M.L. (1991a). Empathy, social cognition, and moral action. In W.M. Kurtines & J.L. Gewirtz (Eds.), *Handbook of moral behavior and development*. Hillsdale, NJ: Lawrence Erlbaum Associates Inc.

Hoffman, M.L. (1991b). 'Toward an integration of Kohlberg's and Hoffman's moral development theories': Commentary. *Human Development*, *34*, 105–110.

Holstein, C.B. (1972). The relation of children's moral judgment level to that of their parents and communication patterns within the family. In S. Smart (Ed.), *Readings in child development and relationships*. New York: Macmillan.

Holt, E.B. (1931). *Animal drive and the learning process*. New York: Holt.

Hook, J., & Cook, T. (1979). Equity theory and the cognitive ability of children. *Psychological Bulletin*, *86*, 429–455.

Horney, K. (1924). On the genesis of the castration complex in women. *International Journal of Psychoanalysis*, *6*, 37–53.

Horney, K. (1926). The flight from womanhood: The masculinity complex in men and women. *International Journal of Psychoanalysis*, *7*, 324–329.

Huang, I., & Lee, H.W. (1945). Experimental analysis of child animism. *Journal of Genetic Psychology*, *66*, 69–74.

Hudson, L. (1968). *Frames of mind*. London: Methuen.

Hunsberger, B., Lea, J., Pancer, S.M., Pratt, M., & McKenzie, B. (1992). Making life complicated: Prompting the use of integratively complex thinking. *Journal of Personality*, *60*, 95–114.

Ibrahim, F.A., & Kahn, H. (1987). Assessment of world views. *Psychological Reports*, *60*, 163–176.

Inhelder, B., & Piaget, J. (1964). *The early growth of logic in the child*. London: Routledge & Kegan Paul.

Irigaray, L. (1985). *Speculum of the other woman*. Ithica, NY: Cornell University Press.

Isaacs, S. (1930). *Intellectual growth in young children*. London: Routledge.

Jacobi, J. (1968). *The psychology of C.G. Jung (7th edition)*. London: Routledge & Kegan Paul.

Jahoda, G. (1979). The construction of economic reality by some Glaswegian schoolchildren. *European Journal of Social Psychology*, *9*, 115–127.

Jahoda, G. (1981). The development of thinking about economic institutions: The bank. *Cahiers de Psychologie Cognitive*, *1*, 55–73.

Jaques, E. (1986). The development of intellectual capability: A discussion of stratified systems theory. *Journal of Applied Behavioral Science*, *22*, 361–383.

Jennings, M.K., & Marcus, G. (1986, August). Yuppie politics. *ISR Newsletter*. Ann Arbor: Institute for Social Research, University of Michigan.

Johnston, M. (1989). Moral reasoning and teachers' understanding of individualized instruction. *Journal of Moral Education*, *18*, 45–59.

Jung, C.G. (1952). *Symbols of transformation. Collected works*, *Vol. 5*. London: Routledge & Kegan Paul.

Kant, I. (1785). *Foundations of the metaphysics of morals*. (English translation by L.W. Beck, 1959, Indianapolis: Bobbs-Merrill.)

Kant, I. (1788). *Critique of practical reason*. (English translation by L.W. Beck, 1956, New York: Garland.)

Karniol, R. (1978). Children's use of intention cues in evaluating behavior. *Psychological Bulletin*, *85*, 76–85.

Katz, Y.J. (1986). Conservatism of Israeli children. *Journal of Social Psychology*, *128*, 833–835.

Katz, Y.J. (1989). Conservatism of Israeli junior high school students, *Psychological Reports*, *65*, 635–641.

Kaufman, R.V. (1983). Oedipal object relations and morality. *Annual of Psychoanalysis*, *11*, 245–256.

Keasey, C.B. (1978). Children's developing awareness and usage of intentionality and motives. In C.B. Keasey (Ed.), *Nebraska symposium on motivation*. Lincoln, NE: University of Nebraska Press.

Keil, L.J., & McClintock, C.G. (1983). A developmental perspective on distributive justice. In D.M. Messick & K.S. Cook (Eds.), *Equity theory: Psychological and sociological perspectives*. New York: Praeger.

Kerlinger, F.N. (1984). *Liberalism and conservatism: The nature and structure of social attitudes*. London: Lawrence Erlbaum Associates Ltd.

Kitwood, T. (1990). *Concern for others: A new psychology of conscience and morality*. London: Routledge.

Kline, P. (1981). *Fact and fantasy in Freudian theory (2nd edition)*. London: Methuen.

Kluckhohn, F.R., & Strodtbeck, F.L. (1964). *Variations in value orientations*. Evanston, IL: Row Paterson.

Kofman, S. (1985). *The enigma of woman*. Ithica, NY: Cornell University Press.

Kohlberg, L. (1958). *The development of modes of moral thinking and choice in the years ten to sixteen*. PhD thesis, University of Chicago.

Kohlberg, L. (1963). The development of children's orientations to the moral order: I. Sequence in the development of moral thought. *Vita Humana*, *6*, 11–33.

Kohlberg, L. (1964). The development of moral character and ideology. In M.L. Hoffman & L.W. Hoffman (Eds.), *Review of child development research. Vol. 1*. New York: Russell Sage.

Kohlberg, L. (1969). Stage and sequence: The cognitive–developmental approach to socialization. In D. Goslin (Ed.), *Handbook of socialization theory and research*. Chicago: Rand-McNally.

Kohlberg, L. (1971). From Is to Ought: How to commit the naturalistic fallacy and get away with it. In T. Mischel (Ed.), *Cognitive development and epistemology*. New York: Academic Press.

Kohlberg, L. (1974). Education, moral development and faith. *Journal of Moral Education*, *4*, 5–16.

Kohlberg, L. (1976). Moral stages and moralization: The cognitive–developmental approach. In T. Lickona (Ed.), *Moral development and behaviour: Theory, research and social issues*. New York: Holt Rinehart & Winston.

Kohlberg, L. (1981). *The philosophy of moral development: Moral stages and the idea of justice*. San Francisco: Harper & Row.

Kohlberg, L. (1984). *The psychology of moral development: The nature and validity of moral stages*. San Francisco: Harper & Row.

Kohlberg, L., & Kramer, R. (1969). Continuities and discontinuities in childhood and adult moral development. *Human Development*, *12*, 93–120.

Kohlberg, L., Levine, C., & Hewer, A. (1983). *Moral stages: A current formulation and a response to critics*. Basel: Karger.

Kohut, H. (1971). *The analysis of the self: A systematic approach to the psychoanalytic treatment of the personality disorders*. London: Hogarth.

Kohut, H. (1977). *The restoration of the self*. New York: International Universities Press.

Kohut, H. (1978–91). *The search for the self: Selected writings of Heinz Kohut. Vols 1–4*. New York: International Universities Press.

Kuhn, T. (1970). *The structure of scientific revolutions (2nd edition)*. Chicago: University of Chicago Press.

Kurtines, W.M., & Gewirtz, J.L. (Eds.) (1991). *Handbook of moral behavior and development. Vols 1–3*. Hillsdale, NJ: Lawrence Erlbaum Associates Inc.

Kurtines, W.M., & Greif, E.B. (1974). The development of moral thought: Review and evaluation of Kohlberg's approach. *Psychological Bulletin, 81*, 453–470.

Laak, J. ter, & Aleva, L. (1991). Distributive justice in children: Social psychological and developmental psychological perspectives. In R. Vermunt & H. Steensma (Eds.), *Social justice and human relations. Vol. 1*. New York: Plenum Press.

Lamb, M.E., Thompson, R.A., Gardner, W., Charnov, E.L., & Connell, J.P. (1985). *Infant–mother attachment: The origins and developmental significance of individual differences in strange situation behavior*. Hillsdale, NJ: Lawrence Erlbaum Associates Inc.

Lane, R.E. (1968). Political education in the midst of life's struggles. *Harvard Educational Review, 38*, 468–494.

Langford, P.E. (1987a). *Concept development in the primary school*. Beckenham, UK: Croom Helm.

Langford, P.E. (1987b). *Concept development in the secondary school*. Beckenham, UK: Croom Helm.

Langford, P.E. (1987c). *Moral judgement scoring manual*. Melbourne: La Trobe University.

Langford, P.E. (1991a). The assessment of moral autonomy within a multidimensional approach to the development of moral reasoning. *Journal of Moral Education, 20*, 55–78.

Langford, P.E. (1991b). Ethical and metaethical reasoning as an educational problem. *International Journal of Educology, 5*, 106–126.

Langford, P.E. (1992a). Refining a non-Kohlbergian decision making approach to the production of justifications for moral judgements. *Psychological Reports, 71*, 883–895.

Langford, P.E. (1992b). Depth of processing in moral judgement interviews. *Genetic, Social and General Psychology Monographs, 118*, 221–248.

Langford, P.E., & Claydon, L.F. (1989). A non-Kohlbergian approach to the development of justifications for moral judgements. *Educational Studies, 15*, 261–279.

Langford, P.E., & D'Cruz, J.V. (1989). A new way of scoring moral judgement interviews. *Journal of Moral Education, 18*, 118–130.

Langford, P.E., & Hunting, R. (1994). A representational communication approach to the development of inductive and deductive logic. In A. Demetriou & A. Efklides (Eds.), *Mind, reasoning and intelligence: Structure and development*. Amsterdam: Elsevier Science.

Langford, P.E., Lovegrove, H., & Lovegrove, M.L. (1994). Do senior secondary students possess the moral maturity to negotiate class rules? *Journal of Moral Education, 23*, 387–407.

Laupa, M., & Turiel, E. (1986). Children's conceptions of adult and peer authority. *Child Development, 57,* 405–412.

Laupa, M., & Turiel, E. (1993). Children's concepts of authority and social contexts. *Journal of Educational Psychology, 85,* 191–197.

Learner, M. (1988). *Moral development: A new method for scoring moral judgment interviews.* Unpublished B.Ed project report, School of Education, La Trobe University, Melbourne.

Lerner, E. (1937a). The problem of perspective in moral reasoning. *American Journal of Sociology, 43,* 249–269.

Lerner, E. (1937b) *Constraint areas and the moral judgment of children.* New York: Baillieu.

Levine, J.M., & Moreland, R.L. (1986). Outcome comparisons in group contexts: Consequences for the self and others. In R. Schwarzer (Ed.), *Self-related cognitions in anxiety and motivation.* Hillsdale, NJ: Lawrence Erlbaum Associates Inc.

Levine, J.M., & Moreland, R.L. (1987). Social comparison and outcome evaluation in group contexts. In J.C. Masters & W.P. Smith (Eds.), *Social comparison, social justice and relative deprivation.* Hillsdale, NJ: Lawrence Erlbaum Associates Inc.

Levine, J.M., & Moreland, R.L. (1989). Social values and multiple outcome comparisons. In N. Eisenberg, J. Reykowski, & E. Staub (Eds.), *Social and moral values: Individual and societal perspectives.* Hillsdale, NJ: Lawrence Erlbaum Associates Inc.

Lickona, T. (Ed.) (1976). *Moral development and moral behavior: Theory, research and social issues.* New York: Holt Rinehart & Winston.

Lieberman, E.J. (1985). *Acts of will: The life and work of Otto Rank.* New York: Free Press.

Likert, R. (1932). A technique for the measurement of attitudes. *Archives of Psychology, 140,* 55.

Light, P. (1985). *Artful work: The politics of social security reform.* New York: Random House.

Liu, A.Y. (1992). *Two studies of the moral reasoning of Chinese tertiary students in Australia.* Unpublished paper, School of Education, La Trobe University, Melbourne.

Loevinger, J. (1970). *Measuring ego development. Vols 1 & 2.* San Francisco: Jossey Bass.

Loevinger, J. (1976). *Ego development.* San Francisco: Jossey Bass.

Loevinger, J. (1979). Construct validity of the sentence completion test of ego development. *Applied Psychological Measurement, 3,* 281–311.

Loevinger, J. (1983). Personality: Stages, traits and the self. *Annual Review of Psychology, 34,* 195–222.

Loevinger, J. (1985a). Ego development in college. *Journal of Personality and Social Psychology, 48,* 947–962.

Loevinger, J. (1985b). Revision of the sentence completion test for ego development. *Journal of Personality and Social Psychology, 48,* 420–427.

Loevinger, J. (1987). *Paradigms of personality.* New York: W.H. Freeman.

Loevinger, J. (1993). Measurement of personality: True or false. *Psychological Inquiry, 4,* 1–16.

Lyons, D. (1965). *Forms and limits of utilitarianism.* Oxford, UK: Clarendon.

Lyons, D. (1991). *In the interest of the governed (2nd edition).* Oxford, UK: Clarendon.

Mackie, J.L. (1977). *Ethics: Inventing right and wrong*. Harmondsworth, UK: Penguin.

MacRae, D.Jr. (1954). A test of Piaget's theories of moral development. *Journal of Abnormal and Social Psychology, 49*, 14–18.

Magowan, S.A., & Lee, T. (1970). Some sources of error in the use of the projective method for the measurement of moral judgment. *British Journal of Psychology, 61*, 535–543.

Marcus, P., & Wineman, I. (1985). Psychoanalysis encountering the holocaust. *Psychoanalytic Inquiry, 5*, 85–98.

Martin, M., & Murray, A. (1983). Distributive injustice and unfair exchange. In D.M. Messick & K.S. Cook (Eds.), *Equity theory: Psychological and sociological perspectives*. New York: Praeger.

Masling, J. (Ed.) (1983–6). *Empirical studies of psychoanalytic theories. Vols 1 & 2*. Hillsdale, NJ: The Analytic Press.

Mayo, B. (1986). *The philosophy of right and wrong: An introduction to ethical theory*. London: Routledge & Kegan Paul.

McCloskey, H.J. (1969). *Metaethics and normative ethics*. The Hague: Nijhoff.

McFarland, D. (1993). *Animal behaviour: Psychobiology, ethology and evolution (2nd edition)*. Harlow, UK: Longman.

Mead, M. (1929). *Coming of age in Samoa (1st edition)*. London: Cape.

Menaker, E. (1982). *Otto Rank: A rediscovered legacy*. New York: Columbia University Press.

Messick, D.M., & Sentis, K. (1979). Fairness and preference. *Journal of Experimental Social Psychology, 15*, 418–434.

Messick, D.M., & Sentis, K. (1983). Fairness, preference and fairness bias. In D.M. Messick & K.S. Cook (Eds.), *Equity theory: Psychological and sociological perspectives*. New York: Praeger.

Mill, J.S. (1861). *Utilitarianism*. London: Longmans, Green.

Mitchell, J. (1974). *Psychoanalysis and feminism*. London: Allen Lane.

Mitchell, J., & Rose, J. (Eds.) (1982) *Feminine sexuality: Jacques Lacan and the école Freudienne*. London: Macmillan.

Modgil, S. & C. (Eds.) (1986). *Lawrence Kohlberg: Consensus and controversy*. Philadelphia: Falmer Press.

Murphy, G. (1947). *Personality: A biosocial approach to its origins and structure*. New York: Harper & Row.

Murphy, G. (1968). Psychological views of personality. In E. Norbeck (Ed.), *The study of personality*. New York: Holt Rinehart & Winston.

Murphy, G., & Kovach, J.K. (1972). *Historical introduction to modern psychology (3rd edition)*. New York: Harcourt Brace.

Murphy, G., & Murphy, L. (1966) Human nature and human potentialities: Imagination and the imaginary. In H.A. Otto (Ed.), *Explorations in human potentialities*. New York: C.C. Thomas.

Murphy, G., Murphy, L., & Newcomb, G. (1937). *Experimental social psychology: An interpretation of research in the socialization of the individual*. New York: Harper.

Musgrave, P. (1989). Social and personal development of students. In P.E. Langford (Ed.), *Educational psychology: An Australian perspective*. Melbourne: Longman.

Nagel, T. (1988). The foundations of impartiality. In D. Seanor & N. Fotion (Eds). *Hare and critics: Essays on moral thinking*. Oxford, UK: Clarendon.

Nias, D.B.K. (1972). The structuring of social attitudes in children. *Child Development, 43*, 211–219.

Nietzsche, F. (1899). *A genealogy of morals*. London: Fisher Unwin.

Nilsson, I., & Ekehammar, B. (1990). A new Swedish social attitude scale. *Scandinavian Journal of Psychology, 31*, 55–64.

Nilsson, I., & Ekehammar, B. (1991). Reliability and construct validity of a Swedish social attitude scale for children. *Swedish Journal of Psychology, 32*, 208–217.

Nilsson, I., Ekehammar, B., & Sidanius, J. (1985). Education and sociopolitical attitudes. *Scandinavian Journal of Educational Research, 29*, 1–15.

O'Brien, E.J., Shank, D., Myers, J.L., & Rayner, K. (1988). Elaborative inferences during reading: Do they occur on-line? *Journal of Experimental Psychology: Learning, Memory and Cognition, 14*, 410–420.

O'Neil, W.M., & Levinson, D.J. (1954). A factorial exploration of authoritarianism and some of its ideological concomitants. *The Journal of Personality, 22*, 449–463.

Perry, W.G. (1970). *Forms of intellectual and ethical development in the college years*. New York: Holt Rinehart & Winston.

Peters, R.S. (1975). A reply to Kohlberg. *Phi Delta Kappan, 56*, 678–679.

Petri, H.L. (1991). *Motivation: Theory, research and applications*. Belmont: Wadsworth.

Piaget, J. (1929). *The child's conception of the world*. London: Routledge & Kegan Paul.

Piaget, J. (1932). *The moral judgement of the child*. London: Routledge & Kegan Paul.

Piaget, J. (1952). *The origin of intelligence in the child*. London: Routledge & Kegan Paul.

Piaget, J. (1972). Intellectual evolution from adolescence to adulthood. *Human Development, 15*, 1–12.

Piaget, J., & Inhelder, B. (1969). *The psychology of the child*. London: Routledge & Kegan Paul.

Pittel, S.M., & Mendelsohn, G.A. (1966). Measurement of moral values: A review and critique. *Psychological Bulletin, 66*, 22–35.

Plamenatz, J. (1966). *The English utilitarians (2nd edition)*. Oxford, UK: Blackwell.

Power, F.C., Higgins, A., & Kohlberg, L. (1989). *Lawrence Kohlberg's approach to moral education*. New York: Columbia University Press.

Pratt, M.W., Hunsberger, B., Pancer, S.M., & Roth, D. (1992). Reflections of religion: Aging, belief, orthodoxy, and interpersonal conflict in the complexity of adult thinking about religious issues. *Journal for the Scientific Study of Religion, 31*, 514–522.

Prawat, R.S., Chancelli, A., & Cook, B. (1976). A developmental study of constructive memory. *Journal of Psychology, 92*, 257–260.

Prentice, D.A., & Crosby, F. (1987). The importance of context for assessing deservingness. In J.C. Masters & W.P. Smith (Eds.), *Social comparison, social justice and relative deprivation*. Hillsdale, NJ: Lawrence Erlbaum Associates Inc.

Quigley, C. (1963). *The evolution of civilizations*. Glencoe, MN: Free Press.

Quinton, A. (1989). *Utilitarian ethics (2nd edition)*. London: Duckworth.

Rank, O. (1931). *Psychology and the soul*. New York: Perpetua Books.

Rank, O. (1968). *Art and artist: Creative urge and personality development.* New York: Agathon Press.

Ray, J.J. (1976). Do authoritarians hold authoritarian attitudes? *Human Relations, 29,* 253–260.

Ray, J.J. (1981). Authoritarianism, dominance and assertiveness. *Journal of Personality Assessment, 45,* 390–397.

Ray, J.J. (1982). Authoritarianism/libertarianism as the second dimension of social attitudes. *The Journal of Social Psychology, 117,* 33–44.

Ray, J.J. (1988). Why the F-scale predicts racism. *Political Psychology, 9,* 671–679.

Ray, J.J. (1989) Authoritarianism research: A review. *The Psychological Record, 39,* 555–561.

Ray, J.J., & Lovejoy, F.H. (1990). Does attitude to authority exist? *Personality and Individual Differences, 11,* 765–769.

Rayner, K., & Pollatsek, A. (1989). *The psychology of reading.* Englewood Cliffs, NJ: Prentice Hall.

Reich, W. (1933). *The mass psychology of fascism.* New York: Farrar.

Renzetti, C.M. (1987). New wave or second stage? Attitudes of college women towards feminism. *Sex-Roles, 16,* 265–277.

Rest, J.R. (1973). The hierarchical nature of moral judgment. *Journal of Personality, 41,* 86–109.

Rest, J.R. (1979). *Development in judging moral issues.* Minneapolis: University of Minneapolis Press.

Rest, J.R. (1983). Morality. In J.H. Flavell & E. Markman (Eds.), *Handbook of child psychology.* New York: Wiley.

Rest, J.R. (1986). *Moral development: Advances in research and theory.* New York: Praeger.

Rest, J.R. (1989). With the benefit of hindsight. *Journal of Moral Education, 18,* 85–96.

Rest, J.R., Turiel, E., & Kohlberg, L. (1969). Level of moral development as a determinant of preference and comprehension of moral judgment made by others. *Journal of Personality, 37,* 225–252.

Rich, J.M., & DeVitis, J.L. (1985). *Theories of moral development.* Springfield, IL: C.C. Thomas.

Robinson, P. (1993). *Freud and his critics.* Berkeley, CA: University of California Press.

Rokeach, M. (1973). *The nature of human values.* New York: Free Press.

Rokeach, M. (1979). *Understanding human values.* New York: Free Press.

Rokeach, M., & Fruchter, B. (1956). A factorial study of dogmatism and related concepts. *Journal of Abnormal and Social Psychology, 53,* 356–360.

Rowley, D.J., Ross, J.G., & Harvey, O.J. (1992). The effects of belief systems on the job-related satisfaction of managers and subordinates. *Journal of Applied Social Psychology, 22,* 213–231.

Rushton, J.P. (1980). *Altruism, socialisation and society.* Englewood Cliffs, NJ: Prentice Hall.

Rushton, J.P. (1981). The altruistic personality. In J.P. Rushton & R.M. Sorrento (Eds.), *Altruism and helping behavior.* Hillsdale, NJ: Lawrence Erlbaum Associates Inc.

Rushton, J.P. (1982). Social learning theory and the development of prosocial behavior. In N. Eisenberg (Ed.), *The development of prosocial behavior.* New York: Academic Press.

Rushton, J.P. (1984). The altruistic personality: Evidence from laboratory, naturalistic and self-report perspectives. In E. Stuab, D. Bar-Tal, J. Karylowski, & J. Reykowski (Eds.), *Development and maintenance of prosocial behavior*. New York: Plenum Press.

Rushton, J.P. (1988). Epigenetic rules in moral development: Distal–proximal approaches to altruism and aggression. *Aggressive Behavior, 14*, 35–50.

Russell, B. (1946). *History of Western philosophy and its connection with political and social circumstances from the earliest times to the present day*. London: Unwin.

Saltzstein, H.D. (1991). Why are nonprototypical events so difficult, and what are the implications for social-developmental psychology. *Monographs of the Society for Research in Child Development, 56* (2), 104–116.

Sanyal, B.S. (1970). *Ethics and metaethics*. Delhi: Vikas.

Sayers, J. (1987). Freud revisited: On gender, moral development and androgyny. *New Ideas in Psychology, 5*, 197–206.

Schaffer, H.R. (1971). *The growth of sociability*. Harmondsworth, UK: Penguin.

Schaffer, H.R. (1984). *The child's entry into a social world*. London: Academic Press.

Schrader, D., Tappan, M., Kohlberg, L., & Armon, C. (1987). Coding moral types: Instruction manual. In A. Colby & L. Kohlberg (Eds.), *The measurement of moral judgment, Vol. 2*. Cambridge, UK: Cambridge University Press.

Schroder, H.M., Driver, M.J., & Streufert, S. (1967). *Human information processing: Individuals and groups functioning in complex social situations*. New York: Holt Rinehart & Winston.

Schumaker, F. (1990). *Wings of illusion: The origin, nature and future of paranormal belief*. Cambridge, UK: Polity.

Seif, B. (1993). *A comparison between Tanzanian and Australian children's concepts of school and schooling*. PhD thesis, La Trobe University, Melbourne, Australia.

Selman, R.L., & Schultz, L.H. (1989). Children's strategies for interpersonal negotiation with peers. In T.L. Berndt, & G.W. Ladd (Eds.), *Peer relationships in child development*. New York: Wiley.

Shayer, M. (1980). A Piagetian approach to science education. In S. & C. Modgil (Eds.), *Towards a theory of psychological development*. Slough, UK: National Foundation for Educational Research.

Shayer, M. (1990). Accelerating the development of formal operational thinking in middle and high school students. I. *Journal of Research in Science Teaching, 27*, 267–285.

Shayer, M. (1992a). Accelerating the development of formal operational thinking in middle and high school students. II. *Journal of Research in Science Teaching, 28*, 81–92.

Shayer, M. (1992b). Accelerating the development of formal operational thinking in middle and high school students. III. *Journal of Research in Science Teaching, 29*, 1101–1115.

Shayer, M. (1993). Accelerating the development of formal operational thinking in middle and high school students. IV. *Journal of Research in Science Teaching, 30*, 351–366.

Shultz, T.R., Wright, K., & Scheifer, M. (1986). Assignment of moral responsibility and punishment. *Child Development, 57*, 177–184.

Shweder, R.A. (1978). Rethinking culture and personality theory: I. *Ethos, 6,* 139–172.

Shweder, R.A. (1979). Rethinking culture and personality theory: II. *Ethos, 7,* 279–311.

Shweder, R.A. (1980). Rethinking culture and personality theory: III. *Ethos, 8,* 60–94.

Shweder, R.A. (1986). Divergent rationalities. In D.W. Fiske & R.A. Shweder (Eds.), *Metatheory in social science: Pluralisms and subjectivities.* Chicago: University of Chicago Press.

Shweder, R.A. (1989). Post-Nietzschean anthropology: The idea of multiple objective worlds. In M. Krausz (Ed.), *Relativism: Confrontation and interpretation.* Notre Dame, IN: Notre Dame University Press.

Shweder, R.A. (1990). In defense of moral realism. *Child Development, 61,* 2060–2067.

Shweder, R.A., & Miller, J.G. (1985). The social construction of the person: How is it possible? In K. Gergen & K. Davis (Eds.), *The social construction of the person.* New York: Springer-Verlag.

Sidanius, J. (1976). *Further tests of a Swedish scale of conservatism.* Reports from the Department of Psychology, University of Stockholm, No. 467.

Sidanius, J. (1985). Cognitive functioning and sociopolitical ideology revisited. *Political Psychology, 6,* 637–661.

Sidanius, J. (1988). Political sophistication and political deviance: A structural equation examination of context theory. *Journal of Personality and Social Psychology, 55,* 156–173.

Sidanius, J. (1990). Basic values and sociopolitical ideology: A comparison of political experts and political novices. *Perceptual and Motor Skills, 71,* 447–450.

Sidanius, J., & Ekehammar, B. (1983). Sex, political party preference, and higher-order dimensions of political ideology. *Journal of Psychology, 115,* 233–239.

Sidanius, J., Ekehammar, B., & Brewer, R.M. (1986). The political socialisation determinants of higher order sociopolitical space: A Swedish example. *Journal of Social Psychology, 126,* 7–22.

Sidanius, J., & Lau, R.R. (1989). Political sophistication and political deviance: A matter of context. *Political Psychology, 10,* 85–109.

Sidgwick, H. (1922). *The methods of ethics (7th edition).* London: Macmillan.

Siegal, M. (1980). Kohlberg versus Piaget: To what extent has one theory eclipsed the other? *Merrill-Palmer Quarterly, 26,* 285–297.

Sigel, R.S. (Ed.)(1989). *Political learning in adulthood.* Chicago: University of Chicago Press.

Simpson, E.L. (1974). Moral development research: A case study of scientific cultural bias. *Human Development, 17,* 81–106.

Singer, P. (1988). Reasoning towards utilitarianism. In D. Seanor & N. Fotion (Eds.), *Hare and critics: Essays on moral thinking.* Oxford, UK: Clarendon.

Slipp, S. (1993). *The Freudian mystique: Freud, women and feminism.* New York: New York University Press.

Sluckin, W. (1972). *Imprinting and early learning.* London: Methuen.

Sluckin, W., Herbert, M., & Sluckin, A. (1983). *Maternal bonding.* Oxford, UK: Blackwell.

Smithers, A.G., & Lobley, D.M. (1978). The relationship between dogmatism and radicalism/conservatism. In H.J. Eysenck & G. Wilson (Eds.), *The psychological basis of ideology*. Lancaster, UK: MTP Press.

Sniderman, P.M., Brody, R.A., & Tetlock, P.E. (1991). *Reasoning and choice: Explorations in political psychology*. Cambridge, UK: Cambridge University Press.

Sniderman, P.M., & Tetlock, P.E. (1986) Interrelationship of political ideology and public opinion. In M.G. Hermann (Ed.), *Political psychology*. San Francisco: Jossey Bass.

Spengler, O. (1926). *The decline of the West*. London: Allen & Unwin.

Srivastava, S., & Ramani, P. (1988). The effect of sex, age and socioeconomic status on the value patterns of adolescents. *Manas*, *35*, 43–53.

Steckenrider, J.S., & Cutler, N.E. (1989). Aging and adult political socialisation. In R.S. Sigel (Ed.), *Political learning in adulthood*. Chicago: University of Chicago Press.

Stephen, L. (1900). *The English utilitarians. Vols 1–3*. London: Duckworth.

Steward, J. (1979). Modes of moral thought. *Journal of Moral Education*, *8*, 124–134.

Stouffer, S.A, Suchman, E.A., DeVinney, L.C., Star, S.A., & Williams, R.M. (1949). *The American soldier. Vol. 1*. Princeton: Princeton University Press.

Suedfeld, P.E. (1985). The APA presidential address: The relation of integrative complexity to historical, professional and personal factors. *Journal of Personality and Social Psychology*, *49*, 1643–1651.

Suedfeld, P., & Tetlock, P.E. (1977). Integrative complexity of communications in international crises. *Journal of Conflict Resolution*, *21*, 169–184.

Sullivan, H.S. (1953). *The interpersonal theory of psychiatry*. New York: Norton.

Sutton-Smith, B. (1982). A performance theory of peer relations. In K.M. Borman (Ed.), *Social life of children in a changing society*. Hillsdale, NJ: Lawrence Erlbaum Associates Inc.

Sutton-Smith, B. (1986). *Toys as culture*. New York: Gardner Press.

Sutton-Smith, B. (1990). School playground as festival. *Children's Environment Quarterly*, *7*, 3–7.

Szirmai, A. (1991). Explaining variations in attitudes toward income equality. In H. Steensma & R. Vermunt (Eds.), *Social justice in human relations. Vol. 2*. New York: Plenum Press.

Tappan, M., Kohlberg, L., Schrader, D., Higgins, A., Armon, C., & Lei, T. (1987). Heteronomy and autonomy in moral development: Two types of moral judgments. In A. Colby & L. Kohlberg (Eds.), *The measurement of moral judgment. Vol. 1*. Cambridge, UK: Cambridge University Press.

Tarr, H., & Lorr, M. (1991). A comparison of right wing authoritarianism, conformity and conservatism. *Personality and Individual Differences*, *12*, 307–311.

Teevan, R.C., Heinzen, T.E., & Hartsough, W.R. (1988). Personality correlates between need for achievement and subscales of the F-scale for authoritarianism. *Psychological Reports*, *62*, 959–961.

Tetlock, P.E. (1986). A value pluralism model of ideological reasoning. *Journal of Personality and Social Psychology*, *50*, 819–827.

Tetlock, P.E. (1990). Some thoughts on fourth-generational models of social cognition. *Psychological Inquiry*, *1*, 212–214.

Tisak, M.S., & Ford, M.E. (1986). Children's conceptions of interpersonal events. *Merrill-Palmer Quarterly, 32,* 291–306.

Tisak, M.S., & Turiel, E. (1984). Children's conceptions of moral and prudential rules. *Child Development, 55,* 1030–1039.

Tisak, M.S., & Turiel, E. (1988). Variation in seriousness of transgressions and children's moral and conventional concepts. *Developmental Psychology, 24,* 352–257.

Tomlinson, P. (1980). Moral judgement and moral psychology: Piaget, Kohlberg and beyond. In S. & C. Modgil (Eds.), *Toward a theory of psychological development.* Slough, UK: National Foundation for Educational Research.

Toynbee, A. (1951–61). *A study of history (2nd edition).* Vols 1–7. London: Oxford University Press.

Trainer, F.E. (1977). A critical analysis of Kohlberg's contributions to the study of moral thought. *Journal for the Theory of Social Behaviour, 1,* 41–63.

Trainer, F.E. (1982). *Dimensions of moral thought.* Sydney, Australia: University of New South Wales Press.

Trainer, F.E. (1983). Ethical objectivism–subjectivism: A neglected dimension in the study of moral thought. *Journal of Moral Education, 12,* 192–207.

Trainer, F.E. (1991). *The nature of morality: An introduction to the subjectivist perspective.* Avebury, UK: Aldershot.

Turiel, E. (1977). Distinct conceptual and developmental domains: Social convention and morality. *Nebraska Symposium on Motivation, 8,* 77–106.

Turiel, E. (1983). *The development of social knowledge.* Cambridge, UK: Cambridge University Press.

Turiel, E., & Davidson, P. (1986). Heterogeneity, inconsistency and asynchrony in the development of cognitive structures. In I. Levin (Ed.), *Stage and structure: Reopening the debate.* Norwood, NJ: Ablex.

Turiel, E., Hildebrandt, C., & Wainryb, C. (1991). Judging social issues: Difficulties, inconsistencies and consistencies. *Monographs of the Society for Research in Child Development, 56* (2), 1–117.

Turiel, E., Killen, M., & Helwig, C.C. (1987). Morality: Its structure, functions and vagaries. In J. Kagan & S. Lamb (Eds.), *The emergence of moral concepts in young children.* Chicago: University of Chicago Press.

Turner, D.B. (1987). *Literature and moral education in the primary school.* M.Ed thesis, Melbourne, La Trobe University.

Turner, M.E. (1957). *The child within the group: An experiment in self-government.* Stanford, CA: Stanford University Press.

Vine, I. (1983a). Sociobiology and social psychology—rivalry or symbiosis? The explanation of altruism. *British Journal of Social Psychology, 22,* 1–11.

Vine, I. (1983b). *The human nature of self-deception.* Bradford, UK: Interdisciplinary Human Studies, University of Bradford.

Vine, I. (1986). Moral maturity in sociocultural perspective: Are Kohlberg's stages universal? In S.& C. Modgil (Eds.), *Lawrence Kohlberg: Consensus and Controversy.* Lewes, UK: Falmer Press.

Vine, I. (1992). Altruism and human nature: Resolving the evolutionary paradox. In P.M. Oliner, S.P. Oliner, L. Baron, D.L. Krebs, & M.Z. Smolenska (Eds.), *Embracing the other: Philosophical, psychological and historical perspectives on altruism.* New York: New York University Press.

Vogelaar, A.L.W., & Vermunt, R. (1991). Allocation standards: Equity, equality and asymmetry. In R. Vermunt & H. Steensma (Eds.), *Social justice and human relations. Vol. 1.* New York: Plenum Press.

Wallwork, E. (1991). *Psychoanalysis and ethics.* New Haven: Yale University Press.

Weiner, B. (1992). *Human motivation: Metaphors, theories and research.* London: Sage.

Westermarck, E. (1939). *Christianity and morals.* London: Dent.

Whaley, J.F. (1981). Readers' expectations of story structure. *Reading Research Quarterly, 17,* 90–114.

Whitford, M. (1991). *Luce Irigaray: Philosophy of the feminine.* London: Routledge.

Wilderom, C.P., & Cryns, A.G. (1986). Authoritarianism/dogmatism as a function of age: A relevant yet forgotten area of research. *High School Journal, 68,* 424–428.

Williams, N. (1969). Children's moral thought. *Moral Education, 1,* 3–12.

Wilson, G.D. (Ed.) (1973). *The psychology of conservatism.* London: Academic Press.

Wilson, G.D., & Patterson, J. (1968). A new measure of conservatism. *British Journal of Social and Clinical Psychology, 7,* 264–269.

Wilson, J. (1973). *The assessment of morality.* Slough, UK: National Foundation for Educational Research.

Wispé, L. (1991). *The psychology of sympathy.* New York: Van Nostrand.

Withey, S. (1965). The U.S. and the U.S.S.R.: A report on the public's perspective on United States–Russian relations in late 1961. In D. Bobrow (Ed.), *Components of defence policy.* Chicago: Rand McNally.

Woodrum, E. (1988). Determinants of moral attitudes. *Journal for the Scientific Study of Religion, 27,* 553–573.

Author index

Subject index